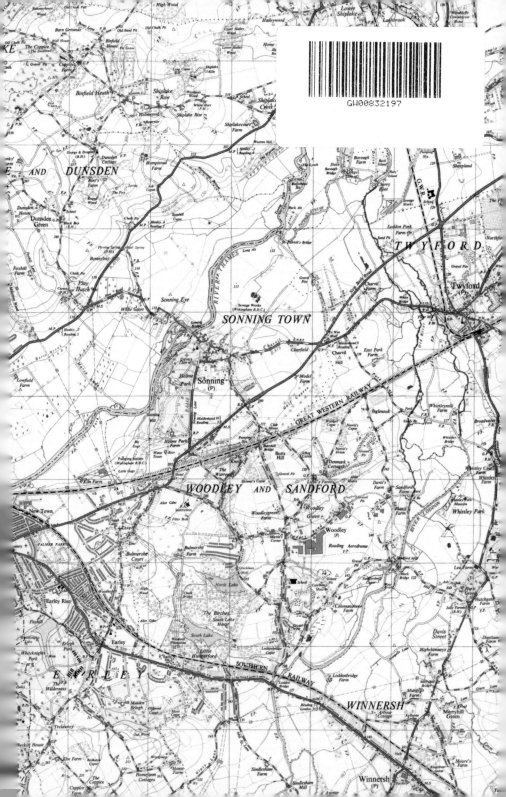
GW00832197

A THAMES PARISH
MAGAZINE

The London Arch built into the churchyard wall of Sonning's church. The bricks used had been reclaimed from London houses destroyed during World War II bombing raids.

A Thames Parish Magazine

The History of
The Parish Magazine
serving Sonning and sometime
Charvil, Dunsden, Earley, Woodley

VOLUME TWO

1946 – 1985

GORDON NUTBROWN

© Parochial Church Council,
St Andrew's Church, Sonning 2016

First published in Great Britain 2016 by
The Parish Magazine
Serving Charvil, Sonning and Sonning Eye

All rights reserved. No part of this publication may be reproduced,
stored in a retrieval system, or transmitted in any form or by any means,
electronic, mechanical, photocopying, recording or otherwise,
without the prior written permission of the copyright owner.

Text typeface:
Goudy Old Style

ISBN: 978-0-9933448-1-7

Printed and bound in Great Britain

Contents

Illustrations

Preface

Volume two of this three part work concentrates upon the forty years following World War II, as seen through the reporting of everyday life and events in Sonning and its near neighbouring parishes. As with World War I, a quarter of a century earlier, Britain had altered quite dramatically over the six long years of conflict. Post World War II Britain was to see unprecedented change, much of which could not have been envisaged even a few years previously.

The next four decades would present immense challenges to Britain which had to reassess her role in the world order. The rapid pace of technological development would impact, for good but sometimes for ill, upon the British population; no longer could "this scepter'd isle" stand alone as an island. The impact of change would be felt throughout local communities, which is graphically unfolded within the valuable store of information that thankfully exists in the past issues of *The Parish Magazine*.

All three volumes of this work draw extensively from passages contained in original issues of the magazine. These passages, which are often abbreviated to contain space, are enclosed with single quotation marks and are reproduced adopting mostly the original use of upper case and lower case type and punctuation.

Gordon M. Nutbrown
Sonning
February 2016

SONNING PARISH MAGAZINE

JANUARY, 1946.

SERVICES AT THE PARISH CHURCH. SONNING.

Sundays.—Holy Communion at 8 a.m. and as below.

Mattins and Sermon at 11 a.m.

Children's Hour at 2.45 p.m.

Evensong and Sermon at 6.30 p.m.

Weekdays.—Holy Communion on Wednesdays at 7.30 and on Thursdays at 10.

Churchings, Holy Baptism, Marriages and Burials by arrangement, after notice to the Verger, Mr. Adnams

Sonning Vicarage,
January 3, 1946.

My Dear People,

I must apologise for the magazine this month; unfortunately I have only just learnt that the copy I sent to the printer on December 20 never reached him. I can, therefore, only just insert a few notices, and express my regret to the Women's Institute and any other correspondents whose contributions have been lost.

I hope that you have all spent a happy Christmas and will have every success and joy during 1946.

Yours sincerely,

S. J. S. GROVES.

Church Notes for the Month

January 6—The Epiphany of our Lord.
Holy Communion at 7 a.m. and 8 a.m.

" 11—Children's Christmas Party.

" 13—1st Sunday after the Epiphany.
Holy Communion at 8 a.m. and 12 noon.

" 20—2nd Sunday after the Epiphany.
Holy Communion at 8 a.m.

" 25—Conversion of S. Paul.
Holy Communion at 8 a.m.
Vestry and Annual Meeting at 7.45 p.m. in the Schools.

" 27—3rd Sunday after the Epiphany.
Holy Communion at 8 a.m.
Sung Eucharist at 10 a.m.

February 2—Presentation of Christ in the Temple.
Holy Communion at 8 a.m.

" 3—4th Sunday after the Epiphany.
Holy Communion at 7 a.m. and 8 a.m.

Church Collections.

January 6—Children's Party.

" 13—Church Expenses.

" 20—Diocesan Sunday School Association

" 27—Choir and Church Music Fund.

Vestry and Annual Meeting

This combined meeting will be held in the Schools on Friday, January 25, at 7.45 p.m., and should be attended by all whose names are on the Electoral Roll of the Parish. We have to appoint the Churchwardens and Parochial Church Council for the year, and transact the other necessary business of the Church.

Thanks

(a) *Post-War Savings Week.*

Those who distributed and collected the envelopes. Those who organised the Church Shop. The Hon. Secretary, Mr. Hoyle.

(b) *Christmas.*

The Decorators. The Organist and Choir, who spent so much time in preparing for the Carol Service.

Church Registers

Holy Baptism

December 2—Gillian Alice Lund.

" 8—Anne Rosina Curteis Warren.

" 19—Mervyn Richard Cotterill.

Burial

November 23—Annie Wilkinson, aged 75.

Front page: January 1946. (23.5 x 17.5cm)

CHAPTER ONE

1946 - 1950

Post war issues of *The Parish Magazine* continued with the same format as those published during the war years; contained to just one leaf of two printed pages and without advertisements. The brevity of what appeared to be a modest newsletter was due to the continuing paper supply difficulties as a result of the war.
[*see: page 8 – Front page January 1946*]

At the dawning of 1946, Britain, and the greater part of the rest of the world, was faced with the consequences of six years of war, unparalleled in the history of this planet. Many British families suffered the loss of family and friends during the hostilities and large numbers had seen their homes and most valued possessions destroyed by enemy bombing. Whilst Sonning and other near villages had been spared bombing devastation, a number of local residents had been killed or permanently injured on active service during the conflict.

Following the ending of the war in Europe in May 1945, but prior to the ending of the war against Japan during the following August, a general election was held in July 1945. The result was a resounding defeat for Winston Churchill's Conservative party who were removed from office and replaced by a Labour government led by Clement Attlee. The new government was to be faced with a massive task of rebuilding Britain from the ravages of the past six years. Post war shortages of food and all manner of materials resulted in restrictions that continued for several years, particularly food rationing, which did not completely cease until 1954. A notable achievement of the Attlee administration was the creation in 1948 of the British National Health Service.

January 1946

The Vicar's Letter: 'I must apologise for the magazine this month; unfortunately I have only just learnt that the copy I sent to the printer on December 20 never reached him. I can, therefore, only just insert a few notices, and express my regret to the Women's Institute and any other correspondents whose contributions have been lost.'

[*The Rev. S. J. S. Groves who had been appointed to the Sonning ministry at the height of the war in 1942 continued as Sonning's vicar until 1965.*]

February 1946

The Vicar's Letter: 'I must apologise for being off duty for so long as a result of falling a victim to influenza, and am particularly sorry to have missed the Children's Party. Mr. Frederick Hoyle kindly stepped into my place and, with Mr. Harry Chapman's assistance, carried through all the arrangements.'

Carol Service: 'We are most grateful for all the hard work that was put in the preparation for the "Carol Service of the Nine Lessons". Carols old and new were sung, and the combined accompaniment of organ and piano was most pleasing.'

Church Bellringers and Choir: 'It is hoped to revive the pre-war custom of holding a supper for the Church Bellringers and Choir, as a slight mark of our appreciation for all of their voluntary work for the Church. Subscriptions will be gladly received by the Vicar and Miss Kemp; the collections in Church on February 17 have been earmarked for this purpose.'

Women's Institute: 'Mrs. White was unquestionably the outright winner of the "trading with a shilling!" her shilling having multiplied massively to £3 12s 6d.'

March 1946

Organist: 'The Vicar and Church Council have appointed an organist and choirmaster Mr. L. F. B. Davis, who has occupied a similar post at Finchampstead for the last fifteen years. He will start his duties on March 1, and we are sure that he will receive the loyal support of all members of the choir.'

Sonning Parochial Church Council – Report for 1945
The Report of the Vicar and P.C.C. to the Annual Church Meeting
1946 included the following:
'20 candidates were presented to the Bishop of Reading for confirmation.
Mr. W. W. Hoskins resigned his post as organist-choirmaster and his place was
taken by Mr. F. C. Griffin. We regret to record that Mr. Griffin has resigned to
take up similar work at South Ascot.
The Day School has again experienced a change of headmaster,
Mr. F. E. Green having been succeeded in May by Mr. H. C. Chapman.'

April 1946
The Vicar's Letter: 'Please notice that I am returning to the earlier
Sonning custom of holding the first Easter celebration at 6.45 instead
of 7.00. This gives more time for a single handed priest, and also
should allow one member of a family to return to take charged of
children before the other one leaves.'

Holy Baptism: 'Now that life is becoming more normal, I feel that I
should remind Christian parents of their duty to have their children
baptised as soon after birth as possible. It is nowhere *ordered* that the
mother's first outing after childbirth shall be to the Church for her
churching, but it is a beautiful and most commendable custom.'

Women's Institute Meeting: 'Mention was made of the forthcoming
Parish Council Election on April 1, and members were asked to show
more awareness of their responsibility to record their votes.
The cookery demonstration was of great help, being on sauce,
mayonnaise, and that very vexed question – sandwich filling.'

County Council Election: It was announced that Mr. Salter Chalker was
elected as the new representative for Sonning to the Berkshire County
Council.

May 1946
The Vicar's Letter: 'I thankfully take this opportunity of expressing my
gratitude to all those who contributed to the Easter offering, which this
year amounted to £46. It was pleasing that the Easter communicants
numbered 220.'

Pearson Hall: 'No news has yet been received of any definite date for the release of the Hall, but it cannot now be long delayed.'
[*The Pearson Hall had been requisitioned by a government authority for use in connection with the war.*]

Nursing Association: 'The Annual General Meeting of the Sonning and Woodley Nursing Association will be held in the Hut at Woodley on Tuesday May 7 at 3pm. Besides the usual business, a question regarding rates of subscription will be discussed.'

June 1946
The Vicar's Letter: Rev. Groves confirmed that a service of Thanksgiving will be held on June 8 to mark Victory Day. Groves also added the following comment: 'Although the international outlook seems far from bright and there is much to perplex and even to dismay us on the world horizon, yet we must be truly grateful for the fact that we, and not the Nazis and Japanese, were victorious in the long struggle. Memories are short, but we should still be able to imagine the horrors had the issue been decided the other way.'

May Day: 'It is most pleasing to report that the collection in Sonning on May 3 for the District Nursing Flag Day was a record, the total of £16 4s 6d contributed to the cause.'

Women's Institute: 'The May meeting, which in all probability will be the last held in the pavilion for some time, was a very lively affair. After tea, enhanced this time by a cake of pre-war dimensions given by Mrs. Powell, lots were drawn for the contents of a gift parcel which contained eight articles of groceries, the lucky members were more than pleased with this little surprise.'

July 1946
War Memorial: 'The Committee appointed by the Parish Meeting has met and co-opted some additional members. It now consists of the following: The Vicar, Gen. Phipps-Hornby, Messrs Hoyle, Williams, Powell, Huggins, Paddick, White, Chew, Ashcroft, Dale-Harris, Mrs Young and Miss South. Suggestions as to the form the memorial should take will be gladly received.'

Pearson Hall: 'A sum of £75 is estimated as the annual cost of running the Hall, whereas takings at the present rate of charge only amount to £40 or £50. As there is absolutely no endowment of the Hall, and the takings are the only source of income, the Committee has found itself faced with the necessity of increasing charges to those taking the Hall.'

Nursing Association: 'The annual meeting of the Sonning and Woodley Nursing Association was held on Tuesday, May 7, at the Hut, Woodley, the Vicar of Woodley presiding. Mrs. Myres of the Berks County Nursing Association addressed the meeting, on the position of the District Nursing Association in relation to the new National Health Service Bill. She gave it as her view that the need for the District Associations was as great as ever, and that, when the Bill comes into force, it will not destroy the Voluntary Associations, but will use them.'

August 1946
Church Schools: 'We congratulate Paulette Reder and Pat Prior on winning scholarships at the Kendrick School, Reading and the Maidenhead County Girls' School respectively.'

Cricket: 'The Cricket Club has restarted after being in abeyance during the war years. Some of the old players are back again and there is a welcome infusion of new blood. Most of the matches played so far have resulted in "draws". As a batting side the club is strong, but there is a definite need for a good slow bowler. The wicket has been prepared with loving care by Mr. Franklin, and so far has favoured the batsman. There is a good programme of matches yet to come.'

September 1946
Reading Blue Coat School: 'We are all delighted to hear that the Trustees of the Blue Coat School, Reading, have purchased Holme Park.'

Boy Scouts: 'The 1st Sonning Boy Scouts have won the Murray Plate, which is given for the best all round troop in Scouting at camp.'

Women's Institute: A report upon the monthly meeting included the following item: 'Another parcel of groceries had been received from Australia, and lots were drawn for the contents by those present.'

October 1946

The Vicar's Letter: 'We are all agreed that the weather this summer has been most disappointing, and we deeply sympathise with the farmers in the difficulty they are experiencing in harvesting their crops. However, we must still obverse our Harvest Festival, because there are so many other temporal blessings for which we must return thanks.

I believe that unintentionally I may have misled one of you by stating that school dinners would be free this term; this is not so, and I apologise to anyone I have misinformed.'

Sonning Cricket Club: 'The first cricket season since the war has ended, not in a blaze of sunshine or glory, but in regrets that so many games were spoiled by the weather. The club played 31 matches, won 6, lost 8 and drew 17. It was good to see the young cricketers coming on; H. Jeskins, A. Kyle and A. Skey did well and have the making of sound batsmen, and T. Moss also did well as wicket keeper. Many of the old stagers on occasions produced some cricket which it was a real pleasure to watch.'

November 1946

The Vicar's Letter: 'We are glad that we are able to have free use of the Pearson Hall this winter, and it is being well used for many activities. It is also a great advantage that we have Guides as well as Scouts working in our parish.'

Welcome Home Dinner: 'A highly successful re-union dinner for ex-service men and women of Sonning took place at the White Hart Hotel on Friday, October 4. Mr. Clement Williams proposed the main toast "Welcome Home" and Gen. Sir Andrew Thorne replied, emphasising the effect on the morale of the serving soldier of the knowledge that his home was a happy one and his family were being well looked after.'

Church Savings Week: 'Once more we shall be keeping the week in which our patron festival falls as Church Savings for the Post-war Needs of the Church. Two of the objects are especially important, as we hope to realise them in the very near future; purchase of a site and provision of a Church Hut for the Charville (*sic*) area and the purchase of a "discus" blower for the organ.'

December 1946

November Services: 'The Commemoration of All Saints' and All Souls' was followed on November 10 by the remembrance of those who gave their lives for us in the two great wars. The Church was nearly filled for the service at 10.30am when the usual ceremony of the placing of the flowers on the memorial was carried out by the children. This was concluded just before 11am when the two minutes' silence was observed. A feature of the service was the beautiful rendering of the Last Post and Reveille by the bugler.'

Bell-Ringing: 'On Saturday, October 19, a visiting band of the Oxford Diocesan Guild of Change-Ringers came to our church, and in two hours and fifty-five minutes rang a peal of Stedman Triples (5040 changes).'

January 1947

The Vicar's Letter: 'I am most sincerely thankful for the success of the Post War Needs Appeal at the end of November, and deeply appreciate the hard work and generosity of all those who contributed to its happy outcome.
We now hope for a brighter New Year than we have been recently spending. My best wishes to you all, for your homes and your dear ones for 1947.'

Post-War Needs Appeal: The appeal raised £270 12s 10d which included a contribution from the Church Shop of £135.

[*Chaos and power cuts caused by freezing weather spreads throughout Britain.*
The temperature on January 29 falls to minus 16 degrees F.
The Labour government nationalises the British coal industry from January 1.
Radio programmes voted most popular by listeners include Woman's Hour and Dick Barton Special Agent.]

February 1947

Sonning and Woodley Nursing Association: 'On Wednesday, January 15, a very successful concert was held in the Pearson Hall in aid of the Association. Due to the generosity of friends who paid the expenses of the concert, upwards of £27 was handed to the Association's Treasurer.'

Churchyard: 'Much work is being done in the churchyard in order to render it as neat and beautiful as possible. I regret that I am bound once more to appeal to residents to keep their dogs on a lead, if it is really necessary to bring them into the churchyard at all. The churchyard is the garden of God's House and the resting place of our departed ones, and should not obviously be liable to be fouled by dogs.'

Reading Blue Coat School: 'We desire to offer to the Headmaster, Staff and Boys of the Blue Coat School a warm welcome to its new headquarters at Holme Park. The School has a long history and has associations with Sonning through Sir Thomas Rich. It is a pleasure to us all to have them worshipping with us in church and to receive some of their number as choristers.'

March 1947

War Memorial: It was agreed to increase the war memorials situated on the south wall of St Andrew's church by adding further plaques in memory of those local men killed on active service in World War II. [*see: Volume One, pages 296 and 297.*]

Sonning Parochial Church Council – Report for 1946
The Report of the Vicar and P.C.C. to the Annual Church Meeting 1947 included the following:
'27 infants received Holy Baptism; 3 candidates were Confirmed.
The Day School had a year of continued progress under the direction of Mr. Chapman; we are glad to welcome Mrs. Higgs to the Infants' Class.
The St Andrew's Social Club has continued its activities, meeting regularly during the winter months.
The Pearson Hall was re-opened in June.
The Berkshire Education Authority has now issued its "Development Plan" under the Education Acts of 1944 and 1946. In this plan, it is laid down that the Junior School at Sonning must be re-built on a new site at an estimated cost of £20,500, if the school is to be retained as an "aided" voluntary school; that is a fully-fledged "Church School". The amount to be raised by the Church will be approximately £9,000.
The accounts for the past year disclose, unfortunately, an unsatisfactory position, showing a deficit of £37 8s 0d on the general account at the end of the year, as compared with a balance in hand of £34 18s 4d at the beginning.'

April 1947

The Vicar's Letter: 'We are all deeply concerned as to the sorry plight in which the Sonning Eye folk have been plunged by the floods and to a lesser degree by the gale, and can only hope that by the time these words reach your eyes the waters will have gone down and the houses be once more dry and clean, and habitable – but how many houses in Sonning Eye are really habitable? This disaster has shewn up afresh the lack of decencies, not to say the amenities of life, from which our parishioners in the Eye suffer; It seems difficult to believe that either the local authority or the landlords have done their duty to these people; callous neglect stares one in the face on every side. Surely, now that the war is over, such unacceptable conditions must no longer be tolerated.'

Diocesan Inspector: 'The Church School was inspected on February 25 by the Rev. A. J. Watts, General Diocesan Inspector, who spent the whole of the morning at the school. We are glad to say that he gave us a thoroughly satisfactory report.'

The Almshouses: 'The Trustees have been greatly exercised by the condition of the Almshouses. It is necessary that the premises not only be repaired and redecorated throughout, but that they are brought up to a modern standard of decency and comfort. Unfortunately, there is no income available for any of this work. The Charity Commission will loan the Trustees part of the capital which they hold; this means, however, that money for the weekly almshouse pensions will no longer be available. The increased state pension of 26 shillings will amply compensate for this.'

May 1947

The Vicar's Letter: 'I must express my warmest thanks to all those who contributed to the Easter Offering, which amounted this year to £55, both for their continued kindness and for their generous gifts. Different parties come into power and go out, politicians argue with one another and slang one another, but they all unfortunately agree in taxing the Vicar's Easter Offering; they persist in regarding what is a free gift from the parishioners as a part of the parish priest's regular income.'

Rev. S. J. S. Groves (left) officiating at the dedication of Holme Park on June 7, 1947 with the Bishop of Oxford, The Rt. Rev. Kenneth Kirk, shortly after the arrival in Sonning earlier that year of the Reading Blue Coat School.

The Bishop, using his bishopric title of Kenneth Oxon, was known to accept invitations with the use of a postcard upon which he would merely write – "OK, KO".

Organ: 'Messrs: Gray and Davidson have at last been able to obtain and install the "Discus" electric organ-blower, which is to be used for the first time for the services on April 27, and we have every reason to believe that it will give us silent and reliable service.'

Flood: 'The Mayor of Reading has informed us that Sonning has been included in the area to be covered in her Flood Distress Relief Fund. A small sub-committee has been formed, which will investigate the flood damage sustained and report to her in due course.'

Nursing: 'Part-time nurses, trained or untrained, are urgently required by the Berk County Council for work in Hospitals and Institutions. Further details may be obtained from the Vicar.'

Rev. Herbert Wigan: The death was recorded in this May issue of Rev. Herbert Wigan (1863-1947) who came to Sonning as assistant curate in 1903 and later became vicar of All Saints', Dunsden.

June 1947

"Operation Hassocks": 'The Mothers Union have volunteered to make a decided onslaught on the hassocks, cassocks, cushions, mats etc. in the Church, which are in great need of repair. Gifts of suitable material for the purpose will be greatly acceptable.'

Collection of House Refuse: 'Existing arrangements for the collection of house refuse in Sonning have recently been under review by the appropriate committee of the Wokingham Rural District Council. It has not, however, been found possible to alter the existing requirements that the bins of refuse must be placed by householders in immediate proximity to the road, although not on the footpath or road itself. A weekly instead of a fortnightly collection has now been arranged.'

Old Sunning Parish Choir Festival: 'Choristers from St Bartholomew's Reading, St Peter's Earley, St John's Woodley and also All Saints' Dunsden will join our choir in singing Evensong at the Festival of Choirs of the Old Sunning Parish (*sic*) on Saturday, June 7 at 7pm. The revival of this old custom is of particular interest to Sonning people and it is hoped that a large congregation will attend.'

July 1947

The Vicar's Letter 'I must apologise for the regrettable omission of the "Church and Home" inset in the last month's magazine, but unfortunately the copies did not reach our printer in time. I also must apologise that some matter sent to me had to be held over until this month, but paper is still in short supply.'

[*The "Church and Home" inset, which would have been published nationally for distribution with local parish magazines, was one of various publications having a Christian message that had been included with the parish magazine in the past.*]

Brownie Pack: 'It is proposed to restart a Brownie Pack in the village of Sonning during this coming September. Will parents who would like their children to join such a Pack, kindly send particulars of names and ages of the prospective Brownies to Mrs. Knott, Rosemary Cottage, Sonning or to the Vicar. Children between the ages of 7 - 10 years are eligible.'

[*Two years after the ending of the war food rations are still being reduced. Milk allowance is now cut to two and a half pints per week and the weekly tinned meat ration lowered to a twopence-worth. The Government introduce new official notices with the rather blunt slogans – "Export or Die" and "Work or Want".*]

August 1947

Confirmation: The vicar had decided to change the time during the year for preparation of Confirmation candidates and their presentation at the Confirmation service. 'I have come to the conclusion that it will be better to have the preparation during the autumn and the Confirmation service in Advent. The Lent term at school is often so greatly broken up by sickness and infection that, now that the Blue Coat School will provide so many of our candidates, the change seems inevitable.'

St Anne's School: 'We would all wish to congratulate Miss Shore on the attainment by her school of its fifteenth birthday, and to offer her our best wishes for its future success. The little school, overflowing with happy pupils, is a well-known and loved feature of our Sonning world, with its life and teaching based on the Christian faith.'

September 1947
Sonning Lock: 'We offer our congratulations to Mr. Prince on the beauty of his lock gardens this year. In spite of the heavy handicap under which he laboured on account of the floods he has succeeded in producing a beautiful picture which fully maintains the high standard set by his predecessor.'

Miss Wickham Legg: 'The death of Miss Wickham Legg came as a great shock to the members of the Sonning Mother's Union, whose enrolling member she was for many years.
[*Miss Wickham Legg was the sister of Rev Richard Wickham Legg vicar of Sonning 1926-1942*]

Cricket: 'The Rev. C. A. M. Roberts, well known to Sonning friends, brought a team from Woughton-on-the-Green, where he is now vicar, to play Sonning on Saturday, August 26. It was a pleasure to see him in his old role as wicket keeper, even though it was on the other side. Sonning batted first scoring 208 for 5 wickets declared. Woughton were all out for 79 but Mr. Roberts batted throughout the innings and was last man out scoring a valuable 28 runs for his side.'

October 1947
The Vicar's Letter: 'The holiday period has been a time of almost unbroken sunshine for nearly everyone, and should provide many subjects for thanksgiving at the Harvest Festival, which I am sure will be observed with great joy and filial gratitude by you all.
I have appointed the Rev. J. F. Amies, vicar of Ravenstone, Bucks, to the vicarage of Dunsden; we wish him and his family every blessing and happiness there.'
[*James Fraser Amies vicar of All Saints', Dunsden 1948-1963*]

Women's Institute: 'The September meeting was the first to be held in Sonning's Pearson Hall for several months. Following the singing of "Jerusalem" the forthcoming Group Meeting and W. I. Week were discussed.'

[*Austerity in Britain continues with the Government reducing the bacon ration to one ounce per week.*]

November 1947

The Vicar's Letter: 'November starts with the beautiful Festival of All Saints', followed by the commemoration of our departed ones on All Souls' Day, when we shall remember by name at the Altar those whose bodies have been laid to rest in the churchyard during the year past, together with any others whose names you care to hand in writing to the Verger on the previous day.'

Church Savings Week: 'We have now completed the first triennial period of the Post-war Needs Appeal to which we have pledged our support, and have raised the total sum of £1,130. Of the objects in view claiming our support, many remain, of which the Parochial needs may here be cited, as they are our first responsibility: The provision of a Church Room in the Charville (*sic*) area; the lay-out of the new churchyard together with the provision of a suitable entrance; cleaning of the Church and organ; the new school lies in the background of our intentions, though it is, I believe, probable that the date of its completion is considerably postponed.'

[*Potatoes are now rationed to three pounds per person per week. It is confirmed that vegetarians will not receive extra potato rations. The Food Ministry promises more meat, sugar and sweets for this coming Christmas.*]

December 1947

The Vicar's Letter: 'Our Remembrance Service this year was, though I am told it was as impressive as ever, overshadowed by the illness of our beloved General [E. J. Phipps Hornby], who has proclaimed the Roll of Honour for so many years. As bound by respect and affection, we made special mention of him at the service. The Church was well filled, and all concerned performed their various duties admirably.

Confirmation: 'Your prayers are asked for the members of the Blue Coat School who are to be presented to the Bishop of Reading for their Confirmation on Friday, December 12, at St John's Reading.'

Guides and Brownies: 'October 17, will be remembered as a very special day for the 1st. Sonning Brownie Pack, five recruits were enrolled by the District Commissioner.'

January 1948
The Vicar's Letter: 'The outlook for 1948 on the international plane looks rather bleak and cheerless, but I think we may trust that in our own country things have taken a turn for the better. But "seek ye first the Kingdom of God, and all these things shall be added unto you," My good wishes to you all.'

General Phipps Hornby: Following the death of General Phipps Hornby an extensive obituary appeared in this issue. In retirement, and after a most distinguished military career during which time he was awarded the Victoria Cross, he had been a leading figure in local village life. Among the many activities in which he was involved was notably his command of the Sonning Platoon of the Local Defence Volunteer force during the recent world war.
[*General Edmund John Phipps Hornby VC (1857-1947) is interred in the Sonning churchyard – see: Record of Burials etc. Church of St Andrew 2012.*]

February 1948
Christmas: 'The festival was observed in the usual way amongst us, the Church looked festive with its decorations and the services were bright with joy and hope, as we sang the familiar hymns and carols. The Children's Party on January 2 was greatly enjoyed by the one hundred and ten children who attended.'

Church Savings Week: 'The Post War Needs Appeal this year brought in a total of £96 2s 6d, which, after deducting expenses, £7 15s 0d, leaves £88 7s 6d to be added to the amount already in hand. The total in the bank now stands at £1,008 15s 2d.'

March 1948
Scouts: 'We are glad to know that Mr. Harwood, of 26 Park View Drive, Sonning has taken over the post of Scoutmaster, and we wish him every success and happiness in this important work. The 1st Sonning Scouts Group Committee has now been formed (the Honorary Secretary is Mrs. W. Forward, of Preston, Pound Lane, Sonning) to further the Scout movement locally. New recruits will be welcomed any Wednesday evening at the Recreation Ground; it is hoped to arrange camping and sports for the boys in due course.'

Pearson Hall: 'A new piano has been purchased for use in concerts held at the Hall. It has cost a great deal of money and must be treated with every respect by those who use it.

The Committee has recently considered a proposal that alcoholic liquor be allowed at public dances, but recommends no change in the existing regulations be made. I am sure that the Committee is right, and that the carrying out of the proposal would alter the character of the dances and the general standing of the Hall as a village centre. I must ask, therefore, that the following rules be accepted and obeyed by all those who use the Hall: no alcoholic liquor must be brought into the Hall or to any room communicating with it, when the Hall is let for a public dance or other public function. In the case of private parties permission may be granted if application is made to me [Rev. Groves] personally at least a fortnight before the date of the function in question.'

Sonning Parochial Church Council – Report for 1947
The Report of the Vicar and P.C.C. to the Annual Church Meeting 1948 included the following:
'The Choir, under Mr. L. F. B. Davis, has given loyal and devoted service throughout the year; it has been considerably enlarged by the addition of men and boys from the Reading Blue Coat School, whom we were very glad to welcome.

We are glad to report an increase in the numbers attending Sunday School, and should be glad of some extra help in the teaching, as the classes have become too large.

The Girl Guide Company under the devoted leadership of Miss Keefe continues to flourish and make recruits.

The local branch of the Workers' Education Association has recently been turning their attention to local history, in which the records and monuments of the Church which they inspected have been the cause of considerable information and interest. An historical group has been formed and hope to make investigations into the past history. in which, no doubt, the Church will be found to have played no small part.'

The P.C.C. General Account Statement for 1947 included £17 17s 6d as the income from magazine sales and a payment of £14 3s 6d as a magazine payment, presumably for printing.

April 1948

The Vicar's Letter: 'In whatever condition the world finds itself, the various seasons of the Church year always provide an apposite message. Thanksgiving and hope which it brings are the two notes of Easter; they are the antidotes against the pessimism and grumbling which are so rife today.'

Church Fees: 'A new table of Church Fees, approved by the Parochial Church Council and sanctioned by the Lord Bishop, has been fixed by this parish by an instrument of the Ecclesiastical Commissioners and will come into force at Easter. It will be agreed that our present table, which has been in force since the time of Archdeacon Pott, requires revision to bring it into tune with the great alteration in the value of money which has taken place in the last fifty years.'

The list of the new charges included a fee of 24/7d [£1. 25] payable in the vestry after a wedding with organ and choir extra. Burial in an ordinary grave 20/- [£1. 00] or with headstone, cross or kerb would now cost 52/- [£2. 60].

Silver Wedding: 'Our loyal congratulations and best wishes to their Majesties, our King and Queen, who will be celebrating their Silver Wedding on April 26.'

[*The Governments food austerity measures continue with a reduction in cheese allowance from two ounces to one and a half ounces per week. However, the weekly milk ration increases one pint to three and a half pints per week. It is also announced that twelve extra clothing coupons each are to be available from late May until the end of September.*]

May 1948

The Vicar's Letter: 'I wish to take this opportunity of expressing my warmest gratitude to you all for once again contributing so generously to the Easter Offering, which this year amounted to £59 10s 5d.

It was in all respects a glorious Easter. Though it fell so early, the weather was perfect, the flowers were abundant, and the Church looked even more beautiful than ever. The feast came as a climax to a Lent and Holy Week which had been, I think we may say, better observed than usual.'

The Parish: 'With the completion of a dozen or more new houses, the parish is once more starting to grow; again, for one reason or another, the population seems to be continually on the move, and houses change hands rapidly.   For this reason it is becoming increasingly difficult for a single-handed priest to keep in touch with everything that is going on in this wide area and to know of the arrivals of new comers, especially when extra work is continually being expected of him.   For this reason, it is being planned to arrange for each district or group of houses to have someone to act as a link between them and the Vicar, so that news, messages, or anything else, may pass between the two rapidly and efficiently.'

Women's Institute: 'A meeting was held in the grounds of the Blue Coat School on April 13, by kind permission of Mr. Inge.   It was reported that the egg collection for the Berkshire Hospital was a record.   Mrs. Siney acted as tea hostess, and after tea members enjoyed walking round the grounds.'

June 1948

The Vicar's Letter: 'How thankful we are for the glorious spring weather and the bright spring festivals.   How sad that at this time the land of our Saviour's birth and the street and fields that His sacred Feet once trod should be defiled by bloodshed and the horrors of war.'

[*On May 14, Jewish leaders proclaim the new state of Israel leading to conflict with neighbouring Arab countries.*]

The New Churchyard: 'As far as we can judge, opinion with regard to the gate into the new churchyard is uniformly favourable, and we feel that a difficult undertaking has been carried out with taste, judgment and skill; indeed one may even believe that the beauty of the churchyard has been enhanced rather than disfigured by the gateway.

We would all wish to express our gratitude to Mr. Ripley for his kind services in designing and superintending the work, to Mr. Paddick for providing the labour and materials involved in the building of the entrance, notably the old bricks, and the workmen, particularly Mr. W. Dance, the foreman bricklayer.'

[*The London Arch, was constructed from bricks reclaimed from London houses which were destroyed by German bombing during World War II – see: Frontispiece.*]

July 1948

The Vicar's Letter: 'July is as usual one of the busiest of the summer months, and we hope that the weather will be drier and warmer than has been the case in June. On Sunday, July 11, the Blue Coat School will be very much in evidence, reading the lessons, collecting the alms and of course, singing. A special invitation to parents to attend is being issued.'

St John the Evangelist Church, Woodley: 'We offer our best wishes to Rev. H. W. H. Wilkinson, B.Sc, who was licensed as Vicar of Woodley by the Bishop of Oxford on May 28.'

Church Messengers: 'As foreshadowed in the May issue of the magazine we have now enrolled a number of keen Churchfolk who will act as messengers and links between the various parts of the parish and the Church, so as to keep the one in constant touch with the other. Parishioners will thus be able to ask their own particular messenger for any information they require about the Church and its services, while the Vicar will be able to obtain information from them as to new arrivals, cases of sickness and so on.'

Church School: 'The school closes in the afternoon of July 29 for the Summer holidays. The managers hope to be able to get the entire premises redecorated, within and without, this Summer.'

[*The National Health Service commences on July 5. The service offers free medical treatment and prescriptions for the entire population. Dental care, eye examination and glasses, as well as wigs, are now available free.*]

August 1948

Confirmation: 'It is expected that there will be a Confirmation Service in our Church early in December. I should be glad to receive the names of intending candidates, and invite all, who have reached the age of twelve and not been confirmed, earnestly to consider the matter.'

Cleaning: 'The necessary work of cleaning the organ was completed during June, and the Church has been thoroughly vacuum cleaned during July. The whole of the former and half of the latter are charges on the Post War Needs Appeal Fund. We must make another effort for a large contribution to that fund this autumn, as we have still far more important and more expensive jobs ahead of us, such as the Church Hall at Charville (sic) and the new Church School.'

[*The Olympic Games are held in London during August. It is the first Games, known as the "Austerity Olympics", held since Hitler's 1936 Nazi propaganda spectacular in Berlin. Rowing events are contested at Henley with Wembley Stadium and nearby Empire Pool providing the main focus.*]

September 1948

The Vicar's Letter: 'We shall be making our annual appeal for our Post-War Needs Fund earlier than usual this year, and we hope to launch it on Sunday, October 17, following that up with weekly events on each Wednesday from then till the middle of November. We have cheering news as to the site for the Charville Church Hall of which more will be said later.'

Appeal to Parishioners of Sonning 1948: The Rev. Groves, as chairman of the Sonning P.C.C. outlined the financial support expected from the Sonning parishioners for a number of projects: 'The Parochial Church Council once more addresses the parishioners of Sonning in order to secure their collaboration in raising the fifth instalment of the Post-War Budget. Our former appeals have met with a most encouraging response, the total amounting to £1,284, and the Council greatly hopes that this may be augmented by a further £300 this year.' It was noted that former appeals had mentioned the following as the most important projects for which funding was required: Provision of a church hall in the Charville (sic) area, to supply the spiritual and social needs of that district; the building of a new church school and various other objectives including the construction of the London Arch in the Sonning churchyard. Groves announced that the Charville hall scheme had been greatly helped by a generous free offer of an acre of land by Mr. Livanos for the purpose of constructing the hall.

Girl Guides: 'The Guide Company held their first camp at Englefield Park from August 6 to 13, and despite the almost continuous wind and rain the camp was a big success. The spirits of the Guides from

Sonning and Knowl Hill and the two Rangers from S.R.S. Grey Goose were never at low ebb, thanks to the excellent quartermastering of Lieutenant and the effective wasp-sting remedies of Brown Owl!'

October 1948
The Vicar's Letter: 'The Harvest Festival brings to a close the Summer, and October will witness the restarting of many of our winter activities. I hope that every house will decide to send something to Church as their thanks offering to God for the comparative plenty that this country enjoys.'

Confirmation: 'We are glad to be able to announce that the Lord Bishop of Oxford will himself be coming to administer the Sacraments of Confirmation in our Church on Saturday, December 4, at 3pm.'

British Legion: 'The Annual General Meeting of the British Legion's local branch will be held in the Pearson Hall on October 1 at 8.15pm.'

November 1948
The Vicar's Letter: 'Thanks to the generosity of a parishioner who wishes to remain anonymous and to the co-operation of our printer, we are enabled for the future to have four pages at our disposal for publishing local matter. We can therefore send forth a wider invitation to societies and individuals in the parish to send in their news, comments or notices, in order that we may include all parochialia within the orbit of the magazine. I am glad and grateful for this, for it saves me the necessity of turning down, curtailing or postponing insertions sent to me. I invite the co-operation of all in this matter, with the stipulation that all matters for publication must reach me by the nineteenth day of the previous month.
I write this letter as we approach the period of raising our year's quota for the Post-War Needs Appeal Fund and look forward to great successes and happy gatherings.'

Armistice Day: 'The observance of Armistice Day is fixed this year for Sunday, November 7. We had hoped that the War Memorial to those killed in the recent war would be ready for dedication by this Sunday, but, unfortunately, it has not yet been completed.'

Parish Council: 'Two seats have been erected on the towing path between the Lock and the Bridge from money provided by the sale of agricultural pies by the W.V.S. The provision of a concrete bowling pitch for cricket in the Recreation Ground and the Bowling Green were referred back for an estimate of the cost.'

December 1948

St Andrew's Club: 'The winter season has been progressing well, and the membership has been growing. Our new hostess with the co-operation of the committee has arranged some interesting programmes, while the instruction in ballroom dancing has proved most popular. We can look forward to a happy and useful time of varied interest and activity.'

British Legion: 'Captain W. Rotheram has made arrangements for a monthly supply of British Legion journals and will be happy to let members or prospective members have a copy each month if they will kindly let him have their names.'

Royal Birth: 'We express our heartiest congratulations to their Majesties and to Princess Elizabeth and her husband on the birth of our infant Prince, whom God preserve, guide and strengthen with his grace.'
[*Charles Phillip Arthur George was born November 14, 1948.*]

Dispensary Fund: 'An invalid chair has been purchased for the use of those parishioners who require it. Applications for the use of it should be addressed to the Vicar.'

Pearson Hall: 'Crockery has now been bought and will be available at a small charge, to those who hire the hall. Application should be made to the caretaker at the time of booking the hall.'

Sir Thomas Rich Apprenticing Charity: 'The Thomas Rich charity provides premiums and grants towards the cost of tools to boys residing in the Ecclesiastical Parishes of Sonning, Earley, Woodley and Dunsden. Application forms for apprenticeship premiums can be obtained from Miss Kemp, Estate Office, Sonning, and applications for grants for tools should be sent to the same address, together with a testimonial from the employer.'

The Magazine: 'We regret to say that the magazine is now running at a loss, which has to be met from Church funds; we have no alternative, therefore, but to raise the price to three pence from January, 1949.'

[*A Special Roads Bill is published which plans 1,000 miles of "motorways"*]

January 1949
The War Memorial: 'The memorial to the men who fell in the Second World War has now been completed and installed on the south wall of the Church. The work has been carried out by Messrs: Powell and Co., of London, to the design of Mr. C. Ripley, to harmonise with the former memorial which was also made by the same firm.'

Girl Guides: 'The Company's dream of possessing a bell tent for camping became a reality with the sum of over £18 being raised for this very necessary item of equipment.'

Dr. John James Davis: It was reported that Dr. Davis, who had been in practice at Sonning for a short period of time, had died. 'It is difficult to avoid the use of the word "tragedy" when we think of the painful illness and death of our doctor, who made himself so beloved not only to his patients, but many besides. His skill and cheerful encouragement have helped countless sufferers here and elsewhere.'

Robert Palmer Almshouses: 'A few years ago the Trustees, feeling that the Almshouses were not up to the standards of modern decency and comfort that old people should expect, decided to approach the Charity Commissioners in order to obtain their permission to borrow some of the Trust capital for the purpose of making improvements. Permission was given by the Commissioners to the extent of £900. However, when the plans for the alterations were drawn up, it became evident that the sum would not be nearly sufficient for the purpose envisaged. At this moment the Trustees of the Fire Brigade intervened with a most welcome and generous offer, to carry out the proposed improvements by a gift of the £2,100 required.'
The improvements included two baths placed in the existing wash houses, the provision for each house of gas and water, a lavatory, a kitchenette with gas cooker, water heater, larder etc.

February 1949

The Vicar's Letter: 'Christmas and the New Year appeared to have been marked by an unusual bout of sickness of various descriptions; we hope that this will soon have taken its normal course and disappeared.'

The Magazine: 'The whole parish is most grateful to Miss A. Davis, who for so many years has been responsible for the distribution of the Parish Magazine each month, and I desire to take this opportunity of publicly expressing your and my thanks to her for her labours.

From April, Captain W. Rotheram, "Ellesmere" Pearson Road, will be acting as manager of the business side as well as Assistant Editor of the magazine, and will carry out the distribution each month with the assistance of the church messengers and others.'

A Kind Offer: 'Miss Hodgkinson asks us to announce that she will be in her car by the "Wee Waif", ready to drive people to church and take them back again after the service, on the first Sunday of the month at 7.45am and the third Sunday at 10.45am.'

Women's Institute: 'At the monthly meeting on January 11, Miss Waltham gave a very interesting demonstration on Dress Embroidery which was greatly appreciated by all members. The Social half-hour was a Whist Drive, the winner being Mrs. Norcot.'

March 1949

National Savings: 'The village is now fairly well served with Savings Groups and Savings Clubs. One group functions at the school, another at the Women's Institute and a Savings Club is now in operation at the Working Men's Club. The difference between a group and a club is this: the former sells stamps and certificates, the latter accepts contributions and pays out in cash, interest on investments being at the rate of two and a half per cent per annum.'

The County Library: 'It may not be generally known that there is a branch of the Berkshire County Library in operation at the old Girls School. Books may be borrowed, without any fees whatsoever, every Tuesday night between the hours of 6.30pm and 7.30pm. There is a good selection of non-fiction and fiction volumes.'

Sonning Parochial Church Council – Report for 1948
The Report of the Vicar and P.C.C. to the Annual Church Meeting 1949 included the following:

'The Choir, under Mr. L. F. B. Davis, continues to grow in number and to give loyal and devoted service. A festival of combined choirs, totalling 143 voices, was held in the Church on May 22.

Both the Church and the organ have been thoroughly cleaned, and the fabric also well maintained.

The increased members attending Sunday School are well maintained, and we have been glad to welcome two new teachers during the year.

The ordinary Church Accounts show up rather badly as compared with a year ago, an opening balance of £24 6s 1d now converted into a deficit of £5 8s 8d. The thorough cleaning of the Church and organ have been met by special grants from the Caroline Palmer Trust and the Post-War Needs Appeal Fund.'

Sonning P.C.C. Accounts:
Accounts for year ended December 31, 1948 included the following:
'The Post-War Needs Appeal Fund had raised the sum of £1,500 12s 10d during the last five year period.

Sales income from the magazine had amounted to £29 16s 0d with an additional £10 received by donation. The magazine printing expenses were £37 16s 0d plus a further £4 17s 6d charged for extra pages.'

British Legion: 'A variety show was performed in the Pearson Hall on Wednesday, February 16, in aid of the Sonning branch of the British Legion. It was the perfect example of what an amateur show should aim at, as it had wit, beauty and speed.'

April 1949
[*The monthly issues now comprised of eight pages and carried one trade advertisement (Sonning Auto Services Ltd). Under the title "Village Activities," four pages were given over, in this issue and two subsequent issues, to reports upon several local clubs and societies.*]

The Church Working Party: 'The Church working party meets on the fourth Tuesday in each month for the purpose of repairing surplices, cassocks, kneelers, cushions etc. for the Church and for making articles for sale. The whole of the profits from articles sold are placed in a fund to provide materials to make articles for the autumn sale and replacement of necessary articles for the Church.'

Women's Institute: 'At a meeting on March 8, Mrs. Walmsley gave a very interesting demonstration of cold sweets, peppermint creams, fondants etc. which members were invited to taste.'

Sonning Lawn Tennis Club: The annual general meeting was held in the cricket pavilion on March 15. Committee members were elected for the 1949 season and it was noted that membership is strictly reserved to Sonning residents. The subscription for the ensuing year was agreed at £1 5s 0d for the season and 10s 6d for juniors.

Sonning Cricket Club: 'Another enjoyable season this year is being anticipated, especially if more of the younger element in the village can be encouraged to take an active interest. A full fixture list has been prepared including two all-day matches against a "Farmers XI".'

Sonning Football Club: ' The Club is running a team in the Reading and District Institute League Division II, and up to date have done very well, having played 18 matches, with 11 wins, 5 defeats and 2 draws.'

Sonning School Old Boys' Association: 'The Association has now celebrated its first birthday. It has had a most successful year with an ever growing number of members. Its president is Miss Fox who has been assistant in the school for 33 years. The present headmaster, Mr. Chapman, together with three previous heads of the Boys' School are numbered among its vice presidents.'

May 1949
Pearson Hall: 'A meeting of the Advisory Committee was held at the hall on April 4. The accounts for 1948 presented by Mr. C. H. Williams showed an excess of expenditure over income of £145, chiefly due to the purchase of the concert piano and heavy repair bills. It was pointed out that there were no endowments for the maintenance of the hall, that the charges were just meeting the costs, and that the balance still remaining was the result of an accumulation during the war, when the hall was requisitioned for Government purposes. It was reported

that the hall chairs had been repaired, and the fire appliances and a set of crockery had been purchased.'

Reading Blue Coat School Scouts Social: 'On Friday, March 25, this recently formed troop under the directorship of its Scoutmaster, H. A. Nuttal, and fellow Scouters, presented their first public show in the form of a Social in a packed Pearson Hall, Sonning of over 150 people.'

Swimming Club: 'Good news reaches us that steps are underway to re starting the Swimming Club. We hope definite news as to the site and full details will soon be forthcoming.'

War Memorial: 'Through the kindness of Captain W. Rotheram, the Vicar was able to present the next-of-kin with a photograph of the 1939-1945 War Memorial - a gift which, we can assure him, was greatly appreciated.'

June 1949
The Vicar's Letter: 'Our Church and social life is so full of interest and makes such claims upon our time at the moment, just now that we seem to live in a constant whirl of rushing from one interesting and important thing to another. The Christian Education Exhibition has proved a remarkable week of effort and achievement, which redounds greatly - I had almost said solely - to the credit of our Rural Dean, Canon Winter.'

Women's Institute: 'A well attended meeting was held on May 10. The Social half-hour was spent in a singing game comprising of groups of four, each group singing a different song of their own choosing and needless to say arousing much merriment.'

Sonning Cricket Club: 'This season's fixture list shows a good batch of some 38 matches, 24 of which are being played at home. The results of the first eight matches were, 5 won, 1 lost and 2 drawn.'

Sonning School Old Boys' Association: 'Old friends are re joining and new ones coming along to swell the membership. When the Association becomes two years old we hope the membership will have risen to 200.'

July 1949

The Vicar's Letter: 'I can never remember a six month period when there was so much serious illness requiring hospital treatment. Ever since Christmas, there has always been at least one, and usually more, of our number in a local hospital or nursing-home. We can only hope that the summer weather will soon better this unfortunate state of affairs.'

Whitsun Farthings: 'Our collection of farthings for the Diocesan Funds was not so good as usual, 1,848 were collected as against 2,840 last year. On the Tuesday in Whitsun Week Ann Glasscock and David Rawlins were among the hundreds of other children of the Diocese at the Cathedral Church of Christ in Oxford to offer their farthings to the Bishop.'

[*The Labour Government confirms that the National Health Service is costing 2s 6d per head of population each week, 1s 4d more than forecast.*]

August 1949

The Oxford Diocesan Missionary Festival: 'This year the festival was held at High Wycombe and was a triumph of organisation, the proceedings moving without a hitch throughout the day. The 10.30am service of Holy Communion was celebrated by the Lord Bishop of Oxford in the Parish Church. After an "al fresco" lunch in the churchyard our party went to Wycombe Abbey School where a public meeting was held in the School Hall.'

British Legion: 'On May 18 and 19 the annual conference of the British Legion Women's Section, was held at the Albert Hall. 1,887 delegates attended and there was a very large number of Standards. Mrs Polden was our Standard bearer and Mrs. Phipps-Hornby also attended.'

September 1949

The Vicar's Letter: 'The Church Council has agreed with me that it is important that a Church Guild, chiefly for the benefit of the young people, should be formed, to help and encourage them to appreciate and use to the full their Christian privileges.

In October we shall be making our annual effort on behalf of the Post

War Needs Fund, which will this year be concentrated on the building of the new Church Hall at Charville (*sic*). We hope that in October we may be able to make a definite announcement of the plans of the hall and of the time of starting the actual building. All your help will be needed.

Saint Andrew's Club: 'The new season will commence with a dance in the Pearson Hall on Tuesday, September 20, at 8pm. Meetings will subsequently be held every Tuesday evening; new members will be cordially welcomed.'

Sonning School Old Girls' Association: 'A meeting of the former pupils of Sonning School was held recently, when it was decided to form an Old Girls' Association. Membership is open to anyone who has attended Sonning School. The subscription to be 2s 0d per year.'

[*On September 11 the milk ration is cut from three to two and a half pints per week, and cut again on September 18 to two pints per week.*
Britain devalues the pound sterling against the dollar by a massive 30.5 per cent.]

October 1949
The Vicar's Letter: 'The Harvest Festival has been a joy to us all, and the offerings of fruit and vegetables quite surprisingly large, considering the difficulties of the season. The collections came to £15, a useful start for our autumn Post-War Needs Appeal.
As you will see from the appeal, we are concentrating entirely this year on the important parochial project of erecting the Church Hall at Charville, and I claim your real interest and help in this matter. I also venture to suggest that the various societies which benefit by the use of any of our Sonning buildings might be willing to provide some of the necessary furniture or appliances for the new hall.'

The Sonning and Woodley Nursing Association: 'The activities of the Association came to an end on the implementation of the National Health Service Act on July 5, 1948. During the forty years of its existence the Association has had fourteen nurses. Until 1940 one nurse sufficed but in that year another nurse was engaged to serve Woodley.'

November 1949

Firmer Moral Standards – Plea by Princess Elizabeth: 'In an address to the young wives' rally of the Mothers' Union at Central Hall, Westminster, yesterday, Princess Elizabeth spoke of the declining moral standards of this age and pleaded for the establishment of a well-balanced code of right and wrong. Princess Elizabeth said that in spite of our marvellous progress in science, medicine and knowledge of all kinds, the need for movements such as the Mothers' Union was even greater today than at the time since their foundation.'

The New Sonning Churchyard: 'The Church Council has been giving careful consideration to the question of the future care and maintenance of the new Sonning churchyard, in view of the fact that there will shortly be no room for burials in the portion that is being used at present. The new churchyard is a beautiful piece of ground, surrounded by a lovely old wall; its charm should not be defaced by unsightly monuments, which do not suit the surroundings, or by foreign material produced by foreign labour which would destroy its quiet beauty.'

December 1949

The Vicar's Letter: 'Thanks to the loyal and cheerful co-operation of all concerned, we have made a very considerable addition to our Post-War Needs Appeal balance. I want to take this opportunity of expressing appreciation of all the hard work done in the many compartments of our autumn effort. In addition to the money raised locally, I have received the promise of a grant of £50 from the Diocesan Church Extension Committee, and I am still negotiating with the Incorporated Church Building Society for help in building the new hall from them. I hope that this will be regarded as a sufficient proportion of the total cost required for the construction to warrant our going ahead with the building.'

Mothers' Union: 'The Mothers' Union Service was held in St Andrew's Church on Thursday, November 3, twenty-two members being present. Miss Dunstan was again at the organ. The Vicar thanked all the members who had given of their time, energies and money in helping at the Church Sale.'

January 1950

The Vicar's Letter: I suppose that the first half of the twentieth century does not end until next December, so that we cannot say we have reached its halfway mark. No one could claim that the history of these first fifty years of this century have shown that mankind is capable of ordering its affairs intelligently; if mankind can realise that obvious lesson and understand that only in obedience to God's revealed will is there any hope of living sensibly and peaceably then the history of the second half of this hitherto uncomfortable century may show some improvement.'

St Anne's School: 'For reasons of health Miss Shore has been obliged to close St Anne's School this Christmas. She is so very grateful to the parents who combined to give her such a wonderful present – the handbag and cheque. For eighteen years the little school has been at work in our High Street, and it is a sad loss to the neighbourhood that it can no longer be carried on. We shall wish Miss Shore all happiness and better health for the future.

[*Dorothea Violet Shore (1892-1954) is interred in the Sonning churchyard see: Record of Burials etc. Church of St Andrew 2012.*]

Confirmation: 'We are glad to note that quite a number of Sonning parishioners were present at St Laurence's for the Confirmation Service on December 4, to witness this important ceremony and to join in prayer for the candidates. Our fifteen candidates included seven from the Blue Coat School, which has traditional ties with St Laurence's Church.'

February 1950

The Vicar's Letter: 'Now we are faced with another General Election – on February 23, which means the eve of the poll will be Ash Wednesday. This may be unfortunate in some ways, but it does mean that we can use the day as a time of intercession for our country, and particularly for the voters that they may make a right choice.'

[*The Labour Party led by Clement Attlee defeats Winston Churchill's Conservative Party in a closely fought general election. The final number of seats won: Labour 315, Conservatives 298, Liberals 9 and others 3.*]

Sonning Parochial Church Council – Report for 1949
The Report of the Vicar and P.C.C. to the Annual Church Meeting
1950 included the following:
'The fabric of the Church has been well maintained; it is inspected each year
by the Diocean Surveyor at the charge of the Caroline Palmer Charity.
The Church Primary School has had a happy and prosperous year under Mr.
Chapman, a highly satisfactory report on the religious teaching being received.
In January the memorial to those who gave their lives during the Second
World War was unveiled by Gen, Sir Andrew Thorne, the Deputy Lieutenant
of Berkshire. The memorial, designed by Mr. C. Ripley and constructed by
Messrs. J. Powell & Co to conform to the former memorial, consists of
fourteen alabaster tablets bearing full particulars of each of the Fallen,
surrounded by two bands of marble.
The Churchyard has been maintained in a good state of tidiness, though in
high summer it taxes the labour of a half-time man to the uttermost. The new
Churchyard has been opened for burial, and a portion has been levelled and
prepared by some enthusiastic labourers from the Reading Blue Coat School.
The Parish Magazine has been enlarged through the kindness of Captain
Rotheram, who has also reorganised its format and distribution.'

[*The pages of the magazine's monthly issues varied in extent from four to eight pages. A
new title design appeared with the May 1949 issue.* see: page 42.]

March 1950
Dramatics: 'The Reading Blue Coat School Dramatic Group is to be
congratulated on the capital entertainment they provided on February
1, 2 and 3 in the Pearson Hall. Three plays were presented – "The
Gipsy's Warning", "News–All Hot" and "Missus's Hat". The elocution
was good, the broad Berkshire accent seemed to come quite naturally
from the lips of those who played the parts of the farm hands.'

Sonning Working Men's Club: 'The Annual General Meeting was held on
January 26, 1950, in the club room, the President, Mr. C. H. Williams,
being in the chair. Mr. S. Paddick in his report stated that the
membership was 141 and during the year visitors to the club had greatly
increased. The President then presented trophies and prizes:
Rotheram Snooker Cup: A. H. Thomas, Rotheram Darts Cup: J. C. Bunce,
Wimperis Billiards Cup: J. J. Bunce, Crib Prize: J. J. Bunce.'

April 1950

Parish Meeting: A large number of Sonning residents were present at a meeting which was convened on March 16, for the purpose of discussing a proposal of the Reading Borough Council to build a large new sewerage disposal works in the village of Sonning. The meeting was reported in this issue: 'This representative meeting of the inhabitants of Sonning desires to register a most emphatic protest against the scheme recently adopted by Reading Town Council for the establishment of a large new sewerage disposal works in the parish of Sonning, to serve the population of the County Borough, which it intends to oppose, in co-operation with the other local authorities concerned, by every legitimate means. Sonning is known as one of the beauty spots of the Thames Valley, and attracts visitors from all parts of England and from abroad. Such a scheme, if adopted, would not only seriously damage the amenities of the village and disfigure the countryside, but would inevitably depreciate the value of all forms of property, large and small, in the neighbourhood.'

[see: page 56 - April 1952.]

May 1950

Village Items: 'Activity on the old allotments looks as though we are really going to have some new Council Houses at last – have you subscribed to a new tree yet? Or are you waiting for the house first.

A meeting of the Swimming Club was held recently, when it was decided to proceed with a scheme for providing a bathing-place.'

St Andrew's Social Club: 'On April 18, the Dramatic Section of the club gave a concert to a large audience in the Pearson Hall. The club members appeared in four sketches. The cast of each sketch were the Misses: M. Lamb, R. May, G. Moore, P. Prior, D. Russell and M. Russell and Messrs: R. Dymott, J. Faulkner, L. Forward, K. Marcham and H. Shine.'

June 1950

Charville Hall: 'We are glad to be able to report that the Church Council has decided to proceed as soon as possible with the erection of the Hall at Charville. We have roughly £1,500 raised or promised out

St. Andrew's, Sonning

"Know ye not that ye are a temple of God, and that the Spirit of God dwelleth in you?"

Sonning Vicarage,
May 17, 1949.

My dear People,

Our Church and social life is so full of interest and makes such claims upon our time at the moment just now that we seem to live in a constant whirl of rushing from one interesting and important thing to another.

Accounts of the Christian Education Exhibition appear below. The Exhibition has proved a remarkable week of effort and achievement, which redounds greatly—I had almost said solely—to the credit of our Rural Dean, Canon Winter, whose infectious faith and enthusiasm has surmounted every difficulty.

Sonning Church without Adnams! It seems almost impossible, but we have to manage somehow without him for the moment. We are so glad to know that he is at home again progressing favourably after his recent operation, and we hope to see him back very soon at the work he loves and does so well.

Yours sincerely,

S. J. S. GROVES.

Church Notes for the Month

June 1—Diocesan Conference at Oxford, 2 p.m. Sung Eucharist in the Cathedral, 11.30 a.m.

2—Mothers' Union Meeting, 3 p m.

4—Whitsun Eve. Episcopal Visitation, 12 noon, at S. Mary's, Reading.

5— Whitsunday.
Holy Communion at 6-45 a m., 8 a.m. (with hymns) and 12 noon.

6—Monday in Whitsun Week.
Holy Communion at 8 a.m.

7—Tuesday in Whitsun Week.
Holy Communion at 7.15 a.m.

8, 10, 11—Ember Days.

12—Trinity Sunday.
Holy Communion at 8 a m, (Preacher:—Rev. C. P. Lester).

14—S. Barnabas the Apostle.
Holy Communion at 7.15 a m.

16—Thanksgiving for the Holy Eucharist.
Holy Communion at 9.45 a.m (Centenary of the Melanesian Mission.)

18—Sonning Choir Festival, 7 p.m.

19 — 1st Sunday after Trinity.
Holy Communion at 8 a.m.
Sung Eucharist at 11 a.m.
(4th Centenary of the 1st English Prayer Book)

24—Nativity of S. John Baptist.
Ho'y Communion at 8 a.m.

26—2nd Sunday after Trinity.
Holy Communion at 8 a.m.

29—S. Peter, Apostle and Martyr.
Holy Communion at 7.15 a.m.

July 2—Visitation of B.V.M.

3—3rd Sunday after Trinity.
Holy Communion at 7 a.m. and 8 a.m.

Church Services

Sundays (as on cover and as above).
Weekdays:—Holy Communion on
Wednesdays at 7 15
(Except June 8 and 15)
Thursdays at 9.45
Fridays at 8.

Church Collections

June 5—Diocesan Ordination Candidates Fund.

12—Choir and Church Music Fund.

19—Diocesan Moral Welfare Work.

26—Churchyard Fund.

Title page: May 1949. (24 x 18cm.)

of the estimated amount required, which is £2,500, leaving £1,000 at least to be raised. We feel that it would be a mistake to delay the start any longer, we believe that the money will come in faster when the Hall is up and available for use. But this will mean the borrowing of £1,000 as soon as the bills come in. Can anyone lend us £1,000 at a low rate of interest (or better still give it) for this important work?'

St Nicholas', Earley: 'We must congratulate our daughter parish of Earley on their enterprise in building a permanent church for the St Nicholas District (off the lower Wokingham Road). St Nicholas' is our second grand-daughter, St Bartholomew's of course, being the first.'

Church School: 'The school, especially the infants' class, is growing so much that the managers have felt justified in applying for an extra teacher; we hope that our request will be granted and that we may be able to make use of the long room in the old school to accommodate one of our classes.'

July 1950
Choir Festival: 'Once again, on Saturday, June 10, Sonning was the meeting place of six neighbouring choirs who united to sing Evensong in our Church. A united practice in the afternoon, was followed by tea in the Pearson Hall, for which we are greatly indebted to Miss South and her helpers. The choirs formed up on the Vicarage lawn at 6.45pm in perfect weather and then the long procession made its way into the well filled church. The music, with the exception of the Anthem, was mainly congregational and included four well-known hymns.'

[*British troops are sent to Korea as the conflict between North and South Korea escalates.*]

August 1950
Souvenir Year Book: 'Attention is invited to the new Souvenir Year Book of the Church which has been prepared and is now on sale price 3d. This book gives the history of the Church and particulars of interest regarding its restoration in 1852 with much more detail than the old brochure.'

Dancing Display and Sale: A number of fund raising events were in progress in aid of the new church hall at Charville [soon to be referred to as Charvil]. This particular event, which took place on the vicarage lawn, was held on the evening of July 19: 'After a dull and cloudy morning and afternoon the sun came out and we had a perfect summer evening for our effort towards building the Church Hall. We expect to hand over £24 to the fund.'

[*The BBC transmits the first live TV pictures across the English Channel from France on August 27. The two hour programme being transmitted from Calais and presented by Richard Dimbleby.*]

September 1950

The Vicar's Letter: 'I express my own thanks and those of the School Managers and of the many parents and children to Mrs. Higgs for her devoted and highly skilled service in our School with the Infants. We all hope that, after a rest, she will find another post, where she may carry on her work with the same success. We welcome Miss Wilkens and Miss Simmonds who start work with us on September 7.'

The Almshouses: 'The extension to the Robert Palmer's Almshouses made possible by the generous benefaction of the Fire Brigade will be blessed after Evensong on Sunday, September 10. We cannot be too thankful that these improvements have made our Almshouses into really delightful and comfortable little homes.'

Sonning Regatta: 'It is some years now since we last held a Regatta in Sonning and meantime the various challenge cups have remained in the hands of those who won them last. In view of the uncertainty as to when a Regatta will be held here again, it has been thought best to collect the challenge cups and deposit them in a place of safety where they would be available if and when required. They have now been deposited for safe keeping with Barclay's Bank, King Street, Reading.'

Women's Institute: 'An extra meeting was held at the Pippin, by invitation of Mrs. Waide. After tea, members enjoyed going round Mr. Ewen's beautiful garden.'

October 1950

Pearson Hall: The original floor boarding of the hall had been replaced by a new oak flooring at a cost of almost £300. This had put the hall into debt, and it was noted that fund raising functions were to be organised in order to restore satisfactorily the hall's finances.

Choir Outing: 'The junior members of the choir accompanied by the Vicar, Organist and Verger, made a successful expedition to Worthing on September 2, for their annual outing.'

November 1950

The Vicar's Letter: 'I must congratulate Mr. and Mrs. Paddick on the magnificent result of the Rummage Sale for the Charville Hall, the total takings having come to £161. This entailed a great deal of hard work on their part, and some hectic moments on the part of all who so kindly undertook the selling of the articles.

We now look forward to our other efforts for the same good cause, and rely on your co-operation to make a success of them - socially as well as financially.'

St. Andrew's Sonning 1950 – from the Vicar and Parochial Church Council to all Parishioners of Sonning: This extensive item appealed for further donations to fund the new church hall at Charvil. It was confirmed that the site had been secured and that a licence to build had been granted by the ministry concerned. The cost of building was noted as £2,500, of which £1,494 had been received or promised. Various fund raising events were listed, including the distribution of an appeal envelope to every house in the parish urging parishioners to support the building fund.

Choir and Ringers' Supper: 'The supper arranged by our indefatigable organist, was given at the White Hart on October 5, when the sumptuous meal was greatly enjoyed. The toasts of Church and King, the Vicar, the Choir, the Bellringers, having been duly proposed and honoured, a musical programme followed, with everyone contributing to community singing, piano pieces were played by Mr. Davis and solos by Messrs. Evans and Siney.'

December 1950

The Vicar's Letter: 'Rejoice with them that do rejoice, and weep with them that weep. We do so readily with those who have been fortunate or unfortunate in the allocation of our Council houses. We also sympathise with those who have had the invidious task of allocating them.'

Almshouses: The trustees of the Sonning Almshouses had announced that in future they were to be known as "The Robert Palmer Cottages".

Pearson Hall: 'The proceeds of the Dance held on November 3 for the funds of the new floor amounted to £11. We are most grateful to Captain Somerville and those who helped him in arranging such a delightful evening. We note that the Working Men's Club are very kindly devoting the proceeds of their Christmas Whist Drive on December 21 to the same object, and we hope that their effort will be well supported.'

CHAPTER TWO

1951 - 1955

Throughout the early 1950's the magazine mostly consisted of four pages, occasional as many as eight pages. The typesetting, layout and general design of the magazine continued unaltered. The benefaction of a local Sonning resident, Captain Rotheram, gave considerable financial support to the magazine at this time which enabled the selling price to be contained whilst the magazine was able to avoid a serious financial loss.

The early years that followed the war saw great efforts made to recover from the numerous effects of the conflict. Locally, the beginning of a vast expansion of house building, with associated infrastructure, was taking place, particularly in Sonning's neighbouring parishes of Charvil, Woodley and Earley, where a substantial increase in population was beginning to occur. Several sporting and social clubs, within Sonning and neighbouring parishes, which had ceased during the hostilities, had now recommenced.

At a time when the British people were looking forward to a peaceful future, Britain soon becoming involved in another armed conflict with the outbreak of the Korean War (1950-1953), which resulted in a large number of British military service casualties. Furthermore, during this time and for many years hence, the threat of a devastating nuclear war against the Soviet Union, and her communist allies, remained a constant threat from which local residents would not have been immune.

January 1951

Parish Magazine: An article detailing various matters concerning the magazine was included in this issue. It was noted that Captain Rotheram had asked to cease responsibility for distributing, assisting with editing and arranging the printing of the magazine. He had also been responsible for providing financial support for the magazine which he had confirmed would continue. It was also mentioned that the printer, Mr. Cusden, had obtained new type for printing. The vicar, who had written the article, commented that the inset which had accompanied the magazine for some time "Church and Home" was to be replaced with the inset "Sign".

February 1951

St Andrew's Club: 'The St Andrew's Social Club Dramatic Group gave a capital entertainment in the Pearson Hall on the evening of Tuesday, January 16. Mrs. Prior, the producer, is to be warmly congratulated on the marked improvement of the players since their last performance.'

Children's Hour: 'Prizes for good attendance during 1950 were presented on January 7 to the following: Susan Hessell, Clive Benger, Graham Forward, Jill Inge, Angela Goodall, Cynthia Cole, Paula Wright, Ann Ansell, Margaret Hessell, Barry Goddard, Philip Patrick, George Preston, Dennis Eaton, Timothy Forward, Julie Fooks, Penelope West, Molly Butler, Ann Glasscock, Barry Glasscock, Beryl Matheson, Janet Lamb, Judith West.'

[*Considerable rainfall occurred during February 1951 and is recorded as the wettest February since 1870.*]

March 1951

Sonning Parochial Church Council – Report for 1950

The Report of the Vicar and P.C.C. to the Annual Church Meeting 1951 included the following:

'The clock face has been regilded at the charge of Captain Rotheram, to whom we are again indebted.

The Church working party under Mrs. Hoyle has again distinguished itself by making the two new carpets for the Chancel. This was done in under three months and reflects great credit on all the workers.

The Churchyard has been maintained as far as possible in a good state of tidiness throughout the year, Mr. Polden once again coming to our assistance during the summer.

The Church Primary School continues to grow in numbers and has now expanded into the old Girls' School, where Miss Fox's class now pursues its studies.

Our efforts for Post-War Needs this year realised the sum of £445 5s 5d, the largest sum raised in any year since the first year when we raised £506. To obtain this sum had entailed a great deal of hard work, and sacrificial giving of time, money and effort on the part of the whole parish. Our objective now is the building of the Church Hall at Charville, and throughout the year we have bent all our energies towards it.'

Sonning Parish Council: The following matters were reported from the meeting held on January 25:

'The attention of the Chief Constable had been drawn to the speed which lorries and cars were being driven through the village. The Chief Constable had replied that before long it was hoped to have a constable resident in the village.

As the Council felt the occupants of the new Council Houses would use the pathway through the allotments when going to and from the village the Council have asked the Wokingham Rural District Council to pay 1s 0d per annum for wayleave rent, to maintain the path and to fix a gate with an automatic spring at the exit from the Housing site.

It was agreed to write to the surveyor asking for the footpath from the Bull Hotel to the Little Deanery to be repaired as soon as possible. Attention was also drawn to the state of the towpath from the Bridge to the Lock.

Arrangements for the Festival of Britain; it was decided to ask all residents to make a special effort with their gardens.'

April 1951

Charville Hall: 'We have now been able to negotiate a loan of £500 from the Oxford Diocesan Board of Finance; the loan is offered at 1% and is repayable in six half yearly instalments starting on December 31 of this year, With this loan there will still be a gap of £200 between our assets and the estimated cost. A generous offer has come from a resident of Woodley to give £10 if nineteen other persons will do the same. Now then! Sonning must rise to this friendly challenge from Woodley! Three offers are to hand already. Now for the other sixteen. Offers will be thankfully received by Mr. Hoyle or the Vicar.'

May 1951

The Choir: 'For some time we have been wishing that the ladies of the choir could be robed in a manner fitting for the worship of the Church. The attainment of this desire was made possible by an anonymous gift of money for the purpose, and by the skill and devotion of the ladies who set themselves the task of making the new gowns.'

Wedding: 'A wedding is always a happy occasion, and none could have been happier than that of Roland Hunt and June Field on Easter Monday.   Both of them had lived from childhood in the village and had made themselves very popular among their fellows.'

Civil Defence: 'A moderately well attended meeting was held in the Pearson Hall on Tuesday, March 20, when a most interesting and informative address was given by Mr. Belcher, Berks County Civil Defence Officer.   Mr. Belcher explained the dangers and also the limitation of the Atom Bomb.'

[*The King and Queen open the Festival of Britain celebrations on London's South Bank of the Thames.*]

June 1951

The Vicar's Letter: 'We are expecting the Reading Blue Coat School parents to Church on Sunday morning, June 10, and the Freemasons of the Old Sunning Lodge and Chapter on June 24; it would be a help if as many members as possible of our congregation would bring their own Prayer books to Church on those occasions.'

Charville Hall: 'Two more gifts of £10 have come in – eight out of nineteen!   Watch the site, between Park View Drive and St Patrick's Avenue, for important developments.   The contract with Messrs. J. M. Jones of Maidenhead is now to hand for signature.'

July 1951

The Vicar's Letter: 'Most of the houses in Little Glebe are now occupied, and we offer the residents our best wishes for their future health and happiness.'

Scouts: 'The 1ˢᵗ Sonning Scouts and Cubs held their 4ᵗʰ Annual Sports Day on the Recreation Ground on Saturday, June 16. Commencing at 2.30pm a varied programme of events carried on until 7.30pm when the prizes were presented. The Events closed with a Camp Fire Sing Song.'

August 1951

[*The magazine now regularly comprised of four pages with the exception of the August issue which was contained to a single leaf of two printed pages.*]

Lay Reader: 'On June 30 Mr. Hoyle was formally admitted to the office of Parochial Lay Reader. The ceremony took place in the Latin Chapel of the Cathedral at Oxford. There were sixteen candidates, and the Bishop gave each one his blessing and commissioned him for his work, presenting him with a copy of the New Testament.'

Women's Institute: 'The July meeting was convened in the garden of "Heathlands" West Drive by invitation of Mrs. Riding (Vice-President) who was in the chair. A demonstration on "Original Salads" was given by Miss Cumming.'

September 1951

The Vicar's Letter: 'I have informed the Parochial Church Council of the Special Service it is intended to hold at 6.30pm on Sunday, September 16. This will be an act of Thanksgiving for two very special events (1) for the successful outcome of the Battle of Britain, which reached its climax in the middle of September 1940, and (2) for the Festival of Britain, which will be closing officially at the end of the month.'

Charville Hall: 'The walls of St Patrick's continue to rise and give promise of a fairly early completion of the building. A large number of furnishings and accessories will, of course, be required, and we hope that many of these will be gladly given as private donations.' There followed an extensive list of items which included an altar and altar rail, credence table, curtains, carpets, cross, candlesticks, prayer and reading desks etc.,

October 1951

The Vicar's Letter: Sidney Groves made comment of the illnesses which were currently afflicting the Bishop of Reading and also the once vicar of Sonning, Canon Wickham Legg, the latter being a patient in the Old Vicarage Nursing Home at Twyford.   Groves continued with the following news item: 'As we go to press, we learn that His Majesty's illness is more severe than was suspected; bound by loyalty and affection we add him to the list of the sick for whom we pray'.

Sunday School: 'New classes began on Sunday, September 9, and we were very pleased to welcome Mrs. Hamilton and Miss Ann Glasscock as regular Sunday School teachers and Mrs. Scott-Buccleuch as our "reserve".'

The Bells of Sonning: Appearing within this issue were the four verses of "The Bells of Sonning" composed by Ernest H. A. Home which was reprinted by kind permission from the Reading Mercury Newspaper. [*see: page 54*]

[*The General Election held on 25 October results in a clear majority for the Tory Party under the leadership of seventy-seven years old Winston Churchill. The Conservatives win 321 seats, Labour 295, Liberals 6 and others 3.*]

November 1951

Harvest Festival: 'The Harvest Festival was duly observed on September 30, when a rich profusion of flowers, fruit and vegetables bedecked the Church, and we were delighted that larger congregations than we have seen at such an occasion for many years filled the Church.'

Was Sonning ever a Roman Settlement?: 'Built into the tower of Sonning Church, chiefly in the battlements at the top, are a number of red brick tiles.   They bear a remarkable resemblance to similar tiles found in the remains of such Roman buildings as Burgh Castle in Norfolk and Pevensey Castle in Sussex.   The interesting question arises, "are these tiles Roman and, if so, how did they get into their present position"? A fragment picked up in the Vicarage garden is believed to be Roman, but it is too small for certain identification.'

December 1951

The Vicar's Letter: 'We learn with regret that Captain Rotheram finds himself unable to continue his most generous subsidy to the Parish Magazine; we desire him to accept our sincerest and warmest thanks for his most liberal contributions which have enabled us to print all the parish news sent in to us without much omission or contraction. I am afraid we shall find no one to take his place, and therefore shall presumably have to consider the possible alternatives of cutting down the local matter or of increasing the charge.'

Reading Blue Coat School: 'The Headmaster and Staff of the Blue Coat School have decided that, as there is so much difficulty in having their plays performed both in Reading and in Sonning during the same week, they must run them alternatively, one year in Reading and one in Sonning.'

Rangers: 'November 11 saw the first public appearance of the Crew's burgee since its dedication last year, when the Crew was pleased to share in the Armistice Parade organised by the British Legion. After the service, eleven of the Crew, kindly helped by Brown Owl and three Guides, took off their nylons and their best shoes and paddled across the Mill House garden to reach their boats, which they brought out from the now flooded Thames.'

Charville Hall Dedication: 'The sums which have come in this autumn now amount to £409. We regret to say that it seems probable that we shall have to ask the Lord Bishop to postpone his visit to dedicate the hall as the wet weather has seriously affected the progress of the building.'

January 1952

The Magazine: 'For reasons mentioned in the December issue, with the additional reason that the cost of production has again gone up, it has been decided with great reluctance that we must increase the price at once to four pence per copy. We earnestly hope that all readers will continue to support us, knowing that even with this increase, the Magazine will still be running at a loss.'

THE BELLS OF SONNING

The old bells of Sonning
  Ring over river and lea
The kind bells of Sonning
  Scatter their melody
Lavishly as a giver
  Open of heart and hand
And it is to the soul forever
  As rain to a thirsty land

The sweet bells of Sonning
  Up in their ancient tower
Sing of the spotless lily
  The rose and the passion flower
And I think of the bells of Sonning
  That sang to an evening sky
When summer was June and heaven
  Grew suddenly strangely nigh

The glad bells of Sonning
  Are singing again today
And the river that runs through Sonning
  Is bearing their song away
Through league and league of homeland
  Down to the waiting sea
Till the winds and the quiet waters
  Are frightened by melody

The clear bells of Sonning
  They challenge the heart of youth
They speak to the old of blessing
  Of peace and the path of truth
And many there be that sorrow
  And many there be that roam
Who dream that the bells of Sonning
  Are calling the weary home

Ernest H. A. Home, *Komoka, Ontario, Canada*

[*see: page 52*]

February 1952

Richard Wickham Legg – Vicar of Sonning 1926-1942: 'All his friends will have learnt with affectionate regret that our late Vicar and Archdeacon has passed to his rest. Canon Wickham Legg was born in 1867 at West Farleigh in Kent, the son of the Rev. William Legg. He was educated at Harrow and New College and ordained deacon in 1892 and priest in 1893.'

Christmas: 'We are most grateful to those who supplied as well as those who arranged the flowers and greenery for the Church decorations, which combined with the soft glow of the candles at the early Eucharist to help in creating the true atmosphere of the Christmas worship.'

[*King George VI (1895-1952) dies in his sleep at Sandringham House on 6 February. Princess Elizabeth returns immediately from a visit to Kenya and is proclaimed Queen, as Elizabeth II.*]

March 1952

The Vicar's Letter: 'Hardly ever can the news of a King's passing have come with such a sudden shock to the ears of his people! We pray for our late King and for those dear to him at this solemn time; for our Queen we ask God's gifts of wisdom, strength and fortitude to enable Her Majesty to happily and confidently discharge the duties of her high calling.'

Sonning Church Schools: 'The School Managers and the Parochial Church Council have agreed to apply for "Aided" status for our school. This means that the school will continue as a fully-ordered church school as at present, the religious instruction and the appointment of teachers remaining in the hands of the Church. Secular instruction will continue to be the responsibility of the Local Education Authority. The State will share fifty-fifty with us the cost of all repairs and improvements, including the cost of the transfer of the school to its new site to the south of the Recreation Ground. We mean to forward and maintain the trust bequeathed to us by many past generations of preserving the security of a Christian education in a Christian atmosphere for all Sonning children who care to make use of it.'

April 1952
Sonning Parochial Church Council – Report for 1951
The Report of the Vicar and P.C.C. to the Annual General Meeting of
Church Electors 1952 included the following:
'There have been no alterations to the fabric of the Church, which has been
inspected by the Diocesan Surveyor, the cost of his survey and consequent
repairs being defrayed by the Caroline Palmer Charity.
The Church Primary School has had another satisfactory year of work under
Mr. Chapman's leadership, without change of staff.
The Council acknowledges the debt of gratitude owed to Mr. C. Ripley for his
work as Hon. Architect of the Charville Hall. Building operations began on
the site during the summer, and we have arranged for the opening by the Lord
Bishop on March 30.
Towards the end of the year the Council successfully applied for a faculty for
the alteration of the Choirboys' Stalls in the chancel, to a plan again most
kindly designed by Mr. Ripley.'

Sonning P C C Accounts:
Accounts for year ended December 31, 1951 included the following:
'The Parish Magazine account showed an income of £37 6s 5d from sales of
the magazine and in addition donations for extra pages of £36. The cost of
printing was £64 9s 0d and the purchase of the inset "The Sign" £7 1s 8d.'

Sonning Parish Council: The following matters were included within the
report of the meeting held on February 29:
'The glad news that Reading Town Council had abandoned its scheme for
bringing Reading's sewerage to Sonning was generally known in January last.
The clerk reported that she had discussed the question of the bus service
through the village with the Thames Valley Traffic Manager. The Manager
would be glad if anyone left behind would notify him of the day and time.'

May 1952
The Vicar's Letter: 'We are glad that the snow and wintery conditions
did not prevent the Lord Bishop reaching Sonning on March 30 to
dedicate St. Patrick's. We are most grateful to him for coming, for his
conduct of the service and for his sermon. An excellent start has been
made with Church, Sunday School and social activities. I ask your
continued prayers for all the work we try to do there.'

Girl Guides: 'Janet Lamb has made history in the Company this month by being the first Sonning Guide to qualify for the Little House Emblem. This emblem, awarded to the holders of the six Home-craft Badges – Cook, Child Nurse, Homemaker, Hostess, Laundress and Needlewoman – bears the design of the Little House presented to our Queen when she was a child by the people of Wales.'

Sonning Cricket Club: 'At a well attended Annual General Meeting held on March 21, with Mr. C. H. Williams in the chair, it was reported that the 1951 season had shown a good all-round improvement in the club's affairs. Although the actual results of the 29 games played were a little disappointing with 9 won, 10 lost and 10 drawn, nevertheless the cricket was very enjoyable and there were some good individual performances with both bat and ball.'

Mothers' Union: 'The monthly meeting was held at the Vicarage on Thursday, April 3. Mrs. Groves said that arrangements were being made for "Women's Afternoons" at Charvil Hall, and she hoped the first one would be in May.'
[*This was the first occasion within the magazine that the spelling of Charville was replaced with Charvil.*]

June 1952
The Vicar's Letter: 'I am glad to say that the Oxford Diocesan Magazine gave a considerable amount of its space to an account of the Dedication of St Patrick's, passing on to its readers my question whether it is the first Elizabethan Church to be completed.'

Sonning School Aided Status: It was noted that the Diocesan Council of Education had approved the Sonning application for aided status, as reported in the March 1952 issue of the parish magazine. In this June issue details were printed of the funding requirement for the new school. The cost of the project had been estimated at £20,000 of which £4,000 was considered to be the amount for which the school managers would be responsible, after realising an estimated £4,000 via the sale of the existing buildings. A loan under the Diocesan Capital Scheme was envisaged in order to adequately fund the school managers required contribution.

July 1952
Choir Festival: 'Under the enthusiastic inspiration of Mr. L. F. B. Davis our Organist, over one hundred men, ladies, boys and girls of local church choirs assembled at Sonning on Saturday, June 14, to hold their annual festival, representing the choirs of Sonning, Dunsden, Earley, Woodley, Twyford and Caversham.'

Civil Defence: 'I have been requested by the Wokingham Civil Defence Officer, Colonel Galbraith, to make an appeal for volunteers for the Civil Defence Organisation from the Parish of Sonning, both men and women. In time of national emergency Civil Defence would play a vital role, but organisation and training in advance are absolutely essential. This appeal has the full support of Sonning Parish Council.'

August 1952
The Vicar's Letter: 'I am indeed grateful for all the kind messages of good wishes that have reached me on the occasion of my appointment by the Lord Bishop as Rural Dean both from you, my parishioners, and from the clergy and laity of the Rural Deanery.'

Another Increase: 'The Registrar General, Somerset House, announces that by an Order in Council dated May 19, 1952, most fees fixed by the Registration Acts are to be increased by one-half as from July 1. The increased costs which are most likely to affect parishioners are: marriage certificate increasing from 2s 6d to 3s 9d and baptism certificate from 1s 0d to 1s 6d.'

Women's Institute: 'The monthly meeting was convened in the garden at Olde Tudor Place by invitation of Mrs. S. Paddick, on Tuesday, July 8, Mrs. A. Riding being in the chair. The Matron of the Royal Berkshire Hospital gave a talk on nursing as a career.'

September 1952
The Vicar's Letter: 'September will mark the end of the holiday season and the resumption of some of our winter activities. The end and purpose of summer is fitly commemorated in the Harvest Festival. This will, of course, be the very first time this festival has been celebrated at St Patrick's.

The news that the hitherto respected Foreign Secretary has entered into a so-called "marriage" with the Prime Minister's niece during the lifetime of his own wife has come as an outrageous shock to Christian sentiment throughout the land.'

[Anthony Eden, latter to become prime minister, married Clarissa the niece of Winston Churchill on August 14, 1952.]

Pearson Hall: 'The Committee has been investigating the possibility of building a further addition to the Hall in order to provide improved accommodation for the cooking and serving of refreshments. A plan has been prepared involving an estimated expenditure of £500, towards which sum the Committee has received two most generous offers, *viz* £250 from the Sonning Volunteer Fire Brigade Trust and £100 from the Trustees of a war-time fund known as "Salute the Soldier".'

October 1952
The Vicar's Letter: 'The Dedication Festival, on October 5, will afford us all a splendid opportunity of making a real handsome birthday present to our beautiful old Mother Church of St Andrew, and I feel sure that all who love her will do all that is possible in this respect. She has stood here as our spiritual home where the Father dispenses his bounteous spiritual gifts for countless generations. For her and also for her infant daughter, St Patrick's Church, the Church Council urges your generous support.

We learn, that Nurse Rostron will be retiring and leaving the village at the end of September. There can be few houses in Sonning which our good nurse has not entered at one time or another during her many years of devoted service. We bid her our affectionate and grateful farewell.'

Rangers: 'The Crew were placed third in the Berkshire Regatta in July, only two points behind the winners. Mary Franklin, Stella Dyster and Suzanne Crowder won the event for the best style of rowing and boat handling, and will represent the county against all the other counties bordering on the Thames at the Thames Sea Ranger Regatta to be held at Kingston on October 4. We still meet in the Mill Garden and will not be moving to the Sonning Recreation Ground Pavilion until the early days of October.'

November 1952

Coronation of H. M. The Queen: 'A Public Meeting to consider plans for the celebration of Coronation Day [June 2, 1953] in Sonning was held on October 17 in the Pearson Hall. After considerable discussion it was decided to hold our local celebration on Coronation Day itself. A General Committee, to consist of representatives of all village clubs and organisations, with powers to add to their numbers, was appointed. The Ministry of Local Government was expected to authorise a reasonable expenditure out of the rates to defray expenses.'

National Memorial to King George VI: 'At the close of the meeting to discuss Coronation arrangements the Chairman read extracts from a communication he had received from the Chairman of the Wokingham District Council inviting every parish in the district to organise a collection on behalf of the fund. The meeting unanimously agreed to organise a house-to-house collection, and Mrs. Powell very kindly undertook to take the lead in this matter and organise a team of collectors.'

Nurse Rostron: 'A very large and representative gathering met in the Pearson Hall on Friday, October 3, to bid farewell to Nurse Rostron on her retirement from the post of District Nurse at Sonning. Mr. Hoyle took the chair and said that Nurse Rostron came to the village in 1928, in the days of the old Sonning and Woodley Nursing Association, and had served the village well and faithfully for twenty-four years. He then called upon Mrs. Powell to present her with a cheque for £100 which had been collected in the village as a parting gift.'

[*Dwight D. Eisenhower, who spent a period of time in Sonning during World War II, is elected President of the United States of America on November 5, 1952.*]

December 1952

St Patrick's: 'We have received the gift of a beautiful Altar Cross made of white-brass, which harmonises with the candlesticks and is the product of a real craftsman's art. For this gift to the little Church we are indebted to Mr. and Mrs. Cedric Ripley, who have made this splendid addition to all the gifts of Mr. Ripley's valuable time and architectural skill which he has already given to St Patrick's.'

1st Sonning Brownie Pack: 'We welcome two more Brownies to the Pack this month, Susan Blandy, who has joined the Fairy Six, and Heather May, the Pixies. Diane Snowball, Iris Turner and Katherine Bailey have all gained their 1st Year Stars.'

Welfare Centre: 'A Welfare Centre is being opened in the New Year at St Patrick's Hall. It is to be hoped that many mothers and young children will attend from Sonning as well as from Charvil, and all will be sure of a welcome.'

[*Queen Elizabeth II makes her first Christmas broadcast. The Queen also gives permission to have the Coronation televised.*]

January 1953
The Vicar's Letter: 'The year will stand out in importance as the year of the Coronation of Elizabeth the Second, "our gracious Queen and Governor", which will inaugurate with the Divine Blessing and Unction what we hope and pray will be a long and happy reign for Her Majesty and her widely-spread people. We must bend our energies that this country may become what in some measure it used to be, a truly Christian land. Our young Sovereign will not fail in this – we must not let her down by our failure to match our faith and purpose with hers.'

Kneelers: 'We are most grateful to the Vicar and Churchwardens of Woodley who have allowed us to have 120 kneeling-pads out of the stock of 200 which they received in their turn from St Laurence's, Reading. We have divided them between the two churches where they will meet a real need.'

King George VI National Memorial Fund: 'The collection which was made in Sonning for the National Memorial to our late King George realised a sum of £29.'

Church of England Children's Society: 'On November 5 the Sonning branch sent as their representative Evelyn Potter to present a purse to Her Royal Highness the Duchess of Gloucester at the Albert Hall. Mrs. McLaren accompanied Evelyn and they both had a very happy time and felt proud that Sonning was able to contribute to the collection.'

February 1953

Christmas: 'The Churches were, as usual, beautifully decorated for the Feast, thanks to our devoted band of decorators. The early Eucharists were well attended, and the Choir and Organist rendered their parts of the services with their usual zeal. We all enjoyed the little family service at St Patrick's in the afternoon, and the little Nativity Play presented there by the children of St Patrick's Sunday School on the following Sunday.'

The Chapel Hall: 'The trustees of the Congregational Chapel in High Street, having decided that there is at the moment no need for using it as a place of worship for members of their denomination, have leased it to the Vicar and the Churchwardens at a low rental, to be used for religious and educational purposes. The obvious use of it is for a Youth Centre where the boys and girls can hold their Scout and Guide meetings. This is a great boon, and we are indeed grateful to the Chapel authorities for their generous offer.'

[*The government announces the end of sweet rationing.*]

March 1953

The Vicar's Letter: 'I am sorry to have cancelled so many engagements and to have been so long getting rid of the influenza. I gather that I am by no means the only one to have caught this particular plague.

We have all been deeply shocked by the terrible disasters which have followed so closely upon one another at the beginning of this month. We would express our sympathy with all those who have suffered bereavement, loss of house and belongings and health as a result either of the shipping disaster or the floods.'

[*On January 31 a British Rail car ferry sank off Belfast Lough with the loss of 128 lives. Hurricane winds and high tides, during early February, caused devastation to areas of England's East Coast resulting in over 500 deaths and many thousands rendered homeless.*]

The Floods: 'Sonning "Little Comforts" Collection for the East Coast devastated homes. The idea was welcomed by Miss Finch of W. V. S., who hopes to send our contributions to one district as the gifts are very individual. The idea of a collection to be sorted here and the gifts to be placed in small bags of blackout material met with a good response. We group our demand for "comforts" under practical headings of: work basket accessories, toilet requisites, writing needs, top drawer contents. Forty-five bags were duly filled by kind friends and there was a nice case of men's ties, collars, shaving tackle and large handkerchiefs and small combs.'

Sonning Parochial Church Council – Report for 1952
The Report of the Vicar and P.C.C. to the Annual General Meeting of Church Electors 1953 included the following:
'Extensive repairs were carried out to the heating apparatus during the summer, the cost of this, as well as that of the entire insurance premium of the Church, being borne by the Susanna Caroline Palmer Charity.
The beauty of the interior of the Church has been enhanced by the removal of the lectern to the south side of the Church away from the centre, and by the substitution of beautifully wrought oak choir stalls for the iron and wood fixture at which the choirboys formerly knelt.
The chief parochial event of the year was the completion and opening of St Patrick's Church Hall, Charvil. The Hall was built at a cost of £2,635 to the design of our Vice-Chairman, Mr. C. Ripley who acted as Honorary Architect. We desire to express our deep gratitude for the voluntary services of our Lay Reader, Mr. F. J. Hoyle, who now regularly conducts Evensong and preaches at one or other of the Churches every Sunday.
Owing to the opening of the Sunday School at St Patrick's, the Sunday School at the Parish Church has suffered an inevitable decrease in numbers. We are glad to welcome Miss M. Poynter to our staff at St Andrew's, while the staff at St Patrick's consists of Mrs. Denton, Mrs. Hamilton, Miss Brooks, Miss Glasscock, Mrs. Scott-Buccleuch and Mrs. Gale.
The Church Primary School continues to flourish under Mr. Chapman, assisted as before by Miss Fox, Miss Wilkens and Miss Simmonds.'

Sonning P.C.C. Accounts:
Accounts for year ended December 31, 1952 included the following:
'Our Church Account, opened the year with a debit balance of £35 3s. 5d, and closed with a credit balance of £45 3s 5d.
The cost of the new choir stall was defrayed from the Venner Bequest.
The Parish Magazine, previously subsidised by a generous parishioner, shows a very substantial loss on the year, a balance in hand of £15 1s 7d having

become, at the end of the year, a debit balance of £22 19s 0d. The position in regard to this matter will call for careful consideration by the Council.
St Patrick's Hall has so far proved self-supporting and ended the year with a balance in hand of £20 17s 5d.'

April 1953
The Vicar's Letter: 'All our regular worshippers will have heard with great regret of the resignation of our Organist, Mr. L. F. B. Davis, on his appointment as Organist and Choirmaster of Christchurch, Reading. During his seven years' work here, he has really transformed the music of our services out of all recognition. We feel that we are losing not only an organist and choirmaster, but a real friend.'

Confetti: 'Those attending weddings are asked to refrain from throwing confetti in the churchyard; confetti is very unsightly, very difficult to sweep up and causes a lot of extra and unnecessary labour. If wedding guests would kindly restrain or postpone their natural enthusiasm, affection, *joie de vivre*, or whatever it is that causes them to throw confetti, until they are outside God's acre, it would be much appreciated.'

May 1953
The Vicar's Letter: 'May I first express my warmest thanks to you all for contributing once again and so generously to my Easter offering.
We would join in the world-wide tribute of affection and respect to Queen Mary, who has so abundantly earned our gratitude for her example of Christian steadfastness in times of peace and war, through joy and distress, in sickness and in health. God grant her light and peace in Paradise.'
[*Queen Mary of Teck (1867-1953) the widow of King George V and grandmother of Queen Elizabeth II. Queen Mary died in her sleep at Marlborough House, London on March 25, 1953.*]

Women's Institute: 'The monthly meeting was held in the Pearson Hall on April 14, Mrs. T. Edwards presiding. A demonstration on Pressure Cookery was given by Miss Vowles, the cooked rabbit later being won by Mrs. Cox. The Woodley Group Cup was won by Sonning for four hand-made Coronation buttonholes.'

Prayer for Animals: 'The Prayer Book (even the revision of 1928) is completely lacking in any prayer for animals, but the following beautiful prayer appears, with the approval of the Lord Bishop, in the current number of the Oxford Diocesan Magazine:

"Hear our humble prayer, O God, for our friends the animals, Thy creatures.
We pray especially for all that are suffering in any way;
For the overworked and underfed, the hunted, lost or hungry;
For all in captivity or ill-treated, and those that must be put to death
We entreat for them Thy mercy and pity, and for those who deal with them
we ask a heart of compassion, gentle hands and kindly words
Make us able to be true friends to animals and so more worthy followers
of our merciful Lord and Saviour, Jesus Christ"

The rule of man over the lower orders of creation is, of course, in the nature of a trust; for his treatment of them man will have to answer hereafter.'

June 1953

The Queen's Coronation: The June issue of the magazine provided details of the services and events that were planned for the Coronation. On the day of the Coronation (Tuesday, June 2) it was announced that a television was to be made available for viewing during the day in the boys' school. At St Andrew's, a peal of bells was to be rung at the moment that the Queen is crowned. Details of various other events were given which included a fancy dress procession around Sonning, sports at the recreation ground, an evening dance in the Pearson Hall and finally an illuminated procession of boats on the Thames starting from Sonning Lock.

Coronation Decorations in Sonning: 'The Coronation Committee are making arrangements for the decorations of the Pearson Hall and the Sonning Recreation Ground. With these exceptions they appeal to all householders to mark this historic occasion by decorating their own houses according to individual tastes. It is suggested that residents should combine with their neighbours on opposite sides of the roads and hang strings of pennants across the road in order to give a festive air to the village.'

Berkshire Grammar Schools Scholarships: 'Two children from Sonning School were awarded Grade A scholarships; Dennis Eaton is expected to join Maidenhead Grammar and Valerie Kite to the Abbey School,'

Challenge Cups for Swimming: 'There are two Challenge Cups for Swimming, which were competed for at the Sonning Regatta until 1937. Radman Wanamaker Challenge Cup and Canon Holmes Challenge Cup. The first of these is kept in the bank but the Holmes Cup is missing. Information to its whereabouts will be gratefully received.'

July 1953

The Vicar's Letter: Sidney Groves used his *Letter* to provide the following account of Coronation Day: 'The Coronation has come and gone, leaving behind it the memory of a most august service, beautifully and reverently performed, the deep and abiding impression of the devotion and dignity of "our most religious and gracious Queen," and the hoped for sense that our nation has turned the corner into a new and more firmly founded future. One need say no more about the Coronation – every item was faithfully recorded on the wireless and television, so that all our people could take a part in the solemnity. For the future the Church, as always, will exercise her priestly function in offering her continuous prayer on behalf of both Her Majesty the Queen and the Commonwealth.

Our own local celebrations were carried out in accordance with the programme arranged, the rain being not permitted to interfere with any of its details, except that only three illuminated boats were to be seen. We are indeed grateful to all those who helped by long preparation as well as by their exertions on the day to celebrate this great occasion in so suitable style. Especially we must thank the Chairman and Secretary of the Committee who worked indefatigably over a period of many months for our entertainment. We were informed that they were going to be driven around the village together in the famous brougham; we were disappointed in this, though of course we were delighted to see the bevy of beauties – other beauties, I mean – who actually did take their seats in the conveyance!

On the religious side, the pre-Coronation services were well attended, and the Church was well-filled for the Sung Eucharist on the morning of Coronation Day, when there were 110 Communicants.'

August 1953

The Vicar's Letter: Sidney Groves commenced his monthly comments by mentioning the terrible shock felt in the village following the sudden death of two young children. He expressed his deepest sympathy to their parents and prayed that the children would find complete fulfilment and bliss in Paradise.

Groves also expressed gratitude to Miss Keefe, who was no longer living locally, for her devoted work for the local girl guides over so many years. It was noted that Miss Mary Russell had now taken over Miss Keefe's role and the vicar expressed his gratitude to her and wished her every success.

Winter Campaign: 'A Committee is being formed to run once more a Winter Campaign for Church funds. The Church Council is deeply concerned over the financial position and asks the assistance and sympathetic support of all Christian people in the Parish. Unusual expenditure is being incurred in these three directions:-
(1) The Churchyard, where a full-time worker is now employed. (2) Completion of the payments for St Patrick's. (3) Maintenance of Aided Status for our Church School.

September 1953

The Vicar's Letter: 'We have been delighted to rejoice in real summer weather this August, and we hope that this has coincided with the holidays of most of you.
It is worth noting, that, in the old deed of trusteeship relating to the Congregational Chapel, the street in which it is situated was then (1807) known as "Silver Street" – it would be interesting to know when this name was changed to "The Street" or to "High Street".'

St Patrick's Fair: 'We most heartily congratulate all those responsible for running the St Patrick's Fair on August 22. The Fair was opened by Mrs. Groves, who also gave away the prizes. Everyone worked together with a will and a most friendly and enthusiastic spirit. There were darts, hidden-treasure, bowling for a tea-set, excellent teas and all the fun of the fair. We are pleased to be able to report a profit for the Church Hall Building Fund of £41 18s. 0d.'

Sonning Church School: 'The Annual Prize-Day ceremony took place at the Vicarage on Friday, July 24. The Headmaster reported that during the year, two of Her Majesty's Inspectors had visited the school and had commented very favourably on the work that they saw. A very good Scripture report had been received from the Diocesan Inspector and the Local Authority was going to provide a medical inspection room at the Girl's School.'

October 1953

The Vicar's Letter:
'Summer has ended in a blaze of golden glory, and those of us who took late holidays are grateful for the weather we enjoyed. The harvest too has been abundant, we can thank God for all the many blessings of this notable Coronation year.

Scouts and Cubs: 'The 1st Sonning Scouts – with the assistance of their Committee – are at the moment busily engaged in putting in electric light and heat to the Chapel Hall, High Street. When this is completed the Hall will become their headquarters, together with the Rangers, Guides and Brownies.'

November 1953

Sonning C. of E. School: 'The Berkshire Education Committee has decided that the following examinations will be held this educational year: Preliminary Test, Intelligence Test and the Main examination in Arithmetic, English and English Composition.'

Women's Institute: 'Mr. Barnes gave an interesting talk on Perennial Flower Borders and judged the competition of a posy in an egg cup, awarding the prize to Misses M. South, R. Harman and Ann Edwards. Sonning won the cup at the Woodley Group Meeting for articles made from a 22-inch Turkish square.'

Church Flowers: 'Members of the Men's and Women's Sections of the British Legion have now undertaken to provide 34 bunches which are placed below the War Memorial Plaques on Remembrance Sunday.'

[*The new Ford Popular car is released for sale at £390 including tax.*]

December 1953

The Magazine: 'Through financial pressure we are compelled to say goodbye to the Castleden Press, who under this title and that of Messrs. J. Cusden & Co., have been our printers for many years, and we thank the firm for their long period of service. We are now engaging the services of Messrs. Luff & Sons, of Slough, who will be responsible for our printing from next year.'

[*With the exception of the typeface used for the title "St Andrew's, Sonning", the appearance of the magazine remained virtually unchanged following the move of the contract to another printer.*]

St Patrick's Youth Club: 'Our membership has now increased to over forty, and our activities during November have consisted of our Club Nights, a Beetle Drive and a Whist Drive. On the Whist Drive we made a profit, we are glad to say, and wish to thank those who gave the prizes and refreshments.'

The Old Wooden Bridge: An extensive article by F. J. H. appeared in this issue concerning the old wooden bridge which spanned the two streams between the Mill and the French Horn Hotel: 'All that it left now is the iron railing which runs between the road and river from the iron bridge to the Horse Bridge. The first authentic mention of the bridge is dated 1762, when there was a bridge on either side of the backwaters; the bridge on the Mill side being called *Mill Bridge* and the one on the French Horn side *Hall's Bridge.*' From the early 1800's until 1892 when the County of Oxford assumed responsibility for the bridge, the owners of the Mill were financially liable for all repairs. The new steel bridge was constructed at a cost of nearly £8,000. The *Reading Mercury* in March 1904 commented: 'After being closed for nine months the new bridge was opened for vehicular traffic on Wednesday.'

January 1954

Campanology: 'On Saturday, November 28, eight members of the Diocesan Guild of Bellringers rang up the bells of St Andrew's Church a peal of Lincolnshire Surprise Major, 5,024 changes in the space of three hours and seventeen minutes. It was specially arranged in honour of the Patronal Festival, and it was the first time that a peal in this method had been rung in the tower.'

February 1954

The Vicar's Letter:

'May I express my gratitude to the Sonning Fire Brigade and all other Societies who have made possible the building of the new kitchen at the Pearson Hall. We also owe our thanks to the architect, Mr. Hives, and the builder, Mr. Paddick for the satisfactory completion of the scheme.' The cost of the new kitchen, including architect's fees amounted to £566 15s. 4d. A number of donations were received to defray this cost, particularly £350 from the Sonning Fire Brigade and £108 from the "Salute the Soldier" fund.

Winter Campaign: 'Our next item under this heading will be a Concert to be given by the Reading Lady Singers, conducted by Mr. Lusty, which will be held in the Pearson Hall, on Tuesday, March 16. The guest solo pianist will be Auriole Hill, while vocal solos will be contributed by Mary Seymour and Doris Goatley.'

Sonning School: A contribution from Mr. Chapman, headmaster of the school, commented upon improvements that had taken place in both the boys' and girls' schools: 'I am pleased to report that the making of a decent playground at the girls' school has now commenced and should be completed by the end of January. The ground has been levelled, and a good foundation laid which will be covered with tarmac, and concrete paths have been constructed. During the Christmas holidays the proposed alteration to the toilet facilities at the boys' school was finished in a highly successful manner.'

March 1954

Choir and Bellringers' Annual Dinner: 'The Dinner was held at the White Hart Hotel on Wednesday, February, 17 when some thirty-two members sat down together and spent a very enjoyable evening, with the Vicar in the chair. The toast to the Choir and Organist was proposed by the Vicar, who mentioned the great progress which the Choir had made under Mr. L. F. B. Davis and later under Mr. A. H. Lusty who had succeeded him.'

Grit and Grace: The following was reproduced from the *Reader's Digest:* 'A widow, who had been left with six sons to bring up, was asked how she had managed to raise such exceptional sons alone and unaided. "It did take grit and grace" she said, "but I wasn't exactly unaided – the good Lord helped me. Every night I knelt and told Him I'd furnish the grit if He'd furnish the grace".'

Robert Palmer Cottages: 'At the Almshouse Charity Trustees' Meeting on January 27 the application of Miss Ellen Keates for the vacancy was accepted. The Trustees are only sorry that they could not provide all the applicants with accommodation.'

[*It is announced that a television licence will increase from £2 to £3 from June 1. The government introduces a Television Bill to create an Independent Television Authority.*]

April 1954
Pearson Hall: 'The Pearson Hall Committee has regretfully decided that they must now increase the charges for the hiring of the Hall.' There followed a list of revised charges to be made, which included – political meetings £2 10s. 0d, whist drives and socials £1 10s. 0d and private parties at 7s. 6d per hour with a minimum charge of £1 5s. 0d.

Sonning Parochial Church Council – Report for 1953
The Report of the Vicar and P.C.C. to the Annual General Meeting 1954 included the following:
'In the course of the annual survey of the fabric of the Church, carried out at the expense of the Caroline Palmer Charity, the Diocesan Surveyor, Mr. Judd, has discovered the activity of the Death Watch Beetle in the floor and supporting joists of the south side of the Nave of the Parish Church.
St Patrick's Hall has been very largely self supporting, although there is a reduction of £14 in the balance in hand, and our thanks are due to all those who have helped to place this venture on a sound financial footing.
The Parish Magazine has for the last two years been a heavy charge on our Church funds, and an amount of no less than £77 has had to be paid out from the General Account to defray the loss, leaving a net balance in hand of £195 in the General Account. New arrangements have been made for this year's magazine which, it is hoped, will avoid any further loss, while maintaining the magazine substantially in its present form.
The cost of the care of the Churchyard has increased from £178 to £290, due to the provision of extra labour.'

May 1954

Bells: 'In the latest volume of the Berkshire Archaeological Journal there is an article by Frederick Sharpe, (one of a series on the Church Bells of Berkshire), in which he describes our bells. On the top of the Tower roof there is a cupola, in which hangs the bell upon which the Church Clock strikes. Of this bell Mr. Sharpe says that it is a valuable one of the thirteenth century. It was formerly hung for ringing, and retained its clapper and headstock; the latter is incised with the date 1822, and the initials "R. G." probably those of the bell-hanger. The bell is now hung "dead" and is struck by a clock hammer.'

1st Sonning Guide Company: 'For our hike on March 27 we walked to Miss Hodgkinson's farm, and very soon we had four hike fires going, ready to cook our tea. It was quite an adventure for some of the Guides as they had only recently come up from the Brownie Pack.'

June 1954

The Vicar's Letter: 'You will see that I am holding a Quiet Day for the Clergy of the Sonning Deanery here on June 15, when we shall be using the Church for services and addresses and for the quiet times in between – as well as the Vicarage and garden. Please do not disturb this short period of retreat by loud talking in or near the Church between 8am and 7pm.'

Robert Palmer Charity: 'Attention is being drawn to the notices exhibited in various places regarding the forthcoming distribution of the Robert Palmer for the Poor Charity, usually given in coal. Residents of the parishes of Sonning, Woodley, Eye and Dunsden, and Sonning Common are eligible (this includes Charvil of course).'

July 1954

The Vicar's Letter: 'The death of our Bishop [Kenneth Kirk], "K.O." as he was familiarly known in the Diocese, has come to us as a tremendous shock. It has meant more to me than to most of you, because I have had closer contact with him, particularly as Rural Dean and Chairman of the Diocesan Voluntary Education Committee. You will remember his delightful and inspiring Confirmation address as well as his blessing of St Patrick's Church Hall. His sudden death leaves many problems to be solved, and it is doubtful now whether Mr. Knell will be able to take over the Archdeaconry from the present Bishop of Reading on July 1 as planned.'

United Choirs Festival: 'The service was held at St Andrew's Church, when the clergy and choirs of the daughter (and grand-daughter) churches whose parishes have been formed out of the ancient parish of Sunning (*sic*) took place. A most remarkable sermon was given by the Rev. S. C. Robinson, of St Peter's Earley. The occasion had something of the atmosphere of a family gathering and we were happy once again to welcome the Churches of St Peter's Earley, St Bartholomew's Reading, St John's Woodley. All Saints' Dunsden, St Nicholas Earley, and St Patrick's Charvil home for the evening.'

[*All food rationing ends after fourteen years. Meat is the last item to be released.*]

August 1954
The Vicar's Letter: 'We are glad to welcome visitors to our church during the summer months; the Churchwardens, Sidesmen and Verger take pains to see that all have books, seats and hassocks, but all our people should do their best to see that their neighbours in church are at home and have everything that they require – Christian people do not need any introduction to their fellow-worshippers.'

Sonning School: 'For the benefit of those parents whose children are attending the school for the first time, please note that the school uniform is obtainable at Langston's, Friar Street, Reading. This uniform is by no means compulsory, but after all children do have to wear clothes, and school clothes cost no more than any other. We believe that our caps, badges, blazers and ties look smart, and besides that they are distinctive.'

September 1954
Fire Brigade Success: 'The Sonning Fire Brigade competing in the "Extension Ladder and Hose Reel Drill" in the Berkshire and Reading Fire Brigade Annual Competitions on Saturday, June 19, were successful in winning the "Wantage Perpetual Challenge Cup" for the best time by a team consisting entirely of Part Time Firemen.'

The University Farm: 'All of us will be sorry that Professor and Mrs. Sanders will be leaving Sonning, but congratulate Professor Sanders on the promotion which has been conferred upon him.' There followed an interesting account of the history of the Reading University Farm at Sonning. The article was the product of research undertaken by students from the National Federation of Young Farmers' Clubs who had been investigating the history of farming in Berkshire.

October 1954

The Vicar's Letter: The summer weather of 1954 proved to be extremely disappointing and resulted in the following comment by Sidney Groves: 'I do not think that we can defer the Harvest Festival beyond the middle of October. Even though the grain harvest may be poor, there will be much else to be thankful for.'

Historical: A lengthy contribution by F.J.H. appeared in this issue. The purpose of the article was to correct a number of inaccuracies within the article concerning the University Farm which had been published in the September issue. One particular reference was to the name of Pound Lane, Sonning. This article mentions: 'With reference to "Pond or Pound" Lane; the lane derived its name from the pound which stood on the site of the open space in front of the gates to the Sonning Recreation Ground. This was a brick wall in the form of a square about six feet in height with a gate in one side. It was used for "impounding" straying cattle.'

November 1954

The Vicar's Letter: 'I am most grateful for all the support you have been giving to our Winter Campaign Fund, and for the hope which this gives us of our being able to come through "on the right side" after meeting all our numerous expenses.

The "headache" caused by the depredations of the beetle in the church floor, necessitating the re-flooring of practically the whole of the Nave, has been dissipated by the very generous legacy bequeathed to us by Mrs. Rose. It seems a shame to have to put so much money underfoot, but the work must be done.'

[*The Rose bequest was a generous £1,500. The cost incurred due to the ravages of the death watch beetle amounted to somewhat over £1,200.*]

Local Events: 'Ye Olde Busse Stoppe – Congratulations to all concerned in the building of the much needed shelter!

Our best wishes to the occupants of the six new bungalows in the Little Glebe. What delightful little homes they are!

. . . and all good wishes to Mrs. Sellwood, of No. 2, Robert Palmer Cottages, who will be celebrating her 90th birthday on November 11.'

Dancing Successes: 'We are pleased to announce that Kathleen Holland, Rita Farmer and Marion Sawyer were all successful in the Preliminary Ballet Dancing Examination held in London. They are pupils of Miss Dulcie Sawyer who at present is on tour with the Benny Hill Show.'

December 1954

Remembrance Sunday: 'The special Service at 10.30am on this day was performed with the ritual that has now become customary in Sonning, solemn but not lugubrious. The Roll of Honour was proclaimed by General Sir Andrew Thorne and the lesson was read by Major-General Price-Davies. The wreath was placed by Mr. W. Huggins and the "Exhortation" read by Mr. C. White.'

The School: A report was included by the headmaster, Mr. H. Chapman, which included the following: 'The Intelligence Test, the first part of the procedure for the selection of children eligible by age for Grammar School education, took place on November 18. I am pleased to report that all our candidates performed most creditably. The School has received some new furniture; six dual locker desks have arrived. They will be put to use when the chairs come.'

Diocesan Quota: A Sonning Ruridecanal Conference meeting was held on October 23 to hear the secretary of the Oxford Diocesan Board of Finance explain the reasons which have led to the raising of the Diocesan Quota by about 50%. The reasons given were chiefly training for holy orders and the maintenance of the Teachers Training College.

January 1955

The Vicar's Letter: 'Mr. J. Heppell of 141 Loddon Bridge Road, Woodley, has now undertaken to print our Parish Magazine for us, and we hope that we may have a long association with him in this work.

Contributors must assist him by trying to write clearly and legibly and on one side of the paper only, and by sending in their contributions to me punctually on the date stated. We aim to publish as before on the Thursday before the first Sunday of each month.

I wish to thank Miss Kemp for all the trouble she takes in organising the advertising side of the magazine.'

[No advertisements appear in the bound archival copies of the magazine during this period. However, the Sonning P.C.C. accounts for 1954 include an item – Advertisements £44 1s 6d. It would appear that an advertisement section was removed when the archival copy was prepared for binding. see: page 90.]

Stop Press: 'We now learn that both Canon [Harry James] Carpenter, as Lord Bishop of Oxford, and also Rev. E. H. Knell as Bishop Suffragan of Reading, are to be consecrated in Southwark Cathedral by the Archbishop of Canterbury on St Paul's Day, January 25.'

February 1955
Charvil Welfare Clinic: 'The Clinic was opened just two years ago with a register of 35 babies under the age of five years. We now have 137 on the register with an average attendance of 40. The success of the Clinic is greatly due to our excellent nurse and the very helpful committee in whom the team spirit is very strong.'

Rev. C. A. M. Roberts: The death of Charles Aldersey Morley Roberts for twelve years (1930-1942) assistant priest at Sonning was announced.

March 1955
Sonning Parochial Church Council – Report for 1954
The Report of the Vicar and P.C.C. to the Annual General Meeting 1955 included the following:

'Our verger never fails in the discharge of his duties and under his and Mrs. Adnams' care the Church continues to be a model of perfect cleanliness and order. We congratulate Mr. Adnams on having completed 25 years of service to the Church as Verger.

The two Sunday Schools continue to carry on their good work, under the superintendence of Mr. Hoyle and Miss Inge, but more teachers are needed, especially at St Patrick's.'

British Legion – Women's Section: 'The Sonning Branch of the British Legion, Women's Section, held a successful meeting in the Pearson Hall on Thursday, February 10. Mrs. Prior was in the chair, and sixty-seven members, including some from Wargrave, Twyford and Woodley branches, were present.'

April 1955

Divine Healing: Sidney Groves extended the following invitation in this issue: 'I have, with the approval of the Lord Bishop, invited Brother Mandus of the World Healing Crusade, to conduct a Divine Healing Service in our Church on Sunday, April 24 at 4pm. To this, I am glad to say, he has assented. Any parishioner, whether sick or whole, may come and join in intercession with us for those who are sick in body, mind or spirit, while the laying-on of hands is administered to them.'

Rangers: 'Boat painting has now been completed and we hope to get the boats on the river in time to use them over the Easter holidays. Our first weekend camp will be held at Englefield Park over the Whitsun weekend when we hope to meet some American Girl Scouts.'

[*Sir Winston Churchill at the age of eighty resigns on April 5 from the premiership, but stays in the Commons as a backbencher. He is succeeded as prime minister by Sir Anthony Eden.*]

May 1955

The Passion: 'On Passion Sunday at evensong the choir rendered "The Passion", an early work by Handel, in an abridged form. It was the most ambitious work which our choir has undertaken recently.'

[*On becoming prime minister, Sir Anthony Eden immediately called a general election, which the Conservatives won and gained an overall 58 seat majority.*]

June 1955

The Vicar's Letter: 'As Rural Dean, I was privileged to take part in the inauguration of the new church buildings at Bracknell by the laying of the foundation stone by H.R.H. the Duke of Edinburgh, and its dedication by the Lord Bishop. A tremendous task lies before the Church in that area, and we must do what we can to help the Vicar, the

Rev. F. W. Broome, in shouldering his obligations as parish priest to his new vast population.'

Woodley Church School: An extensive article was included in this issue acknowledging the centenary of the school which was opened on May 14, 1855: 'The school had been built on ground given by Robert Palmer of Holme Park, the cost of the building being defrayed by his sisters, Elizabeth, Laura and Caroline. The architect was the same Henry Woodyer who had restored Sonning school in 1862 and was later to design the church at Woodley. The original building consisted of the school house, the schoolroom and the infants' room. The school was enlarged and improved on five occasions, lastly in 1952.'

July 1955

The Festivals: 'The sun shone gloriously to enhance the beauty of the Whitsun Festival, which was reflected in the flowers so kindly given and so beautifully arranged. One of the features of Whitsunday is the offering of the Whitsun Farthings by the children at the afternoon worship; the amount collected this year in the two churches came to 3,500 farthings (£3 12s 11d.). This was taken by Sylvia Ward and Paula Wright to Oxford on Whit-Tuesday who will doubtless remember the offering that they presented to the Lord Bishop as he sat in his chair at the high altar of the Cathedral.'

Organ: 'We congratulate our latest Assistant Organist, Barry Goddard, on having passed with distinction the Grade 3 Examination of the Trinity College of Music; he gained 83 marks out of 100.'

[*Limited reporting of sporting activities had been apparent in this magazine over the last decade. This was noticeable as football, cricket etc had been included regularly during earlier peacetime years.*]

August 1955

The Vicar's Letter: 'One of our annual treats is to welcome the children and parents of our School to our garden for the prizegiving; this year we were favoured with glorious weather which made the afternoon's proceedings doubly enjoyable. In recognition of the fact that Miss Fox has completed forty years' service with the School, she was invited to give away the prizes; she informed us that the time was shortly coming when she would have to sever her connection with Sonning School.'

Fire Brigade: 'Anyone passing the Fire Station during the last few months may have seen four firemen continuously running up ladders for no apparent reason; however, their efforts were not in vain, for Sonning Fire Brigade, competing in the Berkshire and Reading Fire Brigade Annual Competitions in Palmer Park on Saturday, June 25, won the "Wantage" Cup for the second year.'

September 1955
The Vicar's Letter: 'The weather has improved so wonderfully during the second half of the summer months that the Harvest will be in earlier than we at one time expected, so that this Festival too can be brought forward one Sunday and observed on October 2.'

Summer Fair: It was reported that the Fair was held in the grounds of St Patrick's Hall in good summer weather on Saturday, August 6. The afternoon comprised of various activities including games, competitions and opportunities to purchase from a number of stallholders; this was followed in the evening by a dance which included square dancing.

October 1955
The Vicar's Letter: 'We are glad that the work of the church repairs is now completed, and we are grateful to all those who worked so hard in many ways to restore things to normal in such a short space of time. Mr. Harry Russell and his workers must be congratulated on carrying out the work so efficiently, also Mr. Ripley who once more placed his wide architectural knowledge at our disposal.'

November 1955
The Vicar's Letter: 'Our Harvest Festival, making a landmark in the progress of the year, is past and gone. The offerings of fruit and flowers and vegetables were plentiful and beautifully arranged. The Choir rendered the three choral services of the day most beautifully, and we were glad to have Mr. Hoyle's message from the pulpit at Matins. I am also grateful to the Vicar of Woodley, Rev. H. W. H. Wilkinson, for preaching to us at St Patrick's for the festival there on Michaelmas Day.'

School Toys: 'It may be that in some homes there are toys that children have "outgrown". Playthings such as scales, baking boards and rolling pins, pull-along toys and big plastic dolls would be much appreciated. They are intended for the lower class in the School, infants of about five years of age, and the children will make good use of them.'

Sonning C. of E. School: 'The Berkshire Education Committee has published in the local press their programme for Secondary Education for 1956. There will be an Intelligence Test for those children born on or between August 1, 1944 and July 31, 1945. Those who qualify will take further tests during the spring in English, Arithmetic and English Composition and they may be required to attend an interview. Successful children may be offered places at certain Grammar Schools; for Sonning children these are generally Maidenhead County Girls' School, The Holt Girls' School, Wokingham, Woodley Hill Boys' School and Maidenhead County Boys' School.'

December 1955
The Vicar's Letter: 'We have to express our sympathy with Mr. Chettle and Mr. and Mrs. Whitlock, whose dwellings were struck by lightning and received considerable damage during the thunderstorm on the night of November 5-6.'

Blood Donors: 'There is a very great need for more blood donors. Will anyone interested please apply to Mrs. N. A. Smith, Peppers, Sonning who will gladly give more details.'

CHAPTER THREE

1956 - 1960

For many years little change had occurred in the appearance of the magazine. However, the decision had now been taken to include trade advertisements. Captain Rotheram had found it necessary to withdraw his financial assistance, and it was clear that advertising income was needed to help to stem the increasing loss which the magazine would otherwise incur.

Bound volumes of the original magazines from this period, held in the church archives, include no example of an illustrated front page design until January 1957. The following five years saw three photographic illustrations appear on the front page; two external views of St Andrew's church and an internal view featuring the reredos and the altar. During this period the Sonning vicar Sidney Groves continued as editor of the magazine, a role which he had occupied since his Sonning ministry began in 1942.

Whilst few new dwellings were being built within Sonning village, further housing development was taking place within the outer area to the south of the village. The parishes of Earley, Woodley and parts of Charvil were experiencing the construction of large numbers of new properties, the development in Charvil included the new Charvil Hall which had been consecrated as St Patrick's Church in 1952.

Following its move from Reading to a new home at Holme Park, Sonning, the Reading Blue Coat School was now an established part of Sonning life. The school was able to make contributions with both lay readers and a considerable number of choristers, who were warmly welcomed by the Sonning clergy.

January 1956

Confirmation: 'The weather for the Confirmation in the afternoon of Sunday, December 4, proved delightful for the time of year, and helped to increase the joy of this great event in the life of the parish. We were glad to welcome the Bishop of Reading on the occasion of his first Episcopal visit to Sonning.'

Sonning C. of E. School: 'The Managers of our school have very kindly presented us with some toys which will be most useful for the lower infants. This is in response to the appeal made in a recent issue of the magazine.'

February 1956

Women's Institute: 'The January meeting was held in the Pearson Hall, Mrs. Powell presiding. A cookery demonstration on omelettes and soufflés was given by Miss Cummings. The competition for a hand-made apron and tray was won by Miss Atkins and Mrs. Ellis.'

March 1956

Sonning Parochial Church Council – Report for 1955
The Report of the Vicar and P.C.C. to the Annual General Meeting 1956 included the following:
Further details were recorded of the repairs to St Andrew's which were required due to the death watch beetle infestation: 'The re-flooring of the church was carried out during the summer. The wooden floor has been replaced by a cement floor covered with Accotiles, which does not in any way conflict with the beauty and amenities of the church.' It was further reported that the total cost of this work: 'will probably amount to some £1,400 or more, but the final account has not yet been agreed.'
The accounts for the parish magazine resulted in a deficit of £10 17s 2d for the year 1955. Income which comprised of the sale of magazines was £53 2s 10d and advertising income amounted to £49 15s 0d.

Choir Supper: 'This pleasant annual event took place this year on Tuesday, February 7, at the White Hart Hotel. A goodly company of forty-eight, comprising choristers, organists, bellringers, servers, vergers and caretakers – not to mention the Vicar and churchwardens. After a bountiful spread, songs were rendered by members of the Choir.'

April 1956

Best Kept Village Competition: 'The Berkshire Branch of the Council for the Preservation of Rural England is organising a competition for the best kept village in Berkshire and Sonning Parish Council has made an entry on behalf of our parish. A special committee has been formed on which all of our clubs and institutions are represented and will doubtless call on a number of helpers to assist them in their work.' The conditions of the competition included: absence of litter - condition of hedges, fences and walls - condition of churchyard - condition of war memorials (not in church or churchyard) - condition of village centre, village green, playing fields and verges - tidiness of flowers, vegetable gardens, allotments, outhouses and sheds.

St Patrick's Youth Club: 'This being the first publication regarding the Club, the Committee would like it to be known that we commenced the year financially solvent. During this last winter a small billiards table and radiogram were purchased, and each is proving as popular as the other.'

[*On April 17 a new £1 premium bond offering tax free prizes of up to £1,000 was announced by Harold MacMillan, the Chancellor of the Exchequer. The Archbishop of Canterbury commented that these bonds debase the nation's spiritual currency.*]

May 1956

The Vicar's Letter: 'I am most grateful for the renewed kindness in making so generous an Easter Offering, which this year amounted to £70; it is indeed a most acceptable gift.

The Easter services were as bright and beautiful as ever, and we are grateful to the Organist and Choir for their devoted help, and to the givers and arrangers of flowers. The communicants numbered 288, not quite so many as last year.'

Church Officials: A list was printed detailing the name of those who currently held various roles in Sonning parish:

Vicar of Sonning: Rev. S. J. S. Groves - Churchwardens: Mr. S. Paddick
Mr. F. J. Hoyle - Organist: Mr. A. H. Lusty - Verger: Mr. R. R. Adnams
Church Council Secretary: Miss I. Kemp - Church Gardener: Mr. C. May
Caretakers of St Patrick's: Mr. and Mrs. W. Gale.

June 1956

The Diocesan Missionary Festival: The following contribution was included in this issue from The Lord Bishop of Oxford: 'The support of Overseas Missions of the Church is one of our most important spiritual obligations as a Diocese. At our Annual Missionary Festival, to be held in Marlow on Thursday, July 12, we come together to renew our dedication to this work, and to hear more of its needs and opportunities. I hope that Incumbents will make the arrangements for this year's Festival widely known in their parishes, so that we may have a representative gathering at Marlow from all parts of the Diocese.'

Sonning C. of E. School: 'We are pleased to record that Graham Patrick and Hilary Penfold have obtained Grammar School places in the recent selection test. We do sincerely congratulate these children (and their parents) and we trust that their success will be the forerunner of many more to come.'

July 1956

1st Sonning Scouts: 'At the last Committee meeting it was unanimously decided that the Scouts, Cubs, Rangers, Guides and Brownies should start a building fund in aid of their combined new Headquarters. Owing to change of ownership, the present H.Q. will not be available much longer.

It was suggested that the Scouts and Cubs be set a target of £100, as would the Rangers, Guides and Brownies, towards the cost. The new headquarters will be a hut to be erected on the upper part of the Recreation Ground.

It is hoped that the local population will give this future building fund their full support as there are at present approximately 100 young members of the community who take part in Scout and Guide activities, and by whom the new building would be used at least five evenings of every week.'

[*The newly elected Egyptian president Gamal Abdel Nasser seizes the Anglo-French controlled Suez Canal which results in the deployment of Anglo-French armed forces in the Suez campaign. Tension escalates, with threats from the Soviet Union. British action is also opposed by the US causing strained relations between the two allies. The United Nations eventually brokered an end to the conflict.*]

August 1956

Sonning School Old Girls' Association: 'At a recent meeting it was decided to discontinue with this organisation. It was also agreed that the sum of £16 12s 10d should be given to the building fund for a combined headquarters for Scouts, Cubs, Guides, Brownies and Rangers.'

Sonning Football Club: 'The Club celebrated its sixtieth year of formation this year, having been formed in 1896, and one of the oldest clubs in the district. The fortunes of the Club have fluctuated over the years, but the team won the Reading Town Junior Cup in 1930-31 season. The last few seasons have not been good but the enthusiasm of the players has made the continued efforts of the committee worth while. The committee and players of Sonning Football Club hope that people of Sonning will come and support their team both at home and away matches and so help the Club to continue during the coming season.'

September 1956

Sonning Lock: 'Congratulations to our Lock-keeper, Mr. S. W. Adams, who has not only come first in the Local Section Competition for the most beautiful lock, but has also won the Sir Reginald Hands Trophy for the whole of the River Thames. He has now done this on three different locks, Rushey, Whitchurch and Sonning – we believe that this constitutes a record.'

Best Kept Village: A further local success was reported in this issue when Sonning was declared the winner of the Best Kept Village in Berkshire award: 'We are most grateful to the Committee who organised us, and must try to see that our village is always kept in the same good state. Litter is unfortunately a menace wherever one goes in this country nowadays, and one wonders whether people will ever learn any better.'

October 1956

The Vicar's Letter: 'We congratulate Charvil on the splendid success of their Summer Fair on August 25, somewhat marred by a storm at the beginning. There again if we are to provide the amenities desired, such as better chairs, we must have funds. Envelopes will be available for contributions – please help.'

Robert Palmer Cottages: 'On August 25 the residents of the Robert Palmer Cottages and a few of their friends and contemporaries were entertained at Shelvingstone by Mrs. Clement Williams. After a more than adequate tea the visitors were treated to a form of entertainment usually provided for a more juvenile company. This consisted of a conjuring display by Mr. John Barlow which, by its clever and humorous method of presentation, successfully mystified and at the same time delighted all present.'

November 1956

Operation Firm Faith: 'The operation has two confluent objectives –
(1) To make all churchpeople realise their responsibility for the training in the Faith and Worship of the Church all children, not only their own, for whom they are primarily accountable. (2) The smaller units, whom we usually call families, living under one roof, feeding from the same table, physically related one to the other, should also worship together. Will all who value the Christian Gospel and their privileges as members of Christ's Church, pray for the success of this operation and use their influence to bring others into the family life of our parish?.'

Best Kept Village: 'The illuminated "Certificate of Merit" won by Sonning recently and organised for the first time in Berkshire by the Council for the Preservation of Rural England will be presented to the Parish Council by Mr. H. A. Benyon, Lord Lieutenant of Berkshire, in the Pearson Hall on Monday, November 12, at 6.30pm.'

December 1956

Family Sunday Service: A full page notice by Rev. Groves appeared in this issue which promoted the importance of the family as a unit. The opening paragraph comprised of the following: 'One of the most precious and sacred of all human institutions is the Family, the God-given association of father, mother and children. We are born into it, we grow up in it almost unconsciously, we love it naturally – in fact "there's no place like home".' The purpose of this notice was to invite local families to attend a newly planned service on the first Sunday of each month to be known as a Special Family Service at 10.30am.

Remembrance Service: 'Our annual commemoration of those who laid down their lives in the two great world wars and our thanksgiving for victory and peace was held under circumstances of grave anxiety for the crisis in the Middle East and of distress for the sufferings of the people of Hungary; perhaps it was for this reason that the congregation was larger than ever before.'

[*A popular uprising in Hungary against the Soviet Union's domination of the country was brutally crushed by a large military force.*]

January 1957

[*Archival copies of the magazine from this period include a four page cover comprising of a front display page, three pages of advertisements and text consisting of four pages. It is likely that advertisements were introduced in the early 1950's which is supported by an entry in the P.C.C. accounts. see: page 82. The advertisers in this January issue included a grocer, coal merchant, chimney sweep, removals and storage contractor. see: pages 88 and 90.*]

Youth Club: 'A number of lads have asked that a Boys' Club might be formed in Sonning. It will be remembered that the St Andrew's Social Club ran for several years but finally fizzled out for lack of support. Since then the St Patrick's Youth Club has been formed and successfully run by parents and friends of the boys and girls at Charvil. There would appear to be no reason why a similar organisation for boys and girls could not be run in Sonning. Is there anyone who is prepared to give up a few hours each week to run such a club? It would be an important and worthwhile job for someone to tackle.'

[*Sir Anthony Eden resigns as prime minister due to health reasons and is succeeded by Harold MacMillan.*]

February 1957

Christmas: 'Once again we have been privileged to celebrate the feast of the Incarnation and to offer our love and veneration to the little child of Bethlehem. We are grateful to all those who helped us in our worship; all of our services were well attended, and there were well over three hundred communicants.'

JANUARY 1957   PRICE 4d.

Sonning
Parish Magazine

SUNDAY SERVICES AT THE PARISH CHURCH

7.0   Holy Communion (1st Sunday in the month)
8.0   Holy Communion (every Sunday)
11.0   Sung Eucharist (3rd Sunday in the month)
11.0   Matins (other Sundays)
2.45   Children's Hour (every Sunday)
6.30   Evensong (every Sunday)

(For weekday services, see within)

Printed by J. HEPPELL 141, Loddon Bridge Road, Woodley

Cover page: January 1957. (23.5 x 17.5cm)

hear```

Children's Christmas Parties: 'The parties were well attended, we are glad to say, and were fairly well equalled out – the under-nines numbering 61 and the elder ones 77. On both occasions a sumptuous tea was served by Mrs. Lamb and other members of the Mothers' Union, and on both occasions the children received a bag of sweets and a lollipop, the gift of the British Legion.'

March 1957
Sonning Parochial Church Council – Report for 1956
The Report of the Vicar and P.C.C. to the Annual General Meeting 1957 included the following:
'Our parish Church is still kept in its usual condition of cleanliness by our Verger, Mr. Adnams, and all the activities at St Patrick's owe much to the tireless energy of Mrs. Gale. The Churchyard under Mr. May has continued to be a model of good order, which has no doubt contributed to the winning by Sonning of the Best-kept Village in Berkshire competition. Again this year we are grateful for the help given by Mr. Holloway and Alan.
We are greatly indebted to all those who helped with the success of our Winter Campaign. In Sonning this produced a net profit of £345. St Patrick's Winter Campaign and their Summer Fair realised together £99, practically all of which sum was spent on new seats.
The Parish Magazine shows an operating loss of £6 on the year, which is a considerable improvement, and our thanks are due to the advertisers.
The total cost of the repairs to the Church due to the ravages of the death-watch beetle amounted to £1,366, the whole of which has been defrayed from Mrs. Lilian Rose's legacy.

[*On March 25 the Treaty of Rome is signed by France, West Germany, Italy, Belgium, Holland and Luxembourg setting up the European Common Market.*]

April 1957
The Choir: 'On Sunday, March 17, Handel's Passion was rendered by the choir to a large congregation. The most outstanding feature was the fine choral singing by the choir. The solo parts were effectively sung by William Evans (Evangelist), Leonard Siney (Jesus), Leonard Crook (Pilates), Brian Hill and Percy Forward (A Believer). The part of the Daughter of Zion was beautifully sung by Hazel Goatley. The excellent organ accompaniment was by Evelyn Alder. Mr. A. H. Lusty, our organist and choirmaster, conducted.'

For **COAL .. COKE**
ANTHRACITE, BOILER FUEL
WOOD LOGS AND KINDLING WOOD

TOOMERS
(Coal and Coke) Ltd.

RAILWAY STATION, TWYFORD
PHONE - TWYFORD 21

Telephone : Reading 62239.

W. G. COX

Fruiterer and Greengrocer

394, London Road, Earley, Reading

WREATHS & CROSSES MADE TO ORDER.   *Plants of all varieties.*

MAKE BAYLIS YOUR FOOD STORE

BAYLIS — THE GROCERS — LTD.
SHOPS :   BROAD STREET CORNER, READING.   Phone 2251
Abingdon, Caversham, Newbury, Erleigh Road, Reading, Theale and MOBILE

Advertisement page: January 1957. (23.5 x 17.5cm)

Sonning Cricket Club: 'The 1957 season will commence at the beginning of May. The Club has an excellent ground and facilities and a good fixture list has been arranged with local clubs. Given good weather, an enjoyable season's cricket is anticipated. The Club is pleased to welcome new members, and anyone interested is asked to get into touch with the Honorary Secretary, Mr. A. F. H. Crust, Hope Cottage, Pound Lane, Sonning.'

May 1957

Rogations: 'We shall hold our usual service of "Blessing the Crops" on Rogation Sunday (May 26), as has now become traditional. The first part of Evensong will be sung in church, and we shall then proceed to the University Farm, where the outdoor service will begin at about 7.15pm. We ask all members of the congregation to join us in the procession and the Charvil folk to meet us for the service at the farm.'

St Patrick's Youth Club: 'Indoor Club finishes on Friday, May 3. We are hoping to organise the usual outdoor games, cricket and netball. The past winter's activities have been most successful, and our membership has increased over other years.'

June 1957

The Vicar's Letter: 'I am so sorry that it has been found necessary to increase some of the charges for the use of the Pearson Hall, but it is impossible to make two ends meet on the present scale. The hall does not pay its way, and there is no endowment; the present balance is due to a large contribution (£75) made from the Church Winter Campaign Fund in 1955. There is much that could be done to the hall if we had the money.'

Church School: 'The Managers have appointed Miss E. L. Pudduck to succeed Miss Fox as Assistant Teacher in September. Miss Pudduck has been trained at Whitelands College, and we look forward with confidence to her work among our children; we hope that she will enjoy the work and have every success in it. Unfortunately, Miss Fox is still unwell and has not been able so far to resume her duties. We are most grateful to Miss Titley for so efficiently filling the gap.'

July 1957

The Vicar's Letter: 'I am most deeply appreciative of the ready generosity of those who have consented to enter into a covenant for seven years to contribute towards the stipend of a parochial assistant. Our warm thanks are due to our first subscribers. The subscriptions and guarantees, together with the Income Tax recoverable thereon, are estimated to produce about £475pa, in addition we hope for a generous grant from the Diocesan Maintenance of the Ministry Fund. The total amount required in order to fund the cost of the stipend, rent and rates is estimated to be £550pa.'

Miss E. M. Fox: 'As is widely known, Miss Fox will not now be able to resume her duties in our school where she has taught so faithfully and efficiently since 1916. It is indeed sad that a serious illness should have prevented her from seeing the very end of her long service to the school. We would all wish Miss Fox a speedy and complete recovery from her illness, and many happy years more to enjoy her well-earned rest,'

August 1957

Women's Institute: 'Mrs. Powell, very kindly entertained Sonning members in her garden on Tuesday, July 9, and a very happy afternoon was spent with many invited members from Woodley, Earley and Twyford. Miss Pankhurst, of Streatley, gave a very interesting and informative demonstration of flower-making from goose and duck feathers. A fine tea was enjoyed, followed by many joining in folk-dancing organised by Miss Dadley.'

F. J. Hoyle: The obituary of Frederick James Hoyle extended to some three columns in this issue and gave some measure to the loss that the parish had suffered by his passing: 'The death of this great little man on Sunday, June 30, brought sorrow to the whole community, for he was a figure universally beloved and respected. He had been Churchwarden for eighteen years and a chorister and Sunday School teacher almost for the whole of his life.'

[*Frederick James Hoyle (1883-1957) is interred in the Sonning Churchyard. see: Record of Burials etc. Church of St Andrew 2012.*]

September 1957

Captain Langridge: 'The Lord Bishop has now given his formal approval to the appointment of Captain Leonard Langridge, a captain in the Church Army, as Lay Evangelist in the parish, and we hope that he will be able to move in to his new residence, 26 Park View Drive, Charvil, during the second week of September, so as to start his ministry on Sunday, September 15. We extend a most hearty welcome to Captain and Mrs. Langridge and their family, and feel sure that all our readers will do the same.'

Young Wives' Group: 'On Thursday, October 10, at 7.30pm we are holding our first Young Wives' Group meeting at the Vicarage. We shall be glad to welcome all young wives and mothers who have children of 16 years or under. We hope to plan an interesting and varied programme for the next year.'

Women's Institute: 'The members, very kindly invited for the eighteenth successive year by Mrs. Waide, enjoyed a happy afternoon in her home and garden, crowned by a fine tea. The competition for a necklace made from anything but beads was very well supported and was won by Mrs. Dodds, Mrs. Field and Mrs. Penticost.'

October 1957

Best Kept Village: 'The C.P.R.E., who organised the competition has circulated to each competing village for their future guidance a note of the particular points on which they have won or lost marks. The following is a summary of the judges' view on Sonning's showing this year:- Full marks - condition of churchyard, village centre and playing field. A few marks lost - absence of unsightly advertising, condition of hedges, fences and surrounds of buildings including village hall. Substantial loss of marks - Absence of litter and refuse dumps, surrounds to schools, school yards, tidiness of allotments in cultivation.'

Rangers: 'Though our numbers have diminished somewhat during the summer, we have nevertheless had a very full programme. We have been to two weekend camps, one at Tidmarsh, near Pangbourne, and the other at Englefield Park.'

November 1957

The Vicar's Letter: 'The epidemic of influenza, though normally of a mild nature, has made widespread attacks on the health of the nation, and has caused the winter "coughs and sneezes" to start early. The schools have been the worst hit in most communities, and we congratulate Miss Puddock and her class on having stuck it out without having to close.

I call your attention to the Church Sale to be opened at the Pearson Hall on Saturday, November 23, at 2.30pm by Mr. Robert Beatty.'

[*A serious epidemic of Asian influenza afflicted a wide area of Britain with substantial loss of life – with estimates of at least 14,000 fatalities.*
Robert Beatty (1909-1992) a Canadian actor, and a Sonning resident, was well known in Britain where he appeared in films, on television and radio.]

Reading and District Music Festival: 'The Festival was held in the Reading Town Hall on Saturday, October 9 at which Barry Goddard won the Elverson Cup together with a bursary of three guineas for tuition fees for organ playing. Barry has also been appointed Organist and Choirmaster of Wargrave Parish Church and commences his duties there in November.'

December 1957

A Parish Party: 'All parishioners are invited to the Pearson Hall on Thursday, December 5, at 8.15pm to a little function which will give them all great pleasure. The party is to be held in honour of the eightieth birthday of Mr. Clement Williams, to whom we own so much, and to whom a token of our affection and respect will be presented. Light refreshments will be served.'

St Patrick's Letter: A regular item had been introduced under the name of Captain L. O. C. Langridge. The letter included announcements of forthcoming events at St Patrick's and other details of interest to those who worshipped at the church.

Children's Hour at St Andrew's: 'We hope to produce a little play entitled the "Little Bearers" to which parents and friends will be invited on Sunday, December 15, at 2.45pm.'

January 1958

Church of England Children's Society: 'On November 4, Sonning was again represented at the Purse Presentation ceremony in the Albert Hall, London in aid of the Society. Lady Ismay received the purses. There was an address by the Bishop of London, and an attractive dancing display. Mrs. Gale and Mrs. Westley accompanied the purse bearers who were Jill Hiles, Barbara Westley, Jeremy Widdows and Francis McLaren.'

Mothers' Union: 'A meeting was held at the Vicarage on Thursday, December 5. Mrs. Victor Smith gave an interesting talk on Christmas customs. Comparing Christmas of today with that of fifty years ago, she said that much of the fun and excitement of preparing for the season was lost, owing to the fact that so many things in these days could be obtained ready-made. Mrs. Smith pointed out that, although Christmas was quite rightly a festive season, we should never lose sight of its true significance as a Christian festival, to commemorate the birth of Jesus Christ.'

February 1958

The Vicar's Letter: 'With Christmas and 1957 behind us, we have come to the turning-point of the year's revolution, and now look forward to longer days and brighter skies – and, we trust, less illness. Spring brings with it Lent, the time for life's spring-cleaning and renewal.'

Young Wives' Group: 'Everyone survived our last meeting – the party, and 23 members attended our fourth meeting. We were glad to welcome a few new members and hope more will join us. We extend our sincere thanks to Mrs. Atkinson for her kindness in allowing us to use her house in her absence, and to Mrs. Symons for taking the chair. Mrs. Goyder, of Rotherfield Greys gave a very interesting talk on Leisure and Recruitment,'

St Patrick's Letter: 'First of all I must say how grateful we are to Duncan Sanders for making a Psalm number board for the church. Many thanks to the children for doing the Nativity Play. It was good to see the church full with so many parents and friends.'

March 1958

Sonning Parochial Church Council – Report for 1957

The Report of the Vicar and P.C.C. to the Annual General Meeting 1958 included the following:

'It has been impressed upon us that extensive repairs to the Tower are now necessary at an estimated cost of £550. Plans have been drawn up, passed by the Diocesan Advisory Board, and forwarded to the Chancellor of the Diocese for his approval for the issue of the necessary faculty.

The Parish Magazine was again run at a loss in spite of generous support from the advertisers, the loss on the year being £25 18s 10d.'

Parish Magazine: 'In order to avoid difficulties that might arise by publishing on Maundy Thursday, we are arranging to publish the April number of the magazine one week earlier than usual, *viz.*, Thursday, March 27. It will be observed that there is a considerable deficit on the magazine fund; this could be avoided if every parishioner became a regular subscriber.'

Thanks: 'Ten five-pound notes were found in the Church Almsbox on one occasion when it was opened recently. We express our heartfelt gratitude to the anonymous donor of this remarkably large sum.'

April 1958

The Vicar's Letter: 'Work on the Church Tower has now started and is likely to prove more extensive than was first thought. It will be necessary during part of the time to dispense with the pealing of the bells, but the services can, of course, continue as usual.

Charvil is now being recognised as an entity of its own as can be seen from the signs on the road, in which we are glad to see that the name Charvil is properly spelt. The Post Office also recognises it, for the postal address is no longer Twyford, but Charvil, Reading, Berkshire.'

Pearson Hall: 'We are sorry to have to announce the resignation of our caretakers, Mr. and Mrs. Roland Hunt. It will be remembered that they were married on Easter Monday, 1951, and have made the Pearson Hall their one and only married home. We thank both of them for all they have done for the hall, and offer them our very best wishes for the future.'

Sonning Football Club: 'As we draw near to the end of another season it is pleasing to report that, after several seasons of poor league placings, we are now far higher in the league positions, presently lying fifth in the table. The club have scored 100 goals with 67 against, Michael Moss has scored 40 goals, John Moss 16, Peter Goodey 14, Jim Halsey and Bob Turner 10 goals each. Next season we shall be playing in new colours. We have purchased a set of red shirts with white sleeves and collars to replace the green shirts which the club has worn over the past ten seasons.'

May 1958

The Vicar's Letter: 'Once again I have the happy occasion of writing to thank you for your most generous Easter offering, which this year amounted to the remarkable total of £86 19s 0d. I need hardly tell you how helpful this will be towards the necessary heavy expenses of the large house and gardens, nor how sincerely grateful I am to you for this token of your kindness and forbearance.

The weather seems at last to be turning more spring-like and Sonning will soon be putting on all its lovely Easter vesture.'

Rich and Reade Trust: 'The Trustees have this year the right of sending a Day Boy, free of charge, to the Reading Blue Coat School. Particulars and forms of application should be obtained from Miss Kemp as soon as possible; all applicants will be required to attend for a special examination at Holme Park on Saturday, May 10, at 9am.'

Mothers' Union: 'May 6 will be an important date for the Mothers' Union, for Mrs. Groves who is Vice-President of the East Berkshire Archdeaconry has arranged a festival in Bath Abbey, at which there will be an attendance of about 1,100 – a gathering of that size in those beautiful surroundings will undoubtedly prove most inspiring and a truly memorable occasion.'

June 1958

The Vicar's Letter: 'During the month of June we shall have the pleasure of welcoming the members of the Old Sunning Lodge and Chapter and also the Reading Blue Coat School parents to Matins.

Another link with the past is snapped by the death of Mrs.Hendy, who was Organist here for so many years, while her husband was Choir Master. Many old, and young, members of the Choir managed to find time to sing at her funeral on Ascension Eve, which brought much happiness to her family.'

The Verger: Rev. Groves included the following item in this issue. 'At the meeting of the Parochial Church Council on May 13 the members learnt the sad news that Mr. R. R. Adnams felt obliged, through ill-health and advanced years, to resign the office of Verger, which he had held for the past twenty-eight years. I am glad to be able to confirm that Mr. W. F. West has accepted the post of Verger in succession to Mr. Adnams.'

July 1958

The Vicar's Letter: 'We go to press under the shadow of the great loss that has befallen us in the death of our beloved Verger, almost on the morrow of his giving up some of his duties he has performed so faithfully for the last 28 years.'
[*Robert Richard Adnams (1881-1958) is interred in the Sonning churchyard see: Record of Burials etc. Church of St Andrew 2012.*]

Caroline Palmer Charity: It was announced that the administration of this charity had been simplified and greatly improved. The capital would forthwith be held by the Diocesan Board of Finance and the income paid to the Parochial Church Council for the repair and insurance of the church building.

Legacy: 'We are indeed grateful to the late Colonel Gordon Dickson who has bequeathed to the Trustees of the Sonning Church Council the sum of £3,000 for the upkeep of the Churchyard.'

Sonning Football Club: 'The club had a very good 1957-58 season and finished a creditable fifth in the league table. Total number of goals scored was 135 with 99 against. It is hoped that the club will do even better next season although some of the players are now serving in the services.'

August 1958
The Vicar's Letter: We may take this opportunity to heartily congratulate Mr. David Keys, of the Gate House, on his great success in winning the "Brains of Britain" competition of the B.B.C. – a truly remarkable achievement.'

Young Wives' Group: 'Instead of our usual meeting in July, we enjoyed an outing to the Theatre Royal, Windsor, to see a performance of "The Chalk Garden". We were pleased to welcome with us quite a number of husbands, and hope it may be the first of many future summer outings.'

September 1958
The Vicar's Letter: 'Mr. W. F. West was duly installed as Verger on July 27, and we wish him and Mrs. West all happiness in their work for God in His Church.
It will be widely known that the Trustees of the Palmer Cottages have offered the vacant cottage to Mrs. Martin of Sonning Eye – we wish her many happy years to enjoy her new home.'

St Patrick's Letter: Captain Langridge made the following determined appeal for males "with a good voice"! 'How good it would be if we could get some men in the choir, I'm sure there must be some good talent being wasted amongst our youth also, so come and use it in God's service. What a joy there is in singing!'

October 1958
The Vicar's Letter: 'October begins with the Harvest Thanksgiving. While it is true that the grain harvest in this country this year has fallen regrettably short of our hopes and expectations, this has not been so everywhere; again this is a Festival we keep in gratitude for all the material blessings with which the heavenly Father loads us during our earthly lives, and there is ample room for the warmest gratitude.'

Winter Campaign: 'The weather favoured us for the first round of our Campaign with a "Bring and Buy" afternoon in the Vicarage garden. The result was most satisfactory with net income of £46 13s 4d.'

November 1958

The Vicar's Letter: 'I want to thank the Embroidery Guild for the beautiful covers they have made for some of the hassocks in the Lady Chapel; the dedicated workmanship is quite exquisite, and I am most grateful.'

Sonning Working Men's Club: 'On the occasion of a Special General Meeting of the Club held on October 10, the Chairman took the opportunity of warning those present that unless there is an increase in membership and active interest the Club cannot survive. It is sincerely hoped that in face of the intense competition of modern outside attractions, the Club, with renewed vigour, will long survive and continue to fulfil its worth-while functions in our village community.'

Street Lighting: 'A Parish Meeting will be held in the Pearson Hall on Monday, November 17, to consider the provision of Street Lighting in the village. A plan showing the position of the proposed lights and estimates of the cost of installation and maintenance will be available to those attending.'

December 1958

The Vicar's Letter: The "Gordon Dickson" bequest has now been received on our behalf by the Diocesan Board of Finance, who will administer the trust for the upkeep and beautification of the Churchyard. It may not be known to everyone that Colonel Gordon Dickson was the brother of the first Mrs. Neville Player, and that the Colonel's wife was killed in a dreadful road accident. In his visits here he came to love Sonning so much that he wished to perpetuate his wife's memory by making this generous provision for the Churchyard.'

An Invitation: 'Mrs. Clement Williams has asked us to say that she is hoping to entertain her old friends and neighbours from Sonning Town and Sonning Eye in the Pearson Hall on Wednesday, January 14, at 3.45pm.   Husbands, wives, bachelors and spinsters who admit to being 65 or over, are invited to tea and entertainment. Will those who accept kindly write their names in a book provided at the Post Office. Mrs. Williams admits to an 80th birthday herself in December.'

January 1959
The Vicar's Letter: 'We are most grateful to the Bishop of Reading for coming over to take our Confirmations for us, with such kindly pastoral dignity, and we must continue to pray for the candidates that they may remain true and faithful soldiers and servants of Christ throughout their lives.'

Cassocks and Surplices: 'Supply of these garments for the Choir in the past has been plentiful, but the quality has deteriorated due to the passage of time and a quantity of them now require renewal. Would anyone who values the help that the Choir gives to our worship care to provide a cassock and or surplice? The Church Working Party "makes and mends" but even the best of things get beyond repair.'

[On January 29 it was reported that dense fog throughout much of Britain, the worst since 1952, had caused major disruption to transport.]

February 1959
Crisis in the East: 'The Middle East has ever been a region of crisis. During the last few years one crisis has followed another in quick succession. What does it mean and what lies behind all the unrest? How does it affect us? The Christian wants to ask another question still – "How does it affect the Church and her work? The Rev Eric Bishop will be in the Reading Town Hall at the Deanery Festival to tell you. He has been a missionary in Cairo for twenty-three years.'

St Patrick's Letter: 'I am trying to raise funds towards our new room (which we need very much) by having a Saturday night Dance once a fortnight 7.30pm to 10pm – 1/6d. including refreshments.
On Shrove Tuesday, February 10, at 7.30pm we shall be having our Sausage and Mash Supper and Social and Dance. Tickets will be 2/- inclusive.'

Women's World Day Prayer: 'Those who attended this World Day of Prayer Service in St Mary's, Reading last year, will, no doubt, like to come again this year and bring others with them. The service is at 3pm on Friday, February 13, in Broad Street Congregational Church.'

March 1959

Our Vicar Honoured: The following entry from the two churchwardens, Sidney Paddick and Percy Forward, was included in this issue of the magazine: 'We have great pleasure in informing all parishioners of the honour which has been bestowed upon the Vicar. He has been made an Honorary Canon of Christ Church Cathedral by the Bishop of Oxford. When one considers there are six hundred parishes in this diocese and only twenty-four Canonries, one can realise what an honour this is.'

Sonning Parochial Church Council – Report for 1958
The Report of the Vicar and P.C.C. to the Annual General Meeting 1959 included the following:
'The principal item of unusual expenditure has been on the Church Tower, which was repaired extensively in the spring under the direction of Mr. Ripley. Costs attributable to the Parish Magazine totalled £132. 12s. 0d against an income from sales and advertising of £111 18s 4d.
Mr. and Mrs. R. Hunt retired from the Pearson Hall during the year after seven years of caretaking, and were succeeded by Mr. and Mrs. Restall,
We have to record the passing during 1958 of the Verger, Mr. R. R. Adnam, Mr. Leonard Russell a former choirman, bellringer and church councillor, Mrs, Hendy a former organist and Mrs. Capon a former member of the Parochial Church Council.'

Sonning Cricket Club: 'Although it may seem rather early to think of cricket, arrangements have already been made for the season which will commence in May. Last year the club was, unfortunately, short of playing members and it is therefore anxiously seeking to obtain new members for the coming season. The club has one of the best grounds in the neighbourhood with an excellent wicket and has an attractive fixture list of afternoon games on Saturdays and Sundays.'

April 1959

The Vicar's Letter: 'I wish to record my own appreciation of the very beautiful and reverent rendering of Bach's Passion according to St Luke given by the Choir on Passion Sunday, and congratulate all, especially Mr. Lusty and the soloists, on their really splendid and finished achievement.'

The Parish Magazine: 'Mrs. A. Wright feels compelled to give up the work of organising the distribution of the Parish Magazine; we accept her resignation with great regret and with our warmest gratitude for her good work in this respect over a period of many years. We are glad to say that Mrs. Talbot, 9 Little Glebe has kindly consented to take over from her.'

May 1959
Woodley: 'By an Order, made by her Majesty in Council and published in the London Gazette of April 3, 1959, The Ecclesiastical Parish of Woodley has been transferred from the Rural Deanery of Sonning to the Rural Deanery of Reading. The purpose of this transfer is to facilitate the adjustment of the boundaries of the parishes of Woodley and Earley, and to enable the incumbents of both of those parishes to deal more satisfactorily with the large influx of urban population from Reading. Both Woodley and Earley parishes were part of the ancient parish of Sunning (*sic*), and now the only formal link between them and their mother is the fact that the Vicar of Sonning still has the right of nominating the two incumbents.'
[*The right of nomination by Sonning's vicar eventually ceased.*]

Sonning Regatta: 'Attention has recently been drawn to an account of £62 13s 8d standing to the credit of the Sonning Regatta with Lloyds Bank who also hold for safe keeping the various Challenge Cups.
After consultation with the Parish Council the Challenge Cups have been placed in a handsome show case in the Pearson Hall, and the balance of the money has been presented to the Pearson Hall Committee. It is generally considered unlikely that Sonning Regatta, at any rate in its old form, will ever be revived.'
[*Following the event which was held on September 2, 1939, the Sonning Regatta ceased to take place due to the outbreak of World War II. However, it was re-established in 2000 as a biennial event.*]

June 1959
Rogation Sunday: 'The first half of May has been particularly lovely this year and the weather glorious. Unfortunately, however, Rogation Sunday proved too wet for the service of the Blessing of the Crops to be

held in the open air, and we are sorry that this meant that the Sonning Silver Band was unable to escort and accompany us in the accustomed manner.'

Whitsun Farthing: 'We are glad to record that we improved on our Farthing Collection this year, the children of the parish raised a creditable total of 5,116 (St Andrew's 2,800 and St Patrick's 2316). The equivalent of £5 6s 7d. Lesley Fisher and Veronica Miller were chosen to represent the children of the parish and to present the money to our Bishop.'

July 1959

Cassocks and Surplices: 'Since the recent appeal in the magazine for donations towards the replacement of the very dilapidated cassocks and surplices of both the men and the boys, we have received generous subscriptions totalling £30 1s 0d. These gifts, together with the grant from Church funds, have enabled us to purchase fourteen cassocks and the material for seventeen surplices. The Working Party members have done a wonderful job of work in making the surplices. Miss Edwards has, in addition, spent many hours in making new collars for a large number of the existing surplices and this work deserves a special vote of thanks.'

Charvil Summer Fair: Captain Langridge included the following entry in his "St Patrick's Letter" report: 'Well! What a lovely day we had, glorious sunshine and a very genial company who came to support our effort. I think some people saw Charvil and our Church Hall for the first time.'
[*The net proceeds from the sale raised was £80 15s 0d.*]

August 1959

The Vicar's Letter: 'We rejoice that the good news has come through that the Ministry of Education has formally "recognised" the Reading Blue Coat School as a secondary school. This has naturally added joy and confidence to all their end of term festivities and their summer holidays. We congratulate the Head Master and Staff on this national recognition.'

The Sign: This inset, which continued to be supplied with issues of the parish magazine, was unable to be printed due to a printers strike which commenced in London, via the national newspapers in Fleet Street, and spread to a number of general printers throughout Britain during 1959: 'The Sign is one of the casualties of the printing strike. We are fortunate in being able to produce the rest of the magazine.'

[*On August 18 the British Motor Corporations new car is launched – a compact four seater to be known as a "Mini". The cost will be around £500 including purchase tax.*]

September 1959
The Vicar's Letter: 'Now that this glorious summer is drawing to its natural end, we shall be offering our thanksgiving this Harvest-time with greater gratitude than ever. Every household in the parish should be able to send at least one offering, a flower, a fruit, a vegetable to the adornment of the Father's house and the enjoyment of His less fortunate children; every household should be able to send at least one representative to thank the Father for all His many blessings. I think that Prime Minister Harold Macmillan's expression was "we have never had it so good".'

Ist Sonning Wolf Cubs: 'Raymond Fisher and Bryan Benstead have been enrolled as Wolf Cubs. During September some of our Cubs will be leaving us to join the Scout Troup, and so there will be vacancies for little lads of seven and a half years and upwards who would like to join us.'

October 1959
The Vicar's Letter: 'I commend the Dedication Festival on October 4 to your devote and joyful observance. This is the celebration of the birthday of our own Sonning Parish Church. The actual date of the consecration of the church is lost in the mists of antiquity, but in such cases Convocation has recommended that, in accordance with very ancient tradition, this festival should be observed on the first Sunday in October. Our beautiful Church and Churchyard – how grateful we should be and how glad we should be to keep one Sunday in the year to thank God for it!

We must be praying that on October 8 the Parliamentary electors may choose rightly fit persons to represent them in Parliament so that, in the words of the Prayer Book, "all things may be so ordered and settled by their endeavours, upon the best and surest foundations, that peace and happiness, truth and justice, religion and piety, may be established among us for all generations.'

[*The Conservative party was re-elected with a substantially increased majority in the general election. The number of seats in the new parliament resulted in 365 for the Conservatives, 258 Labour, 6 Liberals and 1 other.*]

November 1959

Wargrave-Piggott Founders Day: 'Saturday, October 10, was observed as Founders' Day at the Wargrave-Piggott Secondary Modern C. of E. School, to give it its full but cumbrous title, and in spite of it being a wet afternoon the School Hall was overcrowded. We are lucky to have such a good secondary modern school to take our children after they leave our primary school.'

St Patrick's Letter: A building extension to St Patrick's Hall had been planned and fund raising was underway to meet the anticipated cost of some £800. 'Very important is the extension to the Hall. We still need over £400. It's not an easy job raising funds, but do help when you can. We are hoping one day to see the Church's acre of ground edged with trees, adding beauty to the surroundings.'

December 1959

The Vicar's Letter: 'I wish first of all to express my appreciation of the work of the Choir and Organist for their ready help and their continual loyalty in attending practices and services. The three choral services on All Saints' Day were very beautifully rendered by a full choir; it is disappointing that the congregation did not show an equal realisation of the glory of this great Feast.

The church was as full as usual for the annual Remembrance Service, I am delighted to say that the children "did their stuff" beautifully and reverently.

Soon Christmas will have come and gone again. Will it be for you a Christmas with or without Christ in it? The services will be as usual.'

January 1960

The Parish Magazine: 'Our magazine enters on a new year of its existence. An extra fifty copies have been ordered for 1960, so that there will be plenty of opportunities for new readers. Each distributor will carry spare copies, so that they may be approached for copies as they go round; the subscription is only four shillings per annum.'

Scouts and Guides New Headquarters: 'Building of the new H. Q. on its site so kindly leased by the Sonning Parish Council is proceeding apace. Volunteer builders and helpers have been coming along on Saturday afternoons and the venture is now taking shape. We could still employ more assistance and would be grateful for further helpers.'

St Patrick's Letter: 'It is hoped that in the very near future we shall see the new extension being added to the church, the extra room is needed! When you get sixty or seventy children there on a Sunday morning divided into nine classes at Sunday School, there is not much room to move.'

February 1960

Church Social: 'The Pearson Hall was well filled in spite of slithery conditions outside, on the night of Friday, January 15, for which a Church "Social" had been arranged. A start was made with games to attempt to put everyone at their ease and to make a real mix up of the parishioners present. There followed the first part of a most delightful musical entertainment by the members of the Church Choir, arranged and also conducted by Mr. Crook. Captain Langridge then put on his radiogram which encouraged many, both young and old, to dance some of "the good old favourites." At ten o'clock the large company joined in the singing of Auld Lang Syne and The Queen, following which many apparently wanted some more!'

Young Wives' Group: 'At the January meeting Dr. Bailey spoke to us on children's ailments and gave some very helpful and practical advice and answered innumerable questions.'
[*Dr. Grenfell Moyle Bailey, a Sonning resident, was a partner for many years in a local medical practice.*]

March 1960

Sonning Parochial Church Council – Report for 1959

The Report of the Vicar and P.C.C. to the Annual General Meeting 1960 included the following:

'The Church School continues to flourish under Mr, Chapman's direction; Miss Puddock, who left us to go abroad after two years service, has now been replaced by Mrs. Evry, who has carried on her work with excellent results.

The Reading Blue Coat School continues to provide a large proportion of our boy choristers, as well as a number of servers and three apprentice bell-ringers, and we appreciate all their help and goodwill.

The parish magazine has increased its circulation and reduces its losses this year, We are most grateful to Miss Kemp for arranging the advertisements, to the distributors of each monthly issue, and not least to Mr. Heppell the printer who produces each number with such regularity.'

British Legion, Women's Section: 'The monthly meeting of the Sonning branch was held on Thursday, February 18, at 3pm. Mrs Woods gave a demonstration with a washing machine and spin dryer. Tea was served by Miss Wilkinson and helpers. The competition for the home-grown bulb was won by Mrs. D. Williams and Mrs. Somerville.'

April 1960

Robert Palmer Cottages: 'Mr. Martin McLaren M.P. and Mrs. McLaren are very kindly opening their garden in aid of the amenity funds of the Cottages on Saturday, April 9. The garden will be open from 11am to 5pm and a cup of tea will be provided. There will be a small entrance fee and a collection – The Dower House, Pearson Road.

[*Martin McLaren was Conservative Member of Parliament for Bristol North West.*]

Boy Scouts: 'The new Headquarters is proceeding thanks to the most energetic efforts of the parents' committee and friends of members. We would also like to thank all those who supplied us with items for our rummage sale. The Loddon District show "Bare Knees 1960" is in the final stage of rehearsal, we hope that the show will be better than ever.'

Sonning Ratepayers' Association: 'This association has now been officially formed. Anyone wishing to join or obtain information can get details from Mr. M. Wheeler, Blue Cottage, Park Way Drive, Sonning.'

May 1960

Meet our MP: 'Our Member of Parliament, Mr. W. R. van Straubenzee asks us to give notice that he will be available for interviews at the Woodclyffe Hostel, Wargrave, on Friday, May 13, from 5.30pm to 7.30pm; he feels that there may be some of his constituents who would find it difficult to reach him at Wokingham or Bracknell but would be able to get to Wargrave more easily.'

St Patrick's Letter: 'Believe me, I do not like having to appeal for finance, but we need it, so I do appeal to you. St Patrick's is not a large community and we are not able, as yet, fully to support ourselves. Link up with us, support in every way you can. There is an old saying, "The more we are together the merrier we shall be." Make it come true, enjoy your religion with us.'

June 1960

Sonning Ratepayer's Association: 'The Association is very active and the Officers and Committee are always ready to accept new members; there are quite a number who qualify to join and would be welcome at any time. There are several points being taken up about such items as "Why the increase in rates?", the action which should be taken about the crossing between Bath Road and Pound Lane, as regards pedestrians getting over for the bus halt.'

Lay Reader: 'We are glad to be able to announce that Mr. Donald F. Scott M.A., of the Reading Blue Coat School, having passed the necessary examinations, has been granted by the Lord Bishop his licence as a Parochial Lay Reader; we wish him every happiness in his new work, and we look forward to his ministrations among us. It will be noticed, that since Mr. Hoyle's day, the badge of the Lay Reader has been changed; the blue scarf is now the distinctive garb of the Lay Reader throughout the country.'

July 1960

St Patrick's: A number of gifts had been received of furniture, fittings and equipment for St Patrick's. Two further welcomed gifts were now received, an organ and a hymn board with sets of figures.

A *Notable Tercentenary:* 'The Reading Blue Coat School celebrated its Tercentenary on Wednesday, June 8, with a service of thanksgiving at St Laurence's Church, Reading, at which the Lord Bishop was the preacher. This was followed by the unveiling of a commemorative plaque at the School by Bishop Parham and a luncheon in a large marquee on the lawn. After lunch, a message of congratulations from Her Majesty the Queen was read, and speeches were made in honour of the occasion. The new boathouse was then formally opened by Colonel Burnell the Chairman of the Rural District Council.'

August 1960

The Vicar's Letter: 'I hope that it will be possible for you all to take a holiday sometime during this summer, and I trust that the weather will be kinder in August and September than it has been in July.

I want to express my personal thanks this month to those who have so kindly undertaken the onerous task of canvassing on behalf of the financial side of the Christian Stewardship Scheme, and to take this opportunity to congratulate them on the success which has already crowned their efforts.'

Sonning C. of E. School: 'The annual prize distribution took place on Thursday, July 21 in the Vicarage garden, when the usual thunderstorm somewhat dampened the proceedings, but, fortunately, there are plenty of trees around the garden, and everyone kept reasonably dry. A great feature of the school year had been the good number of "A" passes in the "11 plus examination".'

[*The cost of a pint of beer increases by a penny to 1/7d = 8p.*]

September 1960

The Vicar's Letter: 'This is of necessity a small number of the magazine, as there is little to record during the holiday month of August. I hope that all who have been away have managed to enjoy themselves in spite of the unsettled weather that has been experienced. I am grateful to Captain Langridge, Canon Wardley King and Mr. Phillips for carrying on during my absence, and to those others such as the Churchwardens and Verger, to whom it caused extra work.'

Best Kept Village Competition 1960: 'The Committee of the Women's Institute would like to thank all those who helped with this competition. The Sea Rangers, Girl Guides, Brownies and Boy Scouts all worked hard to help keep the village tidy, and to many others who cooperated in various ways. That Sonning should be amongst the first five out of twenty-five villages is entirely due to the cooperation of all concerned and should be sufficient encouragement to greater success in the future.'

October 1960

The Vicar's Letter: 'We are indeed sorry to be losing Mrs. Cazaly from the Post Office, and we are glad that a presentation has been made to her as a slight recognition of her services to our village for nearly twenty years of service. We now have the pleasure of welcoming Mr. S. W. Adams as her successor.'

Bell Ringers: 'We congratulate our ringers on winning the ringing competition for the Sonning Deanery at Sandhurst on Saturday, September 17.'

November 1960

The Vicar's Letter: 'October has continued the rainy record of 1960, and at the time of writing, the wet weather seems likely to continue.
The British and Foreign Bible Society's Festival in the Town Hall, Reading, on October 19, was the usual inspiring function. We were treated to a vivid address, some hearty congregational signing, and anthems by the Reading Lady Singers under the direction of Mr. Lusty. What a pity more of you were not there!'

Young Wives' Group: 'At our second October meeting, a representative from Hoovers entertained us with a demonstration of the Hoover carpet cleaner, and discussed the various types of carpet.
We have received an invitation to attend the first birthday party of the Twyford Group of Young Wives. They have arranged a very ambitious programme. The guest speaker will be Lana, the famous fashion model, and a mannequin parade will be given by Stuarts of Twyford. This is to be held in the Polehampton Boys' School, Twyford.'

December 1960

The Vicar's Letter: 'I was glad to see so many of you at the Thanksgiving Party on October 28, and I am grateful to all those who contributed to its success.

We are glad to see the new extension to St Patrick's taking shape, but it is not possible, at the moment of writing to say when it will be ready to be blessed and used.'

Wargrave-Piggott Church Secondary School: 'Parents and friends of present children and old scholars, will have learnt with considerable regret that Mr. C. C. V. Bush, who is the only headmaster the school has ever had, is retiring at Christmas after twenty years of service.'

Women's Institute: 'The November meeting was held in the Pearson Hall, Mrs. Welsh presiding. The members greatly enjoyed a Christmas cookery demonstration given by Miss Stibbs from Stork and Spry. There was a very good display of knitted articles made by members for the Christmas market on November 25, and also Christmas stocking presents for the adopted Polish family.'

CHAPTER FOUR

1961 - 1965

The magazine maintained the accustomed format; eight pages which comprised an illustrated self cover, three and a half pages of trade advertising and a further three and a half pages of articles and church service details. The photograph used for the illustrated cover page varied during the early sixties, being either an external view of Sonning church or the earlier used image of the reredos and altar. The printing of the magazine continued to be undertaken by J. Heppell, the Woodley based letterpress printer.

A change of headmaster took place at Sonning's C. of E. School in 1963 when Mr. Thomas Feak arrived as a replacement for the retiring Mr. H. C. Chapman. However, Harry Chapman remained in the locality and in time took over the editorship of the parish magazine from Sidney Groves.

The population expansion of Woodley, Charvil and Earley continued apace during the early years of the nineteen sixties. Sonning also saw the construction of new housing when part of the allotment land was used to build dwellings, which were designed for occupation by elderly residents.

Whilst World War II was permanently etched into the memory of those who as adults had lived through those grim and demanding times, there was now a younger generation who could be forgiven for considering that the war had now to be consigned to history. Inevitably, one strong connection that remained to link the war with the present day came to an end on 24 January 1965 with the death, at the age of ninety years, of the indomitable Winston Churchill.

Perfumery and Cosmetics by Elizabeth Arden, Yardley, Coty, **Max Factor**, Goya, etc., etc.

Kodak Films—Cameras   Complete Stock of Medicinal Wines

•

C. H. PATRICK, Ph.C., M.P.S.

Dispensing Chemist

TWYFORD, BERKS

(Telephone Twyford 201)

•

— The Country Pharmacy with the West End Stock —

We invite your inspection

FABRICS
LIBRARY
HOLMES
OF READING

Three Thousand of the loveliest Furnishing Fabrics— traditional and contemporary— Sanderson Sundour Rosebank Warners Tiber Liberty Heals.

All conveniently arranged for you to look through at your leisure.

J. Heppell, Printer, 141, Loddon Bridge Road, Woodley

Advertisement page: January 1961 (23.5cm x 17.5cm)

January 1961

Electoral Role: 'The Vestry and Annual General Church Meeting has been fixed for Monday, February 13, which means that the Electoral Roll is closed on January 30 until after this meeting. All church folk who have reached the age of seventeen and have not already signed the form of application must therefore do so before January 30; the forms may be obtained from the Verger on leaving church. In preparation for the meeting, the Finance Committee will meet on February 1.'

[*Dr. Michael Ramsey becomes Archbishop of Canterbury on January 19 following the retirement of Geoffrey Fisher.*
On January 20 power passed from the youngest to the oldest ever president when forty-three years old John Fitzgerald Kennedy is inaugurated into the USA's highest office and replaces seventy years old Dwight D. Eisenhower.]

February 1961

The Church School: 'An unfortunate and quite unexpected hitch has occurred in our project for the new school. After all the negotiations which have taken place and the work which has been put in and the money which has been subscribed, the Ministry of Education wrote to the Berkshire Education Authority on January 16, "I am sorry to say that we cannot make an allocation of capital available for this purpose at present." The managers will meet to consider what can be done.'

[*The BBC announces that "Children's Hour" which had been broadcast by radio since 1922 was to end in April.*]

March 1961

Sonning Parochial Church Council – Report for 1960
The Report of the Vicar and P.C.C. to the Annual General Meeting 1961 included the following:
'We deeply appreciate the loyal help and ever-ready support of the Reading Blue Coat School which continues to grow and flourish under Mr. B. G. Inge's capable direction and has just celebrated its tercentenary. The school has now furnished us with a Lay Reader in addition to servers, choristers and ringers. Our Youth Societies and Clubs have been carried on through the year by able and devoted leaders. The Sea Rangers have been temporarily closed down, after twelve successful years under Miss Staley's leadership.

The Church Council and its Finance Committee have met regularly during the year, and Mr. S. Morris has succeeded Mr. C. Williams as Hon. Treasurer.' Abbreviated accounts were included in this March issue which indicated that the parish magazine had incurred a lost for the year 1960 of £25.

April 1961

The Vicar's Letter: 'Mr. Paddick has made the offer to undertake the work of re-decorating the Church at his own cost, and I must here take the first opportunity of expressing my own personal gratitude to him for his great generosity. This means that, by his own wish, the work will start almost immediately; as soon as the necessary plans can be made and the necessary authorities consulted. There is also a certain amount of work to be done to the fabric, as required under the new "Inspection of Churches" measures, which in these circumstances, can now be carried out and paid for at once. By the end of the year, therefore, the Church should be whole and clean outside and in.

I have the great privilege of joining the Diocesan Pilgrimage to the Holy Land this April, so that I shall be taking the greater part of my holiday this month. I understand that there will be thirty-two of us in this party. We are scheduled to spend the first week in Galilee and a further week in Jerusalem, the tour also include a passing visit to Rome and to Athens.'

Hoyle Memorial Room: A new room extension for St Patrick's had been completed, and it was decided that the room should bear the names of the late Frederick and Winifred Hoyle, who had both given outstanding service over many years to the parish. The formal opening of the new room and dedication was performed by Sidney Paddick, appropriately on St Patrick's Day (March 17).

The Holy Scriptures: 'One of the outstanding events of the month of March has been the publication of a fresh translation of the New Testament, couched not in the familiar and beautiful language of the Authorised Version of 1611, but in the "vulgar tongue" of to-day. Once again the Bible has proved to be a "best seller", for the first impression of one million copies was completely sold out before midday on the day of publication.'

May 1961

The Vicar's Letter: Now the new version of the New Testament has been in circulation for a few weeks, the Church Council has suggested that from May onwards it shall be used in church at my discretion and in accordance with the Lord Bishop's instructions.'

Church Decorations: 'The sub-committee have engaged the services of the Warham Guild Artist and Architect, Mr. Colin Shewring, to draw out a scheme for the work of re-decorating the church. His scheme has been submitted to the Parochial Church Council, who have given it their general approval, and has now been passed to the Diocesan Advisory Board for their comments. This re-decoration, so long overdue, will be a large undertaking, and will inevitably cause the successive closing off of the different parts of the Church – a small inconvenience in comparison with the great boon which will be conferred on us.'

St Patrick's Letter: The total funding of Charvil's new hall had yet to be achieved, as witnessed by Captain Langridge's further appeal: 'Summer Fair, it is hoped that this effort will have every support. The proceeds will go to paying off the £300 needed for the extension to our Church and Hall – how pleased I shall be to see this accomplished! Donations can be sent to me at any time.'

June 1961

The Vicar's Letter: 'I return to Sonning deeply grateful for the privilege of having been able to join in the Diocesan Pilgrimage to the Holy Land, for the treasured memories of the services we held together at the Sacred Sites, the daily Eucharists and Evensongs we shared, the joy of being allowed to celebrate the Holy Mysteries myself right in the Holy City as well as near the beautiful Lake of Galilee, the thrill of treading in the Saviour's footsteps in Nazareth, in Jerusalem and in many other places as well.'

Sunday School: 'It is proposed this year to hold a joint outing for the two churches on July 15, the destination being Bognor Regis. Parents will be able to accompany their children at a cost of about ten shillings.'

July 1961

St Patrick's Letter: Captain Langridge was able to report a welcomed contribution to the remaining funds required for the Charvil hall: 'I know that you will rejoice with me at the result of our Summer Fair. A profit of £129. This is a great help towards the £300 needed for our Church Extension. We owe our gratitude to all who helped to make our effort a success. Thank you.'

A Vocational Career for Women: 'The Oxford Diocesan Board of Women's Work is trying to make known the many possibilities for young women to train for full time salaried lay service for the Church. The opportunities for responsible work are various and these include Chaplain's Assistants in the Forces, in hospitals and in universities, Moral Welfare Workers and Parish Workers, as well as work in the mission field. Many parishes in this diocese have vacancies on their staff for trained Women Workers, and suitable candidates are urgently needed.'

August 1961

The Vicar's Letter: 'July has been one of the busiest months that I remember, but now the holiday month is upon us, and with both churches undergoing re-decoration, there are few special events of which to give notice. At the Parish Church, both aisles are completed with a very delightful appearance of brightness and cleanliness, and the difficult problem of the Nave is now being tackled – the work being some weeks ahead of schedule.
I find it has been my good fortune to have been Vicar of Sonning longer than anyone since Canon Pearson – but don't be depressed, I shall not be here as long as he was!'

Sonning C. of E. School: 'The Sonning School annual Prize Day took place on Monday, July 17, in the Vicarage garden. The Headmaster, Mr. H. Chapman, reported on the school in general. Due to reduction in numbers, the Education Committee had not replaced Mrs. Evry, but had provided a part-time teacher, Mrs. Waghorn, for the coming year. The headmaster further commented that the school had done well in the "11+ examination, four children were going to Grammar Schools, and one had obtained the Rich & Reade Scholarship to the Reading Blue Coat School.'

September 1961

The Vicar's Letter: 'The great work of redecorating St Andrew's Church is nearly finished, and should be entirely completed during September. The Church will henceforth be more beautiful than it has ever been in its long and varied history. Our Dedication Festival, the Church's birthday, we will keep on October 1, which will thus be an occasion of rejoicing for us, and thanksgiving to God who put this glorious design and purpose of beautifying His Sanctuary into His servant's heart.

You will all join me in congratulating Mr. Lusty, who this month will have completed fifty years as a Church Organist, nine of which have been spent with us here in Sonning.'

Sonning Parish Council: The Council met on July 25, with Mr. Paddick in the chair. Included within the matters reported were the following: 'It was hoped that the new school would be built in 1961/62 and that it would be necessary to provide an entrance to the site through the Children's Corner. Many complaints had been received regarding the dilapidated condition of the kiosk on the Bridge, and a further approach is to be made to the owners to see if this eyesore could be removed.

The excessive speed of lorries through the village was also discussed.'

New Sonning School: The following postscript from Sidney Groves was included in this issue: 'I am afraid that the Parish Council are unduly optimistic about the building of the new school. The Ministry has not only turned down our application for its inclusion in the 1961/62 programme, but also in that of 1962/63.'

October 1961

Sonning Women's Institute: 'There was a good attendance last week at Sonning W. I. at the first meeting convened after the summer holiday. Miss Dadley read a letter of thanks, for a sum of money from the Institute, which had been received from the adopted Polish family, who are always grateful for things sent to them. Miss Chamberlain gave a very interesting talk on flower arrangement, with demonstrations of treatment for various kinds of flowers.'

St Patrick's Letter: 'To young parents (or anyone else in Charvil). On the Third Sunday of each month beginning October 15 at 10.15am we are to have a forty minute family service at St Patrick's. A number have said that "they are unable to get to evening service etc.," because of the children. At this service you come with the children; if they cry it will not matter. Now do come and make it worthwhile!'

November 1961
The Vicar's Letter: 'I have made arrangements to give my talk on my April pilgrimage to the Holy Land in the Pearson Hall on Monday, November 20, at 7.45pm. The talk will be illustrated by lantern slides and also probably by an epidiascope. I am thinking of dividing the talk into two separate parts – Galilee and Judaea – with light refreshments in between. This will, to a possible extent, take the place of a parish social.'

1st Sonning Girl Guide Company: 'The Company started this year with twenty-six Guides who are working on all parts of the test work. Last year six Guides passed their Tenderfoot test, five gained the Second Class and Pamela Salvage gained her First Class and All Round Cords. Forty eight Proficiency badges were awarded. The Company is very sorry that Mrs. Newman, Lieutenant, is leaving at the end of the year and will miss her very much.'

December 1961
The Vicar's Letter: 'I am most grateful to Mrs. Atkinson and her helpers for arranging the refreshments at my Holy Land talk so capably, and to Mr. Chapman for showing the pictures. I am afraid the talk was rather long, but it seemed a pity to leave anything out.
My wife and I are most happy at the engagement of our daughter, Miriam, to Mr. Donald Scott, our Lay Reader, who has been employed as an Assistant Master at the Reading Blue Coat School for the last four and a half years.'

British Legion, Women's Section: 'A Poppy Day Whist Drive was held in the Pearson Hall on Friday, November 10, when a sum of £13 2s. 0d was raised.'

Remembrance Sunday: 'The usual service was held, in commemoration of the gallant dead of the two world wars, on Sunday, November 12. We were sorry that, owing to indisposition, Major-General L. Price-Davies, V.C. was unable to be with us; in his absence Mr. G. Newman, Chairman of the Sonning Branch of the British Legion, read the Roll of Honour.'

January 1962
The Vicar's Letter: 'A party of thirty-one went to Sunningdale Church to witness the Nativity Play, performed with devoted reverence and almost ineffable beauty of pageantry and music. All of us were deeply stirred by the performance, next year we hope to be able to take a much larger party.'

Sonning Parish Council: A Council meeting was held in the Pearson Hall on Tuesday, November 28. The following were among the items reported in this issue:
'As there are very many vacant allotments, and no further applications are being received, the Parish Council consider it to be a suitable site for housing development, and consequently the Wokingham Rural District Council have been approached.
The present two ton weight restriction on traffic using the bridges is proving satisfactory.
It was noted that various roads and footpaths require repair.'

Parish Magazine: 'It will be noted, first that we have a new photograph and block for our cover. The excellent photograph of the newly-decorated reredos was taken by Mr. May of London Street, and copies of the original will be obtainable. Secondly, we are changing our inset to *Home Words*, which, it is hoped, will prove acceptable to all our readers.'
[*see: pages 122 and 124 – Cover and Text pages January 1962.*]

February 1962
Church School: A letter was printed in this issue from the Ministry of Education. The letter confirmed that the ministry was unable to approve the building of a new school in Sonning at the present time. The limited capital available had been allocated until March 31, 1963.

SONNING
PARISH MAGAZINE

JANUARY 1962   PRICE 4d.

Cover page: January 1962. (23.5 x 17.5cm)

Christmas: The Vicar included the following comments: 'We are most grateful once more to those who decorated the Church so beautifully for the Festival, and to the organist and choir for their services. The attendances on Christmas Eve and Christmas Day were very good, but the weather seriously interfered with our worship on the following Sunday. I have myself to apologise to the people of Charvil for my failure to reach them for the 9am Eucharist, but, despite assistance, I could not get the car up the hill – and there was no time to walk.'

March 1962

Sonning Parochial Church Council – Report for 1961
The Report of the Vicar and P.C.C. to the Annual General Meeting 1962 included the following:
'The Regular staff of the Church Day School has been reduced to three, with one part-time assistant, owing to a fall in numbers, but the work has progressed successfully.
The various youth societies and clubs are still maintaining a high standard, and meeting an urgent need.
The structural repairs to be undertaken to the Parish Church, as required by the Inspector of Churches Measure, are well in hand, and a system of oil-fired heating has been installed at the cost of some £850.'
The parish magazine account for the year 1961 showed a loss of £19.

April 1962

Sonning Parish Council: The annual parish meeting was held in the Pearson Hall on March 12. The report included the following items:
'Repairs to the Tennis Courts on the Recreation Ground have been carried out and re-surfacing which it is hoped will be satisfactory.
The Council has made proposals to the Rural District Council that a portion of the allotments should be used as a site for building twenty-four old people's bungalow homes. The R.D.C. have accordingly agreed to purchase the land for this purpose.'

Boy Scouts Revue: 'The annual Loddon District Scout Show, "Bare Knees 1962" will be staged at the Pearson Hall on Friday and Saturday, April 27, and 28, commencing at 7.45pm. Once again the Sonning Troop has the largest number of any troop in the district in the cast, and we hope you will come along and support your local troop.'

St. Patrick's

Holy Communion on Sundays, January 14 and 28, at 9 a.m.; on Thursdays, January 11 and 25, at 10.15 a.m.; on Fridays, January 19 and February 2, at 7.30 a.m., and on Saturday, January 6, at 7.30 a.m.

Family Service on Sunday, January 21, at 10.15 a.m.

Children's Hour at 11.30 a.m. and Evensong at 6.30 p.m. every Sunday

Women's Afternoon on Wednesday, January 17, at 3 p.m.

Prayer Group on Tuesday, January 23, at 3 p.m.

St. Patrick's Letter

Dear Friends,

A very Happy New Year to you all.

During December the Sunday School children had their Prizegiving and Party. May I say "thank you", to all who sent cakes and refreshment or provided in other ways, and to all who helped in any way. A very nice time was had by all.

At the time of writing Christmas is very near and we are having a Nativity Play; in next month's letter more will be said.

Looking back over the past year we see a few things which have given us happiness, the finishing of the Extension to the Church, the re-decorating, both outside and inside, and new curtains, making it a place of welcome for worship and other activities.

We have had our encouragements and our disappointments, but as we step out into 1962 let us as Christians see that we play our part and do as a Christian ought to do. Let us see that we keep our appointments with God in His House, in our reading of His Holy Word, in our prayer life. If we all did this our churches would be filled, our lives and homes happier places, God's will being fulfilled. The Kingdom of God within.

Will you who read this letter really try, then life will be worth while during this coming year.

Health, Happiness, God's Blessing be with you.

Yours sincerely,
L. O. C. LANGRIDGE,
Captain, C.A.

Magazine

The next number of the magazine is due for publication on Thursday, February 1; all copy should therefore reach the Vicar by Saturday, January 20.

It will be noted, first that we have a new photograph and block for our cover. The excellent photograph of the newly-decorated reredos was taken by Mr. May of London Street, and copies of the original will be obtainable. Secondly, we are

changing our inset to Home Words, which, it is hoped, will prove acceptable to all our readers.

Vestry and A.G.M.

The date for the holding of the Vestry and Annual General Parochial Church Meeting has been fixed for Tuesday, February 20. This means that the Electoral Roll closes on February 6, by which date all new applications for enrolment must have been received. It should be noted that the minimum age for enrolment is now 17.

C.F.Y.

Stands for Christian Family Year, to be observed from May, 1962, to May, 1963. More will be heard of this — meanwhile, is your Family Life Christian?

Mothers' Union

A meeting was held at the Vicarage on December 7, the speaker being Miss Wheeler. For her subject she took the Christmas Story which she illustrated with Flannelgraph.

Mrs. Long welcomed one new member and two prospective members. M.U. members are invited to join the Young Wives at the Pearson Hall on February 6, 1962, at 7.30 p.m.

At our monthly meeting on February 1, 1962, there will be a bring and buy stall, in aid of Christian Family Year.

V.M.L.

Dear fellow members,

I must first of all thank you very much indeed for the beautiful azalea you so kindly sent me for Christmas; it is beautiful and I am delighted with it. Our next meeting is in Church on January 4 at 3 p.m. when the Vicar will continue his talks on "Women of the New Testament". The Prayer Group will be on Tuesday, January 16, in Church at 3 p.m. Please don't forget we are having a "Bring and Buy" at our February meeting when Mrs. Stevens will be telling us about plans and aims for C.F. Year.

The Quarterly Corporate Communion is on January 21 at 8 a.m. (11 a.m. if unable to come at 8 a.m.).

With my very best wishes for your Peace and Happiness throughout 1962.

Sincerely,
Essie M. Long.

Young Wives

January 2, 7.30 p.m. at "Gramarye", Holmemoor Drive, Sonning. Mrs. Atkinson — Photographs of a Bavarian Holiday.

January 11, 7.30 p.m. at "Birchcroft", Glebe Lane. "Working Party".

Text page: January 1962. (23.5 x 17.5cm)

May 1962

The Vicar's Letter: 'I write too early to make any comment on our Easter Services, but I know that I can safely express your and my thanks to the choir, organist and decorators for all they do to help us in our worship. Easter is late, and so is spring, and we seem to have had enough of our wintry weather. This time last year I was enjoying the warmth and sunshine of Palestine – indeed on this date I was bathing in the Sea of Galilee.'

Bishop of Reading's River Trip: The vicar provided an introduction, including details of a service that had been arranged, on the occasion of an unusual visit to Sonning by the bishop: 'I hope that as many of you as possible will gather on the wharf (the piece of grass between the river and the White Hart Hotel) to meet the Bishop of Reading.'

From the Bishop of Reading: 'You will have heard of my proposed river trip from one end of the county (Buscot) to the other (Old Windsor). Along these 110 miles or so of the Thames about forty parishes stretch down to the water and it is my plan to step ashore at every one and, in this way, pay a somewhat unusual type of visit. I hope to arrive in your parish on Wednesday, May 9, at about 3 o'clock, and I look forward to seeing as many of you as possible– *Eric Reading.*'

Warning: 'We are asked to issue a reminder that the old series of £1 notes will cease to be legal tender after May 28. Any savings hoarded in these notes in old socks or boxes must be changed before then.'

June 1962

The Bishop of Reading: 'We all greatly enjoyed the Bishop of Reading's visit to us on Wednesday, May 9, and were pleased to see so many adults joining with the children in welcoming him on the wharf and in the little service in Church. The Mother's Union members excelled themselves in the beautiful tea they provided for us in the Pearson Hall afterwards, which gave everyone an opportunity of having a word with the Bishop. The children apparently enjoyed the afternoon too – not least the "suitable refreshment" provided for them in the School canteen.'

Diocesan Missionary Festival 1962: The Bishop of Oxford provided the following information in this issue: 'This year's Festival will be held in Reading on Thursday, July 12. This annual Festival is a representative act of the whole Diocese in which we pray and think together in order to renew our dedication to the cause of spreading the Gospel through the work of the Church Overseas. There will be a continuous exhibition and showing of films. Services and meetings will be held in the morning, afternoon and evening, so as to make it possible for the maximum number of people to attend – *Harry Oxon.*'

July 1962

The Vicar's Letter: 'The Rogation Service was blessed with a dry, though cool and somewhat cloudy evening, and we were able to foregather at the University Farm in fair numbers, but unfortunately without the aid of the Sonning Silver Band. We were glad to have with us at the Service the Rev. J. G. Graham, the newly-appointed Chaplain to the Reading University.

Yesterday I celebrated the twentieth anniversary of my Institution as your Vicar and I thank you for your help, friendship and forbearance. 1962 seems for me a year of "round-number" anniversaries; forty years a priest, thirty-five years a Vicar, twenty years Vicar of Sonning, ten years Rural Dean of Sonning.'

From The Bishop of Reading: 'I take the earliest opportunity I have had since I stepped ashore two weeks ago to write and thank you and your people for the hospitality and warm welcome you gave me upon my arrival at your port of call. All along the coast of Berkshire I found a pleasant and useful programme laid on in each parish and I was very glad of the opportunity thus presented to meet so many people, and I have returned with a most cheering impression of Church life in all the parishes I visited. – *Eric Reading*'

St Patrick's Letter: 'St Patrick's Summer Fair – what a lovely day we had. God's sunshine smiling upon us. We have not quite settled all of our accounts or received all our money in but I feel confident we shall have cleared off the debt of our Church Extension. So you see, we have much to thank God for.'

August 1962

The Vicar's Letter: 'The weather has been kind for all of our outdoor events this year, including the St Patrick's Fair and the School prize giving. Thanks to the hard work put in, the Fair was a great success and resulted in a balance of £124, which extinguished the debt on the Extension.

The service and tea in the garden on Sunday, July 1, for the families with infant children, provided a very pleasant gathering, and we all enjoyed the tea kindly supplied by the Young Wives.

One of the most interesting events of the past month was, to my mind, the visit to the Houses of Parliament, in which I was allowed to join with the top form of the school. Mr. van Straubenzee, our Member of Parliament, was so kind as to give up two hours of his valuable time to us, and greatly contributed to our enjoyment.

The Diocesan Missionary Festival at St Giles' Church and at Olympia in Reading was remarkable in many ways; in the variety of the day's events, in the number of people who attended it, and in the excellence of the organisation. What a pity that so few Sonning people went!

We congratulate John Cornish on his discovery of a Roman coin in Sonning Eye. The Director of the Reading Museum states, "it was issued by the Constantine dynasty and minted at Trier (Treves) some time between 335 and 350 A.D. It is in splendid condition".'

Women's Institute: 'On June 27, we welcomed a party of old ladies from a club connected with a London church. After tea at the Pearson Hall the visitors were taken round two lovely gardens through the kindness of Mrs. Paddick and Mrs. Williams, and obviously much enjoyed it. Each received a small present, also some sweets and a bunch of flowers.'

September 1962

Sonning Parish Council: A Parish Council meeting was held on August 9, the report included the following items:

Access to the new school was discussed and approval of the National Playing Fields Association is awaited.

Laying of the new sewers through the Recreation Ground has caused flooding. The Chief Engineer of Wokingham R.D.C. has been notified.

Repairs to the iron bridge are complete, we hope that a five-ton limit will be imposed.'

St Patrick's Letter: 'We would very much value financial support through the "My Gift to God and Church" effort. Envelopes are supplied, dated weekly, monthly or as you wish, and are a great help in the work. The amount collected for the Church Army Emblem week was – Charvil £9 6s 0d; Sonning £15. 14s 1d. The Church Army send their thanks for all support given.'

October 1962

The Vicar's Letter: 'We heartedly congratulate Mr. Tomes and all the members of the Parents' Committee of the Local Scouts Association on the completion and opening of their new and very fine hut on the Sonning Recreation Ground, and thank all those who were in any way responsible for erecting this splendid meeting place for our young folks' activities. The opening by Mrs. Powell took place during the course of the Sports' Afternoon on September 15.

Our congratulations to our sidesman, Mr. John Morris, who is to marry another member of our congregation, Miss Diane Chopping.

We are glad and thankful that Miss Amor has very kindly taken over Miss South's task of looking after the choir cassocks and surplices. But we still need someone to volunteer to play the organ for the Mothers' Union services and for the afternoon service on the first Sunday in every month.

Mrs. Allan, of Elveley, West Drive, has kindly taken over the task of delivering the Parish Magazine. We still need a volunteer to organise the Bible Reading Fellowship.'

The Choir: 'We would welcome two ladies (mezzo soprano) also two gentlemen to sing bass. Apply to the Vicar or Mr. Lusty.'

New School Building: 'A further letter from the Ministry of Education states "the capital available for minor works at aided schools is restricted but the Minister will continue to keep the Managers' proposals under review".'

[*The "Cuban Crisis" brought about by Russia establishing a missile base in Cuba, had seized the world's attention with the horrific possibility of a nuclear war. Finally, on October 28, an agreement was reached between the USA's President Kennedy and the Soviet leader Mr. Khrushchev which averted potentially a catastrophic outcome.*]

November 1962

The Vicar's Letter: 'The Bible Society Festival was again as inspiring an event as always – The New Elizabethan Singers gave us of their best, whilst the Bishop of Buckingham's address was most thought provoking and illuminating. The mass of voices singing the hymns is always a delight.

A Deanery Christian Family Year "Any Questions" event was held at Wokingham on October 9 and was a great success, and in spite of fog there was a fair attendance. The panel consisted of:

The Mayor of Wokingham, Dr. Phyllys Pigott (Chairman), Mr. W. van Straubenzee M.P., Mrs. Swinbank, Mrs, May (Moral Welfare Worker) and Rev. J. J. Williams (Rector of St Paul's, Wokingham). Sensible and interesting questions were asked and well answered.'

Sonning Parish Council: A Parish Council meeting was held on Friday, October 16, the report included the following items:

'The Wokingham Rural District Council is arranging to provide and to also maintain a lifebelt at Sonning Wharf.

'A letter had been received from the Wokingham RDC agreeing to purchase approximately two acres of allotment land to build the Old Peoples' Homes.'

December 1962

Remembrance Sunday: 'The usual solemn service of commemoration of the fallen of the 1914 and 1939 wars was held at 10.30am on Sunday, November 11. As General Price Davies, V.C., was unable to perform the duty of proclaiming the Roll of Honour, his place was taken by Mr. W. Huggins, M.M. our oldest Ex-Servicemen and president of the British Legion branch. The service proceeded with its usual dignified solemnity, the two-minute silence being its focal point. The fact that every spare seat in the Church was occupied seems to give the lie to the theory, sometimes expressed, that this commemoration has passed its period of usefulness.'

1st Sonning Scouts: 'It is pleasing to announce that the Scouts and Cubs, Guides and Brownies are now holding their activities in the new Headquarters on the Recreation Ground. One hundred young people belonging to the local Scouting Movement are now able to have a headquarters of their own in which to pursue their various activities.'

January 1963

The Vicar's Letter: 'On November 24, Our Member of Parliament, Mr. W. van Straubenzee, kindly met some of us at the School in response to a request for help in expediting the building of the new School. We greatly appreciate his interest and sympathy, and hope that he may be able to intervene in the right quarters and achieve a successful result for the benefit of our children.

The Parish Party seemed to be enjoyed by the large number of folk who attended it, and the programme of dancing and entertainment, as well as the refreshments, met with universal approval.

We congratulate Mrs. Mellor on being appointed as the new tenant of the vacant Robert Palmer Cottage; I think it is some time since we had a Woodley lady in one of the cottages. Mrs. Mellor has given much time and service to social work in Woodley, and we are glad to be able to offer her this accommodation in Sonning.'

[*Most parts of Britain suffered the worst weather conditions for over two hundred years during the 1962-63 winter. Widespread heavy fog during late November and early December was followed by a sustained intense cold period. A heavy snow fall occurred on Boxing Day and did not thaw until early March in most parts of the country, which included the Thames Valley.*]

February 1963

The Vicar's Letter: 'I hope that, by the time you read these lines, the weather will not be quite so arctic, and that we shall be able to see the green fields again. Unfortunately, the cold and snow have hampered our activities for the last month very considerably.

At Easter my term of service as Rural Dean will expire, and at my request the Lord Bishop will not renew my commission. I think that it is now no secret that Mr. Chapman will be retiring at the end of July as Head Teacher, and Miss Simmons as Assistant. This is indeed sad, alas! inevitable, and the Managers are now engaged in selecting suitable successors.

Meanwhile, Mr. van Straubenzee has been exercising his charm on Mr. Christopher Chataway, but as yet has received no promise about the new School.'

[*Chataway was a Junior Education Minister and one time world class athlete.*]

March 1963

Sonning Parochial Church Council – Report for 1962
The Report of the Vicar and P.C.C. to the Annual General Meeting
1963 included the following:
'The Church building and the oil-fired heating apparatus have stood up well to
the demands made upon them by the intense cold of the winter. The repairs
to the fabric required by the last inspection have been completed, we can look
with confidence to the Surveyor's second survey which is due in 1963.
St Patrick's has been the scene of the usual services and social activities. A
cross has been affixed to the east end of the roof, and a notice board bearing
the list of services has been erected. A Processional Cross made in the work-
room of the Wargrave-Piggott School has been presented and dedicated.'
The accounts for the year 1962 showed a profit for the parish magazine of £3.

Sonning Parish Council: A meeting was held on Wednesday, February 13
and the report included the following items:
'The plans had been received from the Ministry of Transport of the proposed
alteration at the top of Pound Lane in connection with the proposed new
roundabout; these were approved but it is hoped that some of the trees and
shrubs between Pound Lane and Parkway Drive can be retained.
Plans had been submitted to the Wokingham R.D.C. for new bus shelters to
be erected in Pound Lane and Pearson Road.'

Sonning Women's Institute: 'The President, Mrs. Torkington, presided at
the February meeting, which was held in the Pearson Hall. Hearty
congratulations were given to Mrs. Hall whose picture was selected for
the current exhibition at the Art Gallery, and to Mrs. Prior, whose play
was placed fourteenth at the National Competition last year.'

April 1963

The Vicar's Letter: 'The Church Needlework Guild, under the skilled
guidance of Miss Atkins, is doing some splendid work for our Altars,
making and embroidering stoles, burses and veils. For some time now
the members have been meeting regularly at the Green House, at the
kind invitation of Mrs. Ogden.
A bitterly cold night accompanied those who came to see the film
which had been arranged by the Christian Family Year Committee on
February 20, it should have been viewed by a much larger and younger
audience.'

Church School: 'To succeed Mr. Chapman as Headmaster of our School the Managers have appointed Mr. T. A. Feak. at present Deputy-Head of West Green county School in Crawley, Sussex, a mixed Junior School of 300 pupils. Mr. Feak who is married and has two sons, will be taking up his duties here when the autumn term starts on September 10, and, I am sure, will receive a warm welcome from parents and children and from the whole of our community in which he will be having such a responsible position. He is a talented musician and is now organist and choirmaster at Pulborough Parish Church. All good wishes to Mr. and Mrs. Feak for a very happy stay among us.'

May 1963

The Vicar's Letter: 'We would wish to thank the Choir and Organist for their good services, especially in the Passion Cantata on Good Friday evening, and on Easter Day. We are also most grateful to the Reading Lady Singers, who came out to augment the Choir for the Good Friday evening service. The Church again looked beautiful for the Festival, thanks to those who gave and arranged flowers.

We now have to thank the Church Needlework Guild for completing two sets of red stoles, burses and veils, one for the Parish Church and one for St Patrick's, both sets exquisitely embroidered.

A new set of white vestments, with red orphreys, has been purchased out of Church funds for St Patrick's.

Everyone in the Deanery will be delighted that the Rev. F. J. E. Britnell, Vicar of St Sebastian's, Wokingham, has been appointed by the Lord Bishop to succeed me as Rural Dean of Sonning.'

Young Wives: 'A visit to the "Holy Land" was vividly described and illustrated by Canon Groves at our meeting last month to a thoroughly appreciative audience.'

Christian Family Year: 'The concluding service of thanksgiving at the end of the first Christian Family Year takes place at St Paul's Cathedral in London on May22, to be attended by the Queen and the Duke of Edinburgh. Mr. and Mrs. Atkinson have the great privilege of attending this very special service as representatives of the Sonning Deanery.'

June 1963

The Vicar's Letter: 'The chief parochial news this month is, of course, the announcement that the Ministry of Education has given permission for us to re-build our School. The site chosen is the large field to the south of the Recreation Ground, the access to it having been kindly permitted by the Sonning Parish Council. The Diocesan Council of Education has also given its consent, and will be giving us every assistance that is possible.

You must not imagine that an undertaking of this importance and magnitude can be carried through in the twinkling of an eye, and we must all be patient. An architect must be appointed and draw up his plans, which must be approved by many authorities; then the work must be put out to tender – and so on.

We are most grateful to the Local Education Authority, to our Member of Parliament, and to any others who have assisted in obtaining this permission.

The new School will technically be a "transferred Aided Voluntary Primary School", and will eventually accommodate 120 children in four classrooms, with hall, canteen, etc.'

Sonning C. of E. School: 'As we go to press we learn with deep regret of the death of Miss Ethel M. Fox, who taught at Sonning School for over forty years.

It will be widely known that Mr. Chapman and Miss Simmons will be leaving us this term after eighteen and thirteen years' service respectively. We shall desire to give them some tangible tokens of our affection and gratitude for the considerable contribution they have made to the School, a subscription list will be opened.'

July 1963

The Vicar's Letter: The Rev. Groves referred to a letter which the P.C.C. had insisted should be printed in this issue of the magazine. The letter was an acknowledgment of the contribution that Sidney Groves had made to the parish having served twenty-one years as the Sonning parish priest. His was now the second longest Sonning ministry, second only to Hugh Pearson's long forty years of ministry served during the previous century.

New Sonning Primary School: 'The Managers recently spent an interesting afternoon visiting new schools in the neighbourhood; with the approval of the Diocesan Council of Education, they have selected as their Architect, Mr. George Batten, who designed the new Earley School, opened by the Lord Bishop on June 14.'

Women's Institute: 'Mrs. Torkington was in the Chair at the June meeting which was convened in the Pearson Hall. Following the usual discussions of business, and the reading of a letter of thanks from the Polish family, it was confirmed that rug-making classes will commence during the autumn. The financial statement showed that there was a balance in hand of £52.'

Server: 'Philip Arthur Whittaker was admitted to the office of Altar Server on Sunday, May 28, and subsequently performed his duties at the Holy Eucharist which followed.'

August 1963
The Vicar's Letter: The letter reported only two occurrences, the deaths of notable local parishioners. Clement Hilton Williams M.B.E. (1877-1963) had made considerable contributions to the parish having served on many committees which included the chairmanship of the parish council and long time member of the rural district council. William Henry Bale C.B.E. (1883-1963) was a former mayor of Reading and alderman of the borough over a long period of time.
[*Both Clement Williams (1877-1963) and William Bale (1883-1963) are interred in the Sonning churchyard. see: Record of Burials etc. Church of St Andrew 2012.*]

Chiropody: 'The chiropody service which has recently commenced for elderly people in the village is progressing satisfactorily. Mrs. Thorne S.R.N., attends the Pearson Hall fortnightly. Anyone interested should contact either Mrs. Prismall or Mrs. Holland.'

St Patrick's Letter: 'There will be no Evening Services at St Patrick's during August. You are asked to join the services at Sonning. If you board the 6pm bus from Slesta Stores you will get there in good time for the commencement of the service.'

September 1963

The Vicar's Letter: 'We give a warm welcome to Mr. and Mrs. Feak and their family, who will be taking up residence in the School House before the new term starts on September 10, and we wish them every happiness in Sonning. Miss D. L. Caws, I am sure, will also be welcomed as she starts her work among us at the same time.

We were pleased to see both Mr. Feak and Miss Caws at the School Prize Giving at the end of last term, when they put to good use the opportunity of making the acquaintance of some of the parents and children.'

Sonning Parish Council: The following comments from the August meeting of the parish council were included in this issue:

'On the matter of the Sonning Bridges, the Sonning Parish Council are greatly concerned to receive information that the Oxfordshire County Council have decided to carry out further repairs to the Iron Bridge, and when completed it is probable that the existing restriction of five tons will be increased to a ten tons limit. Any increase in the existing limit will entail the return of the large and heavy lorries over the Old Brick Bridge and through the narrow village streets, both of which are unsuitable for this type of vehicle. A letter of protest has been sent to the Berkshire County Council.

Our view of the increasing traffic build-up on the area east of Reading makes the provision of a new bridge between Sonning and Reading an urgent necessity. We suggest therefore it is important that this scheme be proceeded with without delay so as to relieve the present crossings of a traffic load for which they are entirely unsuited.

The sale of Allotment Land to the District Council has been completed, and after repayment of outstanding loans, the provision of new Tennis Court Surround, new Mowing Machine and new Bus Shelters, the balance will be invested in Treasury 5.5% Bonds.

The entrance to the new School Site has been agreed. It was decided to provide and erect a new Children's Slide and new Swings in the Children's Corner, new Sink and Gas Stove in the Pavilion.

Representatives of Cricket and Tennis Clubs tendered thanks to the Council for the facilities extended to them.'

Pearson Hall Accounts: 'It was hoped to obtain relief from the rates on the Hall which would have saved about £23pa but the rates were increased by £13pa The matter is going to appeal.'

October 1963

The Vicar's Letter: 'Thoughts that are uppermost in our minds at this moment are inevitably a mixture of sorrow and thanksgiving – sorrow for the death of our good friend and helper, Mr. Cedric Gurney Ripley, and thanksgiving for all that he has done for us ever since he first came to this parish. I remember being told "a Mr. Ripley has come to live in the Peyman's house – he is an architect" – little did one realise what a charming benefactor had come to live in our village. Alas! we have now lost two Vice-Chairmen of the P.C.C. within a few months.'

Lay Reader: 'We are glad to announce that the Lord Bishop has re-appointed to a Parochial Lay Readership Mr. N. E. Budden, House Master at the Reading Blue Coat School and has transferred his licence back to the Diocese.'

[*Harold MacMillan resigns as Britain's prime minister and is replaced by the Earl of Home who immediately renounces his six titles to become Sir Alec Douglas-Home.*]

November 1963

Sonning C. of E. Primary School: 'Mrs. C. Baigent who has been Cook-in-charge of the School Canteen for over fourteen years has moved from this area. We are very sorry to lose her. On her last day at the Canteen one of the School children presented her with a cheque as a token of appreciation for the high standard of cooking she has maintained.'

St Patrick's Letter: 'We were pleased to see all who came to our Harvest service. The Rev. N. G. May gave an inspiring address. What a lovely lot of flowers and vegetables, so many jars of jam and tins of everything, plus a bunch of bananas. On the following Monday, Mr. Simmonds and I took them to the children's homes at Reading.'

[*The USA president, John F. Kennedy, is assassinated during a visit to Dallas, Texas on November 22. The vice president, Lyndon B. Johnson, is immediately sworn in as the new president.*
The assassination was received with shock in most parts of the world and many people "of a certain age" were still able to recall years later where and when they first heard news of the Kennedy death.]

December 1963

The Vicar's Letter: 'We are all glad to see our good Churchwarden, Percy Forward, in circulation again after his long illness, and we hope that after a time of rest and convalescence in Somerset, he will soon be his old self again. We have all missed him greatly.

I express my thanks to Mrs. Gale for all she has done for St Patrick's ever since its inception and her care of the Sanctuary and vestments.

We now look forward once more to Christmas, I suppose that, with the vast amount of shopping that is now considered necessary, "Father Christmas" has to make his appearance even earlier in the year. It is, however, surely a mistake to start the actual festivities so prematurely. Christmas does not begin until the midnight of December 24/25, even Christmas Eve being a Fast and not a Feast.'

Young Wives: 'In spite of foggy weather there was a good attendance for the first meeting under our new President, Mrs. Johnson. We welcomed the Rev. E. L. King, the Rector of Theale; having been a schoolmaster and head for thirty-four years, he had many varied and entertaining stories to relate! One of his quotations was "Parents are by nature unfitted to bring up their own children!" Undoubtedly he left many thoughts in our minds.'

January 1964

Sonning Churchyard: An extensive article was included in this issue concerning the cost of maintaining the Sonning churchyard and various conditions relating to the form and appearance of individual graves. The list of conditions and the form of action to be taken included the following:

'The grave mounds in the portion of the churchyard known as Bone Orchard will be levelled in order to reduce maintenance time.

All memorials must be of stone quarried in Great Britain, or of English Oak. All designs, measurements and inscriptions must be submitted for approval. No artificial flowers may be placed on any grave.

The surface of the churchyard will be grass and will be kept level and mowed. Grave mounds which are left unlevelled for twelve months may be levelled. Chippings on graves are not allowed.

The churchyard is reserved for parishioners and those who die in the parish. The burial of non-parishioners requires approval and an extra fee is payable.

Sonning C. of E. Primary School: 'All concerned will be glad to hear that progress towards the building of the new school has, we hope, really been made. The managers have decided on the plans drawn up by the architect, Mr. May, of Freeman, Howell and Batten, and these plans have been passed by the Diocesan Council of Education; they must now go to the Berkshire Education Authority and then to the Ministry of Education – then to tender. Thus much still remains to be done before the end of March!'

[*A government calculation states the average weekly wage in Britain is £16 14s 11d.*]

February 1964
Special Lent Arrangements: 'As previously arranged with the Parochial Church Council, and at the request of the Lord Bishop, our chief object of consideration this Lent will be the proposal for re-union between the Church of England and the Methodists.

By way of introduction, Canon S. C. Robinson, the Vicar of St Peter's, Earley, has very kindly offered to come over and give us two lectures, illustrated with slides and tape-recorder, on the outlines of Church History from the Acts of the Apostles to the time of John Wesley. These lectures will be given by him in the Pearson Hall on Mondays, February 10, and 17, at 8pm.'

St Patrick's Letter: 'A very happy afternoon was spent at the Women's Afternoon Party. It was good to see the ladies putting all the home chores in the background and entering into the fun and games. It is also good to see our choir at the moment – the boys had new cassocks and surplices earlier and the girls had their robes for the new year, we are fifteen in number and it is good to have the help of these young people.'

March 1964
The Vicar's Letter: 'We are indeed grateful that this winter has not proved so rigorous as the last one, and that we have been able to get about in reasonable comfort and safety.

The position with regard to the new School is that we have now "gone out to tender", so that we hope that an actual start may be made before the end of March. We are fortunate in having Mr. Peter Johnson, an experienced architect, on the Board of Managers in Mr. Ripley's place.'

Sonning C. of E. Primary School: 'The newly formed Parent-Teacher Association held a social in the School on February 8 at very short notice. In spite of this, nearly fifty parents and friends attended a most successful evening, ably organised by the committee and parents who were co-opted to help with refreshments. Parents who had not met before were able to get to know each other in the informal atmosphere which the games and dancing provided.'

April 1964
Sonning Parochial Church Council – Report for 1963
The Report of the Vicar and P.C.C. to the Annual General Meeting 1964 included the following:
'The Church building has had its quinquennial survey by the Diocesan Architect, showing little need of repair in anything but the smallest details, which, however, add up to a considerable sum.
We owe a debt of gratitude to Mr. S. Paddick our Churchwarden, for his care of our beautiful Church.
Mr. May who had retired on part time duty in the Churchyard, was taken ill at the end of the year and Mr. R. S. Hunt is now employed on a full time basis.
The Vicar and Church Council appeal to all dog-owners to respect the sanctity of the Churchyard as God's acre and the resting-place of the departed.
Our Youth Societies and clubs carry on with their most efficient leaders; we once more acknowledge the ready support given us by the boys of the Reading Blue Coat School in the choir and belfry and congregation.
The accounts for the year ended December 31, 1963, again shows a reduction in income, but also a reduction in expenditure, resulting in a surplus of £91 compared with a deficit of £73 in the previous year.
The Parish Magazine incurred a loss during 1963 of £10.'

All Saints' Church: 'To fill the vacancy, which has been caused by the resignation of the Rev. J. F. Amies, I have nominated the Rev. H. Cutler to succeed him as Vicar of Dunsden our daughter-parish. Mr. Cutler is at present Vicar of Stewkley in Buckinghamshire and is married with three children. They will be going into a brand new vicarage, and we wish them a very happy time at Dunsden.'

Darby and Joan Club: 'The Club now has fifty-one members and meets once a fortnight on Monday at 2.30pm in the Sonning Scout Hut. On March 2, Mrs. Rogers and friends gave a humorous play reading and on March 16, Mrs Body, from Cookham, entertained us with musical interludes.'

May 1964

The Vicar's Letter: 'The Church Needlework Guild has completed a new gold frontlet for the High Altar, and in addition a new white Stole, Burse and Veil with approximately embroidered designs, for which we thank them warmly.

I am also most grateful to Mrs. May, who has made a most beautiful woollen carpet for the pulpit; it must not tempt me to stay there too long!'

1ˢᵗ Sonning Guide Company: 'On Sunday, April 19, the Company joined with the Loddon District Scouts and Guides in a St George's Day parade held at Twyford, our colours being carried by Susan Holland and Frances Pullin. Our next big occasion will be the County Rally at Newbury Racecourse on Saturday, May 23, and preparations for this are well in hand.'

June 1964

The Vicar's Letter: 'June again looks like a busy month, in the parish the chief event will be the Summer Fair on June 13, which I hope will be well supported.

We offer our deepest sympathy to the Matron and Staff of the Chavil Nursing Home, 102 Old Bath Road, on their disastrous fire on April 27. Mercifully there was no loss of life among the old people, for whom alternative accommodation was found without delay; fortunately, too, it was a lovely warm day. We hope the building is restored without undue delay; it has been a privilege to Captain Langridge and myself to visit the patients and to take services for them.

The Lord Bishop held his Whitsun Gift Service on Whit-Tuesday in the Cathedral, which was filled to overflowing. Sonning was represented by Elizabeth Nichols and Susan Cornish, Charvil by Janet Rust and Sylvia Nattriss, who presented the children's offerings to the Bishop.'

Sonning C. of E. Primary School: 'Having successfully cut through yards of every kind of red tape, we believe that we shall see the commencement of the building of the new School early in June. The tender of the Tilbury Construction Company Ltd., has been accepted, all of the necessary approvals having been at last received. We pray for God's blessing on the work - and on the future of our School.'

July 1964

The Vicar's Letter: 'You will have seen that a start has been made on the new School, and the Managers are still busy working out all the problems involved.

The death of Walter Whay has removed from Sonning one whom all who knew him loved and respected. Badly crippled in the First War, he struggled manfully against his disability, and bore pain and discomfort over the years most nobly and without complaint. The death of his wife a few months ago was a great blow, and we cannot but be glad that he has now followed her through the valley of the shadow of death.'

[*Both Walter Whay (1889-1964) and Violet Lillian Whay (1892-1963) are interred in Sonning Churchyard. see: Record of Burials etc. Church of St Andrew 2012.*]

C. of E. Children's Society: 'The Flag Week collection for this Society resulted in £27 13s 6d., an increase on last year of just over £7. The Society is very pleased with the result, and they send their most grateful thanks to the collectors. I also want to thank the donors for their continued generosity and loyal support to this very good cause.'

St Patrick's Letter: 'I want to thank everyone who in any way helped and supported our Summer Fair last month. The weather behaved itself; we had sunshine and smiles, in fact the afternoon was a very happy one. The net profit from the event was £98 15s 0d. The children excelled themselves at the cake competition and miniature gardens and fancy dress - jolly good show!'

August 1964

The Vicar's Letter: 'I regret to say that Mr. L. Crook, who has played the organ beautifully for the Family and Children's services on Sundays for eight year, now feels that he can no longer carry on this valuable work.

Again, most unfortunate for Sonning, Miss Inge is leaving the Blue Coat School on her retirement. For seventeen years she has lived in Sonning, besides her work as art mistress at the school, she has done all that she could to help forward God's work among us.

I am most grateful to Mr. Feak and Captain Langridge who arranged such splendid excursions for the Day School and Sunday School respectively, and to Mrs. Sherwood who organised the St Patrick's Women's afternoon outing to Savernake Forest and White Horse Hill.'

Confetti: 'Please take note – it is now illegal as well as undesirable to throw confetti in the Churchyard (or anywhere else for that matter). It causes a lot of unnecessary work, being very difficult to sweep up.'

Darby and Joan Club: 'For the last fortnightly meeting in June we visited the Royal Horticultural Society's Gardens at Wisley and everyone enjoyed wandering in the gardens and admiring the beautiful flowers. After tea we returned via the Hog's Back.'

September 1964

The Vicar's Letter: 'I do hope that every household will endeavour to send at least some little contribution to the Harvest Festival decorations in token of gratitude to the Heavenly Father for the rich abundance with which he supplies our needs and desires.

We would all like to congratulate Captain Langridge on his completion of forty years' service with the Church Army, and to thank him for all he has done for us here during the last seven years.'

Anglo-Methodist Conversations: 'The report of the "conversations" between representatives of the Church of England and the Methodists has been the subject of discussion at the Ruridecanal Conference and the Parochial Church Council, and the results were reported to the Bishop by the end of July. While all the members were unanimous in favour of re-union for the honour of our Lord and for the improved implementation and extension of His purposes, some of the members considered that the present scheme was far too vague, and did not provide sufficient and necessary safeguards for a number of the important practices, *eg* Confirmation.'

October 1964

The Vicar's Letter: 'I want to draw the attention of all married folk, especially the younger ones, to the great Family Day being held in Reading on October 6. Both the morning services and the afternoon meetings will inevitably concern wives rather than husbands, but the evening meeting at 7.30pm in the Town Hall is intended for everyone. I do urge all Christian parents to make every effort to attend part of the day's proceedings.

All Saints' Day falls on a Sunday this year – so that it can be observed by all, with gratitude to the heroes of our Faith, who gave their lives to preserve our Christian heritage, and in the thankfulness that "our citizenship is in heaven".

We also have a temporary citizenship on earth, and shall be entitled to exercise one of its privileges by voting in the General Election on October 15. We must pray that each and all may be guided in the choice of the new government which is to represent us for the next few years.'

[*The result of the general election returned the Labour Party, led by Harold Wilson, to power after a thirteen years period in opposition, but with a slender majority. Labour polled 317 seats, Conservatives 303 and Liberals 9.*]

November 1964

Sonning C. of E. Primary School: The new headmaster, Thomas Feak, had clearly made a positive impact upon the school, as witnessed by the content of his contributions to the parish magazine:

'The term has got off to a good start and the new entrants have happily settled in.

At the Annual General Meeting of the P.T.A. a new committee was elected and set themselves a target of £50 to be raised during the year which is to be spent on educational equipment.

The second of the lectures on Education will be on November 26 when Mr. Stagles, Headmaster of the new Bulmershe School and Mr. Waghorn of Wargrave Piggott will share the platform. All friends of the School are cordially invited.

The P.T.A. have also organised a Social which will be held at the School On November 14, from 8pm.'

Choir and Ringers: 'The outing of the Choir and Ringers and other Church workers was arranged for Saturday, October 3, and took the form of a visit to the New Theatre to hear the Gilbert & Sullivan opera, "The Gondoliers". We all enjoyed this new departure very much and are most grateful to Mr. Lusty for organising it, and the P.C.C. for financing it.'

December 1964

Sonning Parish Council: A meeting was held on November 3 and the report included the following items:

'The building of the new Church of England School was well in hand and it is hoped that the new entrance and Children's Corner would soon be completed.

Extensive repairs were being carried out to the Cricket Pitch, the cost being defrayed by the Cricket Club.

The owners of Holme Park Farm had lodged an appeal against the Planning Authority refusal to grant permission to develop eighty acres of farm land at Sonning. The Parish Council unanimously support the previous decision of the Planning Authority to oppose the proposed development.

Work was well in hand to the formation of a new roundabout on the A4 at Pound Lane crossing, the work to be completed in nine months. The lighting will be provided by twenty-four 35 feet columns fitted with 200 watt sodium lamps.'

Young Wives: 'Our meeting on November 4 was well attended and we had a most lively and most enjoyable evening. On the Brains Trust we had Mrs. Pittman, whom most of us know and lives in Sonning, Mr. David John, a sculptor and Mr. Ward-Hopkins, Headmaster of St Peter's, Earley. The answers to our questions, some serious and others more light-hearted, were both enlightened and entertaining.'

January 1965

The Vicar's Letter: Rev. Groves had been taken ill, in his letter of December 16 he expressed his apology for the abruptness of his need to cease work, and to leave others to continue his various responsibilities during his absence. Groves explained that he was to undergo a minor operation and would not be "entirely at your service" until February.

It was noted in this letter that the choral music to be rendered in the church on January 31 was to be performed by the Reading Palestrina Choir. The following article concerning the choir was included in this issue.

Palestrina Choir: 'The Choir was formed about twelve years ago largely as a result of a suggestion from Canon Bourne, the then vicar of St Bartholomew's, who was anxious to have occasional recitals of 16th century church music in his church. The choir is based on the University of Reading and its conductor is the Professor of Music, Dr. Ronald Woodham, but its membership is drawn largely from outside the university. The singers are people interested in the rehearsal and occasional performance of church music mainly from the period of the 16th century.'

[*On January 24, the ninety years old Sir Winston Churchill died at his home at Hyde Park Gate, London. A state funeral service was held on January 30 when the Queen led a nation in mourning to a man considered by many to be the greatest Briton ever.*]

February 1965
The Vicar's Letter: 'I want, first of all, to thank everyone for their great kindness, sympathy, interest in my illness, and above all their prayers. I am much better and have quite recovered from the operation, but am ordered not to resume work until March, for which I am terribly sorry.
What a wonderful party I was given for my seventieth birthday! I could not express all that I felt at the time and naturally found difficulty in making an adequate after-Dinner speech sitting down. We had a lovely little party at home the week before with all our children and grandchildren. I was pleased to be able to hobble over to the Post Office to draw my first O.A.P.!'

Sonning C. of E. Primary School: 'The new term has started well and promises to be the last term in the old School buildings. Although we are all eager to move I am sure that many will look back with nostalgia and sentiment on the happy times spent at the old premises. The children, however, are the school and they will soon make the new buildings their own and benefit by the new facilities which will be offered to them.'

Congratulations: 'We congratulate Mr. R. Adlem, B.E.M. for his very well-deserved award for fifty years service in the Gas Industry.'

March 1965

The Vicar's Letter: 'Once more I must express my gratitude to those who have taken my place in Church during this month – notably Captain Langridge and Mr. Budden – and the various clergy, some of whom have come at great inconvenience to themselves. I have to-day had an encouraging medical report and hope to be able to begin some work again in March.'

Sonning Glebe Institute: 'It was full house at the first open meeting of our Institute, when our speaker was Mr. Heath, who gave a most interesting talk, illustrated with coloured slides, on his visit to the Far East.

It was unanimously agreed that the President, Mrs Shaw, should be chosen to accept the invitation to Buckingham Palace garden party in May.'

April 1965

The Vicar's Letter: 'It will now be no secret to you that, as I announced to the Parochial Church Council on March 9, I have decided that I must resign my privileged position as your Vicar, and thus break what has been to me a very long and happy partnership of some twenty-three years. I have arranged with the Lord Bishop that my deed of resignation will be dated at the end of August. There is therefore no question of saying goodbye as yet. Meanwhile we have just heard this morning that our offer for a small bungalow at Goring-on-Thames has been accepted. Matters of procedure in connection with my resignation are dealt with below.'

Resignation and Appointment of Vicar: A statement by Rev. Sidney Groves to the P.C.C. was printed which informed them of his decision to resign his living at St Andrew's due to ill health.

A further statement to the parishioners from the churchwardens, Sidney Paddick and Percy Forward, was also printed in this issue. This statement, on behalf of the P.C.C. announced the resignation of the vicar and expressed on behalf of the parishioners their warmest good wishes to Canon and Mrs. Groves and wished that Sidney Groves would soon be restored to good health.

A detailed explanation of the procedure on the resignation of a vicar and the appointment of a successor was also included in this issue.

Sonning Parish Council: A council meeting was held on March 8, and the following matters were reported in this issue:

'The Advisory Committee had approved a speed limit for the village and the matter was now in the hands of the Ministry of Transport.

The amended plans of the proposed roundabout at the Wee Waif junction was considered and approved.

The attention of the Council was drawn to the damage still being done to the old brick bridge, the condition of the wharf and the footpath in Thames Street and these matters were being dealt with.'

Sonning C. of E. Primary School: The headmaster reported that the move into the new school premises would take place on April 9: 'We shall spend the last two days of the term acclimatising ourselves to the new surroundings. The P.T.A. are busy painting and re-polishing furniture and helping in many other ways.'

May 1965
The Vicar's Letter: 'I must thank all those who have assisted me in the Sunday services – in which I hope to be able to play an increasing part in the few months ahead. The Bishop of Reading has very kindly promised to take the morning services on Whitsunday.

One of the outstanding events of May will be the opening of the new School on Wednesday, May 26. Those concerned all feel that it is a delightful building – in fact to adopt the vivid language of some of those who will be using it – "it's real smashing". We wish the teachers and children every possible success and happiness in their work at the new School.'

Appointments: 'At Matins on Sunday, March 14, the ceremony of the investiture of Mr. T. A. Field as Verger took place. He was presented by Mr. S. Paddick to the Vicar who admitted him to office investing him with his gown and virge.'

Sonning Parochial Church Council – Report for 1964

The Report of the Vicar and P.C.C. to the Annual General Meeting 1965 included the following:

'The Church Bellringers, and indeed the whole parish, have suffered a great loss in the death of Mr. Frank Cox, their captain and the Keeper of the Belfry. Mr. Norman Willis, a ringer of long experience, has stepped into his place. Mr. W. F. West has resigned as Verger on the advice of his doctor. We are fortunate in finding a worthy successor in the person of Mr. T. A. Field.

The new Church Aided School building adjoining the Recreation Ground will be dedicated by the Lord Bishop on May 26.

The Church fabric is in excellent order, a humidifier having been installed to prevent any further deterioration in the organ.

The accounts for the year 1964 resulted in a parish magazine loss of £31.'

June 1965

The Vicar's Letter: Following very soon after the announcement of the vicar's resignation, in this issue Captain Langridge also announced his intended retirement at the end of this year:

'You will read of Captain Langridge's impended departure with great regret; he has been a most loyal colleague to me, always willing to do anything asked of him, including shouldering the burden of the children's work at the Parish Church during my illness; to the people of Charvil he has proved a most faithful minister in spiritual and social matters.

We congratulate the people, especially the young people, of Charvil on the possession of their new Recreation Ground, which was opened by Mr. W. van Straubenzee M.P. on April 24.'

St Patrick's Letter: Captain Langridge included his forthcoming retirement in this report: 'For a few years now it has been known that the Church Army have a retiring age. I hardy like to think I shall be a pensioner at the end of the year, but it is so; Mrs. Langridge and I will be in our ninth year with you and will leave at the end of December.

We are trying to improve the outlook round St Patrick's Church; inside the floor has been sandpapered and polished and looks very nice and worthwhile; outside we are going to have brick pillars with link chains between, this will be a vast improvement, the existing hedge will then be removed.'

July 1965

The Vicar's Letter: 'We were pleased to welcome the Chaplain and some students from the University of Reading to our Rogation Service, and we are grateful to Mr, Stansfield for the welcome and help given to us by the agricultural faculty.

The services on Whitsunday and Trinity Sunday were very lovely, and I was glad of the help of the Bishop of Reading and the other priests.

Mr. Budden, has been appointed to the role of deputy headmaster of a very important Village College near Cambridge, and will be leaving the Reading Blue Coat School at the end of July. His ministrations as Parochial Lay Reader have been most acceptable throughout the years he has been with us in Sonning. We warmly thank him and wish him God-speed!'

Opening and Dedication of the New School: 'Over two hundred children, parents and invited guests filled the School Hall for the opening and dedication of the new building on May 26. Mrs. Groves officially declared the school open, after which the Bishop of Oxford dedicated the school and spoke of the importance of a village school in the community.

The ladies of the P.T.A. committee and the kitchen staff had organised refreshments in the form of tea and biscuits for the guests, and the children were given cordial and crisps through the generosity of the Managers.'

August 1965

The Vicar's Letter: 'I again have to express my gratitude for much help given me in the church services and also my regret that I have to be so greatly dependent on other folk.

The Almshouse Charity Trustees were very sad at having to accept Mrs. Clement Williams' resignation after years of service.

Mrs. Groves and I shall be leaving the Vicarage early in August, so that any alterations to the house can be started as soon as possible, but I am your Vicar until the end of the month and shall be over here nearly every day. After August the parish will be in charge of Sequestrators, the Rural Dean and Churchwardens, until such time as a new Vicar has been appointed and instituted.'

Sonning C. of E. Primary School: 'The new building has now been in use for a full term and has thoroughly proved its worth; the outside has still to be put in order, and is the responsibility of the L.E.A.

The old schools were put up to auction and sold at the Great Western Hotel, Reading, on July 8. After some keen bidding the buildings were "knocked down" to Mr. S. Paddick, at the price of £7,500 for the infants' block and £8,000 for the Thames Street house and school. Prices much in advance of the valuation and reserved price.'

September 1965
The Vicar's Letter: 'As I said at the "Farewell Party" on July 24, I cannot possibly enumerate all the kindness and help I have received here during the last twenty-three years or make any sort of list of those to whom I owe so much for the very happy days spent with you in Sonning.

The Farewell Party itself was something so marvellous that it really baffles description – so wonderfully well organised and so very well attended. The album presented to us will be a constant reminder of our Church, our Home and Parish; while the breathtaking cheque for £340 – well, what can one say of that? We shall certainly use part for a longer holiday than usual and the rest for things we require for our new home.

Finally, God bless you all, good folk, and grant that under your new Vicar you may all go forward in greater solidarity towards the higher prize of our calling.'

The Vicar-Designate: 'The Lord Bishop has appointed, as Vicar and Rector of Sonning, the Rev. Robert Springett Brutton, M.A., Vicar of Radley since 1957. He is married with three children. It is hoped that the new Vicar will take up his ministry in Sonning by the end of November.'

Sonning's Double First: 'Heartiest congratulations to our Lock-keeper, Mr. V. P. Dyer, on winning the Sir Reginald Hanson Challenge Cup for the best-kept lock garden in the whole of the Thames Conservancy's area. Also, to all those in Sonning who took the trouble of helping Sonning to win the Shield for the best-kept large village in Berkshire.'

October 1965

The Parish Magazine: 'Mr. H. C. Chapman the retired headmaster of Sonning school, has agreed to undertake the editing of the magazine during the interregnum period.'

St Patrick's Letter: In his monthly comments, Captain Langridge paid tribute to the achievements of Sidney Groves during his long ministry in Sonning. He then outlined some arrangement which had been agreed concerning forthcoming services to be held at both Sonning and Charvil: 'I was glad to get Captain J. Benson to take most of the evening services at Sonning during October, and also Captain B. Fairbrother to take the Harvest service at 6.30pm at Charvil.' It was clear that until the new incumbent was installed into St Andrew's, Captain Langridge would be expected to take on further commitments. However, Langridge was also to retire from his position at Charvil by the end of the year, and was no doubt anxious to use the short period left to ensure that the future pastoral responsibilities at St Patrick's were secure before his departure.

November 1965

A message from Mr. Brutton: 'This is just to say how much my family and I look forward to meeting you all. We have already been given a warm welcome by the Churchwardens and Parochial Church Council and we no longer feel complete strangers. It will take me some time to visit you all in your homes but, after the Institution and Induction on December 2, I hope that you will contact me at the Vicarage if I can help in any way. I should perhaps explain that we will not be moving in to the Vicarage for a week or so, but I will be in the Study on most mornings.'

The Vicarage: It was reported that the Parochial Church Council had agreed to have carried out various improvements to the vicarage prior to the arrival of the Brutton family. The work involved included the installation of a central heating system and domestic hot water, an additional bath and the modernising of the kitchen. Further work required due to dilapidation was also necessary and included electrical re-wiring and renewal of sanitary fittings. The cost of the work would be partly borne by the Church Commissioners.

Sonning C. of E. Primary School: In his comments concerning Sonning school, Thomas Feak noted that there were nearly ninety children on the school role: 'This term we have, unfortunately, lost Mrs. Covington who has taught P.E. at the school for some years. Mrs. Williams has taken her place as a half-time teacher.'

December 1965

Vicar's Notes: 'By the time you read this, the Institution and Induction will have taken place. Unfortunately, in spite of a great effort all round, the Vicarage will not be ready for occupation until December 16 at the earliest, so I will have to live in Radley and come over in the afternoon to start visiting you in your own homes.

This is going to be a most exciting Christmas for me and my family. If any of my plans seem a bit "mad" please be patient. Some of the changes may worry you, but if we all join in the worship at this lovely church (Charvil too) then it will become more that worship – it will be a happy occasion and a meeting place for friends all over the parish. To make it succeed we need *you* and your *family*, do come!'

St Patrick's Letter: This final monthly report from Captain Langridge concentrated mainly upon thanking the parishioners prior to his retirement from the Charvil ministry: 'I have been forty-one years in the Church Army, and my retirement comes at the end of December in my ninth year with you in this parish. There are so many people (I mention no names) who have been so kind and helpful in my ministry, giving loyal support in the work of the Church. My wife too, has enjoyed working in your midst. May you all be much blessed as you continue to uphold the work. It is a joy to know that I have been a help in God's work in your midst; it has not been all easy work, there is much I would have loved to have done.

I am anxious about teachers for Charvil Sunday School. Seventy or more children need help and guidance. We need three teachers to take my place also, my daughter's. We have had to join classes together, sometimes having twenty-four children in a class. Is there a man who could help? This work is very important and should not be let down.'

CHAPTER FIVE

1966 - 1970

The page extent of the magazine had remained constant with a total of eight pages all of which were printed on the same paper. However, from January 1969 a heavier paper was included for the outer four pages. The cover design again altered during the later sixties; in 1967 a drawing of a medieval knight was displayed and later in 1969 a replica of the first cover design from January 1869 was used in celebration of the magazine's centenary. [*see: pages 164 and 178.*]

After twenty three years as vicar of Sonning, Sidney Groves had retired and the Sonning living was taken up by Robert (Robin) Springett Brutton. Robin Brutton had been involved in his family's brewing business before taking Holy Orders in his early forties. The content of the magazine during Brutton's ministry was markedly different to that of the Groves era. Whilst the content under the editorship of Rev. Groves included a relatively small number of regular contributors, the new editor, Harry Chapman, one time headmaster of Sonning school, doubtless with the encouragement of Rev. Brutton, developed a wider content with reports from an expanded range of clubs and societies.

In Sonning, with the notable exception of a massive increase in vehicle traffic passing through the village, for which another Thames bridge had been appealed for on numerous occasions, the village remained quintessentially English. St Andrew's Church and the Pearson Hall continued to provide for the spiritual and social needs of the parishioners. The parishes of Woodley and Earley were continuing to develop and now included a wide range of retail shops, banks, medical centres etc. The population of Charvil had also greatly increased; in 1970 Charvil was recognised by being awarded parish status.

1865   CENTENARY YEAR   1965

A. F. JONES

Monumental and Masonry Craftsman

Established since 1865

Specialists in all stone restorations and Garden materials

Head Office and Works : Bedford Road, Reading. Tel. 53537

Henley Office and Works : as E. T. Shephard, Reading Road, Henley, Oxon. Tel. 460

FUNERAL DIRECTORS

Tomalin & Son, New Street, Henley   Tel. Henley 370   Private Chapel

---

K. LOCK

Vacuum
Chimney Sweep

with Brushes and Scraper

**PILGRIMS FARM,
BURGHFIELD, BERKS.**

Write, Call or Phone anytime.

Telephone — Burghfield Common 372

C. & G. AYRES Ltd.

REMOVALS .. STORAGE

EXPERT STAFF
MODERN VANS
ESTIMATES FREE
FINE DEPOSITORIES
HEATED IN WINTER

*Royal County Depository
Friar Street . Reading*

Telephone : 55139

UPHOLSTERY

We have a comprehensive range of beautiful fabrics from the best of British, French and Italian Houses. Patterns at your house, or we can arrange a visit to any London showroom.

We specialise in modern and antique upholstery, recovered and repaired, carpets supplied and fitted. Curtains and Pelmets.

W. MacBAIN

21 WARREN ROAD, WOODLEY, READING

Telephone: SONNING 2647

Advertisement page: January 1966. (23.5 x 17.5cm)

January 1966

Vicar's Notes: 'The reactions to my services during my first two Sundays were most encouraging. People are obviously ready to give these shorter services a fair trial, and if they do leave the church a little breathless, they are putting up with it for patience and understanding. I am most grateful to all of you who have given the Morning Service in its present form the benefit of the doubt.

What a lot goes on in Sonning just before Christmas! A regular whirl of parties and entertainment. I only wish that I could have accepted all your kind invitations. I have much enjoyed my visits to your homes and have appreciated your warm welcome.'

I am grateful to Mr. Chapman for continuing his work as editor of the magazine.'

Sonning Bell Ringers: 'On Saturday, 27 November, the Sonning Ringers rang, for the Confirmation Service, a quarter of a peal of Grandsire Triples, being 1260 changes. This is the first time in at least eight years that an all-Sonning band has rung a quarter peal. The conductor was Norman Willis, captain of the ringers.'

1st Sonning Brownies: 'On November 19, we were pleased to welcome Mrs. Bevan, the Charvil Tawny, who came to enrol Patricia Malkin.

We enjoyed the Christmas Fair on December 3. Our grateful thanks to all those who supported us. We have now been able to add £6. 7s. 0d to our funds.

[*Mrs. Patricia Grove, nee Malkin, was later appointed verger of St Andrew's, Sonning.*]

February 1966

Vicar's Notes: Completion of various improvements to the Vicarage were delayed and the Brutton family eventually took residence on February 3.

'At a meeting on January 4, at St Patrick's Church, Charvil it was agreed, after discussion, that for a trial period of six months, Charvil would join in corporate worship at the Parish Church (Charvil of course being in the ecclesiastical parish of Sonning), and that a coach should be laid on to take people to the 11am Morning Service and 6.30pm Evensong.'

as follows: —Treble bell, Ivor Newell; second bell, David C. Willis; third bell, Mrs. Jean Busby; fourth bell, Alfred W. Burton; fifth bell, Charles Williams; sixth bell, Geoffrey M. Harvey; seventh bell, A. Norman Willis; tenor bell, Stephen J. Atkins. The conductor was A. Norman Willis, captain of the ringers.

Wanted

Occasional Typing for the Sonning Deanery Lay Council. This should be very interesting. If you would like to help please contact Mrs. Nutter, Sonning 3291.

Sonning Deanery Lay Council

At the first meeting on 23 November, the Rural Dean explained his reasons for calling us together, saying that there was a widespread feeling that lay-men must have greater opportunity for service in the church. The real work was done when priest and people worked together, and some of the laity had special gifts which the church should be able to use.

An entirely lay committee was being formed to discuss ways of improving the spiritual life of the Deanery and to report from time to time to the Ruridecanal Conference. Two representatives from each parish were asked to attend.

Officers were appointed, after which the Rural Dean retired and left us to discuss how the committee should function. There was a good deal of discussion, and we shall be very glad of further suggestions from anyone who is interested.

For the next meeting on 25 January, a question was taken to be discussed beforehand in each parish, conclusions to be written down and collected together for the Lay Council.

Question (a) Why does the Church mean nothing to the vast majority in England? and (b) What can we do about it?

Will you please give comments to Mrs. Nutter, York Cottage, Pearson Road, Sonning, and attend, if possible, a meeting to be arranged during the second week in January (date to be announced).

J.N.

Mothers' Union

The monthly meeting was held on December 8

in the Pearson Hall. We were very pleased to welcome our new Vicar who, after the prayers, spoke a few words before leaving. He said it was difficult to express all it meant to a new Vicar to find such a well established Mothers' Union in the parish. He went on to say that the M.U. stood for the stability of family life and that where there are stable homes it is like having houses 'built on rock' and this, of course, was a very good thing to have in a parish.

Mrs. Sutcliffe then gave a very interesting talk on the Chinese New Year with all its ancient customs and mysticism. She had a considerable number of exhibits displayed. A vote of thanks was proposed by Mrs. Brown. Mrs. Long then kindly presented me with a very useful gift — a Pyrex covered bowl, for which I again express my sincere thanks to you all and repeat what I said then, "that service is not one-sided — if one gives one usually receives three-fold" and for any service I give to the Branch I most certainly receive a wealth of friendship from you — the members.

I would like to thank our chauffeurs, Mrs. Dobbs and Mrs. Long, who so willingly collect and take home our more elderly members each month. Also I am extremely glad to have our Secretary and Treasurer — Mrs. Eggleston — back again and thank her and all the Committee members for their work and loyalty to the Branch and to me.

The next meeting will be in the Pearson Hall on Thursday, January 6, at 3 p.m. Corporate Communion January 23. Prayer Group in Church January 18, at 3 p.m.

E.A.C.

Sonning Women's Institute

The December meeting was held in the Pearson Hall, with Mrs. Welsh in the chair.

Business included the announcement that a letter had been written to the County Council about the suggested speed limit in Pound Lane.

There are still vacancies in the art classes in Sonning, and the cake icing classes to start at Burchetts Green on February 9. Transport available.

Miss Gowring and Miss Dadley gave lively and interesting accounts of their visits to Denman College.

The birthday posy went to Mrs. Piper, the raffle to Mrs. Bowmer, and the competition for the best mince pies was won by Mrs. Morris.

Text page: January 1966. (23.5 x 17.5cm)

Mr. T. Cowley has very kindly supplied new chains to complete the fencing by the Deanery Wall in the Churchyard – these chains replace the original ones removed during the last war.

Induction of the Rev. R. S. Brutton: 'On Thursday evening, December 2, the Rev. Robert Springett Brutton was instituted and inducted as Vicar of Sonning by the Bishop of Oxford and the Rural Dean of Sonning.'

Major-General Price-Davies, V.C. (1878-1965): The death of General Price-Davies was recorded in this issue. Price-Davies and his wife came to live at Sonning in 1952. He was a distinguished soldier who was awarded the Victoria Cross during the Boer War (1899-1902).
[*Llewellyn Albru Emelius Price-Davies (1878-1965) is interred in Sonning churchyard. see: Record of Burials etc. Church of St Andrew 2012.*]

March 1966
Sonning Parish Council: A council meeting was held on February 8, and the following matters were reported in this issue:
'Owing to building alterations at the Old School in Pearson Road, it will be necessary to remove the post-box, and it is hoped to arrange with the Postmaster to re-fix this in a new position.
A letter has been received from the County Council regarding the application from the Parish Council for a 30 mile speed limit in Pound Lane. The position is that the Highways and Bridges Committee agree to impose a speed limit of 30 miles per hour in Pound Lane which is subject to the agreement of the Ministry of Transport.
It was decided to purchase a new motor mower at a cost of £285.'

Sonning Cubs and Scouts: 'Congratulations to S. Malkin, R. Bennett, S. Ridout and C. Humphreys on their investiture as Scouts. A "big welcome" to J. Lister, who has just joined the Troop, and to C. May, having passed through his Cubbing, now takes a big step into the adventure of Scouting.'

St Patrick's Women's Meeting: 'A meeting was held in January which was well attended, despite the very cold day. We were delighted to welcome Mrs. Brutton, who came to speak to us, and took us on a wonderful tour of Greece, by way of colour slides.'

[*Labour's Prime Minister Harold Wilson declares a General Election for March 31; the Labour Party are returned to power with an increased majority of 96 seats.*]

April 1966

Vicar's Notes: The coach used to transport Charvil worshippers to Sonning for Sunday services received the following comment from the vicar:

'The coach is proving useful to an ever growing number of people – all thirty-six seats have been occupied on occasions for the morning service. I am grateful to those helping with the organisation – we are so glad that so many are coming to the Parish Church to join in the corporate worship.

Mr. W. Townsend is taking on the upkeep of the Churchyard and he can be sure of a warm welcome from the people of Sonning and hundreds of visitors who enjoy the beauty of our Church and its surroundings.

The Vicarage garden is always open after the services on Sunday to any member of the congregation who may care to use it, and my wife and I hope it will be the scene of many social gatherings.'

Sonning Parochial Church Council – Report for 1965
The Report of the Vicar and P.C.C. to the Annual General Meeting 1966 included the following items:

'Mrs. Ripley and Mrs. Rogers have each presented £50 in memory of their husbands, Mr. and Mrs. Clement Davies have presented an antique oak table, which has been placed under the War Memorial, Canon Groves gave many of his books to start a Church Library and Mr. and Mrs. W. S. Field provided a bookcase for them.

The income from the Caroline Palmer Trust amounts to £216 and as the expenditure was only £19 the balance of the fund increased by £197 to £487. It must be remembered however, that this can only be used for repairs to the fabric of the Church and is not available for general expenditure.

The 1965 accounts showed a loss for the Parish Magazine of £65.'

May 1966

Chiropody Clinic for Old People: 'The Sonning Clinic has been run with the help of the Woodley Volunteer Committee for Old People, but an independent Sonning Chiropody Committee has now been formed.'

Sonning Parish Council: Report to the Annual General Meeting held March 29, 1966 included the following:
'The competition for the "Best Kept Village" was won by Sonning this year with 88% of possible marks.
Mr. Tom Lindfield, the groundsman on the Recreation Ground has retired after many years of good service. Mr. Arthur Norcott has been engaged as the new groundsman.
The homes of the aged in Little Glebe are nearing completion and will shortly be ready for occupation.'

June 1966
Vicar's Notes: 'Mrs. W. G. Wallace has very kindly given to the Church twenty-five chairs designed to stack neatly when not in use. The chairs are stacked in the vestry ready for immediate use.
A new monthly magazine "Sunday" has now made its appearance and should be of much interest to church-goers, though it is also intended to appeal to people who do not go to church. Its price is a shilling. Its organisers say that it "will attempt to be a lively and vigorous medium for a positive Christian – but not "churchy".'

Ballroom Dancing: 'Dancing classes are held at the Pearson Hall on every Friday evening – three shillings a lesson. Can you dance the Samba, Waltz, Cha-cha-cha, Slow Foxtrot, Quick Step, Boston Two-Step, the March of the Mods?
– NO, then come to the Pearson Hall – Boys and Girls aged 13 to 18.'

[*Barclays Bank launch the Barclaycard, the first British credit card.*]

July 1966
Vicar's Notes: 'From all accounts that I hear the Church Social on June 10, achieved its objective of giving the "congregations" a chance to get to know each other, and I am very grateful to you all for entering into the spirit of the thing so enthusiastically, and for moving around cheerfully at the clang of the bell!
The first Men's Meeting will be on Tuesday, October 18, in the Pearson Hall. The first object of these meetings will be to give men who come to our Church an opportunity to get to know each other, they in turn will quite likely bring a friend and so the group will develop.

The monthly Abingdon Deanery News used to contain a "story" from the Rev. Tindall Hart. He has kindly allowed me to make use of these, so here goes with this month's "story" –

One cannibal chief said to another, "we boiled a missionary for our dinner the other day, but he was so tough we simply couldn't get our teeth into him". "Oh" replied his friend, "you made a great mistake with him. He wasn't a boiler, he was a Friar" . . . Which reminds me, we need a Missions' Secretary – any volunteers?'

Young Wives: 'On June 1, a party of thirty Young Wives went by coach to The Theatre Royal Windsor to see the comedy play "Cat among the Pigeons" everyone in the party enjoyed it and had a good laugh. Our next meeting is July 6, at Wildwood, Warren Road. We shall have a lecture from the Milk Marketing Board and the emphasis will be on "Milk in the Diet".'

[*July 30, England win the World Football Cup played at Wembley Stadium, defeating Germany by 4 goals to 2 after extra time.*]

August 1966

Vicar's Notes: 'My forecast of a better-than-ever Summer Fair did not make due allowance for the weather, which was awful! Considering the weather, the financial result was amazingly good, £112 12s 11d. A sincere thank you to all those concerned and particularly to the chief organiser Mrs. Brown.

Several people have asked if we can have another Church Social. It looks like being a sort of Christmas Party and I should be glad to receive some bright ideas from anyone. Last time it was cheese and wine; What's it to be this time? sausage and beer? port and pasties? coffee and cakes?'

St Patrick's Women's Hour: 'For our June meeting we went by coach to Coventry Cathedral, which was enjoyed by all. In July we were to have held a Garden Party in Mrs. Temple's garden, but the recent rain made that impossible. However, we did have tea and competitions etc., in the hall.

This will be the last meeting of our Women's Hour. Many thanks to all those who have helped in the past few months.'

Sonning C. of E. Primary School: 'The swimming pool was in operation six weeks before the end of term and during that time, with daily swimming, forty per cent of the children in the school have started to swim. Please note that the pool will be in operation during the whole of the summer holidays.'

September 1966

Vicar's Notes: Robin Brutton included with his notes a current list of the "Top Ten" hymns as published in *Contact*, the Bristol ecumenical monthly:

'Abide with me – The Lord's my Shepherd – O love that wilt not let me go –
The day Thou gavest, Lord, is ended – Dear Lord and Father of mankind –
Lead, kindly light – My song is love unknown – Guide me, O Thou great
Redeemer – And now, O Father, mindful of the love – How sweet the name of
Jesus sounds.'

Sonning Lock: 'The Parish Council and parishioners congratulate the lock-keeper, Mr. Eric Schofield, on winning first prize for the best lock on the Thames (Boulters to Caversham). The gardens are very beautiful and greatly admired by everyone.'

Church Disaster: The following "Stop Press" announcement was included in this issue:

'It is with regret that we announce that the Church was badly damaged by fire on the night of Sunday, August 28. Due to the efforts of the Berkshire & Reading combined Fire Brigades, the fire was confined to the roof of the East end of the North Aisle. Their work prevented the Church from total destruction. Much damage, of course, has been done and the cause of the fire is at present the subject of a police enquiry. An attempt was made to break open the safe containing money and silver but this failed. It appears that the beautiful old Jacobean Chair and Table in the vestry have been practically destroyed and vestments are also a total loss.'

October 1966

Vicar's Notes – The Fire: The Vicar's Notes were totally given over to an attempted burglary and arson attack on St Andrew's Church. The following is a summary of Robin Brutton's comments:

'We now have an opportunity to express our gratitude to those, especially the Fire Brigades, whose prompt action saved the Church from complete disaster. The roof at the East end of the North Aisle has been burnt out, necessitating a temporary galvanised iron structure to keep out the weather. An inventory of our losses in the vestry has been compiled and estimates for repair work are being prepared. In the meantime services carry on as usual with a minimum of inconvenience. We are grateful to all those who worked so hard to clear rubble and mess and then to spring clean the Church, which was in a sorry state after the fire had been extinguished – and the fact that now it is clean and shining is entirely due to the relays of helpers who shovelled and brushed and scrubbed and dusted and polished for days on end.

Our services on the first Sunday after the fire were a strange mixture of sadness and thanksgiving, of sadness because the fire was so pathetically unnecessary; of sadness because we can't understand anyone breaking into, let alone desecrating, the house of God; of thanksgiving because, in spite of all, the greater part of the Church was saved.'

November 1966

Sonning Glebe Women's Institute: 'The meeting on Monday, October 17, was unusually well attended because members were eager to watch the splendid cookery demonstration given by Miss Vowles. We all learned something from her lucid and entertaining presentation.

The flan, made by Mrs. Manning-Press for the re-staged exhibit for the County Show, was raffled and won by Mrs. Sawyer,'

Sonning Football Club: 'We are on our way with the season's programme. As at present five league games have been played, one won, two drawn and two lost. Not exactly an inspiring start, but certainly better than the previous season when we went five games before collecting a point. The Club will soon enter into the rounds of cup matches, and on November 5, we shall have a very attractive fixture in the Berks and Bucks Junior Cup against a team from Reading University, the match will be played at the "Rec".'

Sonning Darby and Joan Club: 'On Monday, October 3, a Darts Match was held, after which members recounted "it happened to me" stories.'

December 1966
Vicar's Notes: 'Our Songs of Praise went very well, and we hope to have another similar service on January 15. The modern tune to "Now thank we all our God" was especially enjoyed by the great majority of people. Those who found it almost unbearable will, I know, grin and bear it for the sake of the others.'

Sonning Surgery: 'The Doctors and receptionists at the Sonning Surgery gave Mrs. Cox a presentation last week on her retirement after fifteen years. Mrs. Cox is most grateful for their kindness.'

Sonning Youth Club: 'The support and enthusiasm for the club has been most pleasing and enlightening. Membership now stands at sixty. Several matches have been arranged for the football team, the first game took place on November 12, when the lads, ably captained by Terry Clarke, played well against an experienced Battle Athletic Youth League side, how pleasing to have so many supporters encouraging Sonning Youths.'

January 1967
Vicar's Notes 'We have now completed our first year together in this parish and I want to thank you all for your help and kindness. You have been ready to give me the benefit of the doubt and give new ideas a fair trial, and those who have disliked some of the changes have, with very few exceptions, "stuck to their Church" and been prepared to "grinned and beard it!"'

Sonning Scouts, Guides, Cubs and Brownies: 'We all had a very enjoyable Christmas Party in the Scouts hut on Saturday, December 17, when over sixty Scouts, Guides, Cubs and Brownies joined in the games, and after tea tucked into a huge, Scout-embossed, Christmas cake given by Mrs. Waring.'

Badminton and Table Tennis: 'Commencing on Wednesday, January 4, Table Tennis can be played at the Pearson Hall each Wednesday at 3/6d per evening. A Badminton night will be arranged when sufficient funds are available to purchase the necessary equipment.'

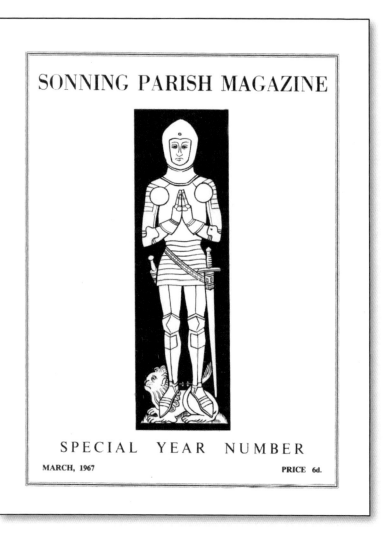

SONNING PARISH MAGAZINE

SPECIAL   YEAR   NUMBER

MARCH, 1967   PRICE 6d.

Cover page: March 1967 (23.5 x 17.5cm).

The drawing of a knight-in-armour was taken from an effigy engraved into brass on the chancel floor in St. Andrew's Church. The figure appears to represent Laurence Fyton who died March 29, 1434.

[*see: Record of Burials etc. Church of St Andrew 2012.*]

February 1967

Vicar's Notes: 'In Lent we should take ourselves by the scruff of the neck and shake hard! It is time for making a Big Effort to do the things required of every committed Christian – come to Church at least once a Sunday, say your prayers (talk to God) every night without fail, have charity toward all people.

Let's make a big effort in Lent! – start next Sunday.

Our First Year: Robin Brutton acknowledged the contribution made by advertisers and distributors to the parish magazine with the following item: 'I would like to thank all our advertisers for their much valued support, and also to all those conscientious distributors who take this magazine to our houses month after month, We are very grateful to them all.'

Winston Churchill Memorial Scholarship: 'Our congratulations to Mr. Malcolm Stansfield of the University Farm on winning this scholarship which has given him the opportunity to visit North America to study farm management from December to April. We shall miss him at the morning service at which he sometimes read the lesson – but he returns in the spring.'

Sonning Village Year 1967: 'All our village organisations have agreed to co-operate during 1967 to carry out a number of voluntary activities which will be of direct benefit to the village. It is their intention to encourage every person in the community to help in his or her own way to make our village more pleasant, more interesting and more beautiful to live in.'

March 1967

Vicar's Notes: 'This special "Village Year" number of the Sonning Parish Magazine will be taken to every house in the Parish, by hand, by our loyal team of distributors. We are glad of the opportunity to give new readers the latest information about the Church and the various local organisations.'

[*A new front cover design for the purpose of publicising the "Village Year" and depicting a knight-in-armour was featured from the March 1967 issue. – see: page 164.*]

Sonning Parish Council: A council meeting was held on February 13, and the following matter was reported in this issue:
'Repairs are again being carried out to the old Brick Bridge and it seems that the only likely solution of saving the Bridge from destruction would be the installation of traffic lights. A new road was planned some forty years ago to relieve the heavy traffic over Sonning Bridge, this road was to branch off near the top of Sonning Lane, over the river to Henley Road and Oxfordshire to the West. A letter has been sent to the County Surveyor suggesting that this scheme should, if possible, be revived and proceeded with as early as possible.'

April 1967

The Vicar's Notes: 'Our new lay reader, Mr. Hugh Grainger preached his first sermon in Sonning Church on Palm Sunday. For some time past he has been giving valuable help in this parish, with the Sunday School at Charvil, by administering the Chalice at Communion and as a member of the Parochial Church Council. He can be sure of very genuine support from us all as he starts this new and vitally important work.'

Sonning Parochial Church Council – Report for 1966
The Report of the Vicar and P.C.C. to the Annual General Meeting 1967 included the following items:
'The Choir has grown and they are now about fifty strong. It is with great regret that we are losing Mr. W. Evans who has been a member for twenty-five years.
Flood lighting of the tower has been set up and has been much admired.
Services have been held at St Patrick's, Charvil, on Harvest Festival, St Patrick's Day, etc., and Communion is celebrated there on alternate Thursdays.
The Treasurer reported that the total receipts from the fire insurance claim amounted to £8,500.
The Parish Magazine incurred a loss during 1966 of £80.'

May 1967

Vicar's Notes: 'Whitsunday is one of the first most important days in the Church Year, do come and join in our worship. The Festival celebrates the coming to the disciples of the Holy Spirit in the form of tongues of flame and a rushing of wind. It is called Whit or White Sunday because in the old days many people were baptised at this time and wore white clothes.

If the church clock has been a little erratic of late you must blame it on the pigeon which chose to build its nest behind the number "6" on the dial. The minute hand was, therefore, handicapped at the half hour by various sticks and feathers. At least one egg was hatched successfully – the fledgling got so used to the creeping hand that he occasionally perched on it and got a free ride!'

Sonning Parish Council: A council meeting was held on March 2, and the following matters were reported in this issue:
'A thirty mile per hour speed limit for the village has been agreed and will shortly be put into operation by the Ministry of Transport.
Experimental traffic lights have been in operation on the Old Brick Bridge and, if they prove to be successful, permanent ones will be installed.
Several locks on the Thames have been mechanised and a letter has been sent to the Conservators asking that when the modernisation of Sonning Lock is carried out the old beams and gates should, if possible, be retained, thus preserving its traditional character and charm.'

June 1967
Vicar's Notes: 'It is difficult to avoid untidy corners in a church, but the new screen in the vestry under the Tower has improved matters enormously, and the men and boys in the Choir will now have a first class hanging cupboard and a room not entirely dominated by the Rich Memorial and the broom cupboard!'

Darby and Joan Club: 'There was no meeting on April 17, as a visit to the Black and White Minstrels had been arranged on that day. This was a great success and much enjoyed by everyone.'

Sonning Football Club: 'The posts have been taken down and the nets safely stored away until next September. Thus ends another season of the Club, one in which we have experienced anxiety, when we were so close to being among the candidates for relegation, and relief when our position in the league improved and we left this relegation bogey behind. Thanks to a successful April, in which we won four matches and drew one out of the six matches played, we finished nearly half-way up the league table. The Club officials thank all the players who have served the Club so well during the season.'

July 1967

Vicar's Notes: 'Three hundred and sixty pounds for the Pearson Hall! Under Mrs. Goodyear's dynamic influence the show at the Vicarage on June 8, produced this amazing contribution towards improvements in the Village Hall, and gave much enjoyment to a lot of people.

A fascinating Embroidery Exhibition together with an embroidery demonstration was arranged by Lady Hamilton Fairley.

The Summer House was used for a most attractive display of plants, articles for flower arranging etc. – all of which sold.

I think most of you are aware that this Hall is not a Church Hall, though the Vicar is, as it happens, sole trustee. The Church is not called upon to give any financial help, and the Hall is dependent on the booking fees received and a most generous contribution from the Fire Brigade Trust.'

Sonning C. of E. Primary School: 'A most successful sports day was held on Saturday, June 10. This is the first occasion it has been held on Saturday and, judging by the attendance, it will be well worth repeating. The swimming season is now in full swing. All the children going to Secondary Schools this year are able to swim.'

August 1967

Vicar's Notes: 'I wish more families would take advantage of the crèche at the Vicarage when it re-opens on August 6. Mothers can leave their babies or very young children in the charge of the Young Wives and come themselves to the Morning Service. My renewed thanks to the Young Wives for this valuable help and also their help with the Church cleaning.'

From the Editor: An item by Mr. Chapman was included in this issue which mentioned various matters of interest to readers of the magazine: 'Congratulations to Mr. E. Scholfield, Sonning Lock Keeper. His garden around the lock was judged equal first with the one at Bray.

Another item of news has just reached me – litter baskets of a more substantial type are to be placed at various points in the village and I'm sure that the Parish Council wishes that they shall be used in the proper fashion.'

St Patrick's: 'No Sunday School in August. Children and Parents are invited to use the coach which leaves from St Patrick's Church at 10.30am for the half-hour Family Service at Sonning – No Charge! The coach also leaves St Patrick's at 6.00pm for the 6.30pm Evensong at Sonning.'

September 1967

Vicar's Notes: 'On Sunday morning, September 10, the Bishop of Reading, himself at the piano, will play, sing and lead a selection of modern hymn tunes in our Church. His contribution toward brighter music is widely acknowledged, and it must be unique to have a Bishop leading this rather gay [merry, joyful] sort of music from a grand piano at the chancel step! We all know the Bishop fairly well (such is his friendly personality) and he can be assured of a spontaneous and most warm welcome.'

Working Men's Club: 'The land purchased at the rear of the existing premises has been named the "Williams Garden." Groups of members have been digging and levelling the site prior to laying a lawn, and a French window has been installed in the Club room allowing access to the garden.'

October 1967

Sonning Parish Council: Some important matters were reported in this issue concerning the construction of new roads which would have an impact upon local communities, particularly in Sonning, Woodley and Earley:

'New Thames Bridge – The Parish Council is greatly concerned regarding the increased traffic through the Village and over the old bridge, it is considered the building of a new bridge over the Thames is the only way to relieve the situation.

Link Roads – At a joint meeting of the Parish Council and the Ratepayers Association the following resolution was passed. It was decided to favour the route leading from Suttons trial grounds to Loddon Bridge. It will mean the demolition of many houses, but this seems to be the only satisfactory route. It was noted that all property owners who are affected by this route should be properly compensated.

[*The link road was later constructed and is known as the A329(M).*]

November 1967

Vicar's Notes: The new Holy Communion Service was introduced into St Andrew's by Robin Brutton with the following comments: 'For over three hundred years the Church of England has remained faithful to the Book of Common Prayer, but now, for an experimental period, we have a new form of service for the Holy Communion. It has been drawn up by a Commission consisting of bishops, scholars, clergy, lay men and women. The whole Church, clergy and laity alike, have had an important hand in this service which is intended for the whole Church to use.'

Pearson Hall: 'The Hall has been closed until early December for redecoration and improvements. The stage will have decent curtaining and the Hall lighting will be increased by the provision of wall lights. The kitchen will be greatly improved with a wider serving hatch and better equipment.'

December 1967

Amen: The vicar explained some understanding of the origin of the word "Amen" in this issue: 'The use of this word links our worship with that of the Jews. A Hebrew word meaning "firmly" it was used by the Jews to express assent at the end of prayers, hymns, creeds and other religious formulae. Our Lord's emphatic "Verily, verily" is in the original "Amen amen." It passed into Christian use in the very early days. It is obviously desirable that the word should be said together, convincingly, loud and clear. Too often it sounds like a stifled grunt!.'

The Magazine: The editor, Mr. Chapman, used this December issue as an opportunity to express his thanks to those who regularly contributed to the magazines monthly appearance: 'I would like to pay tribute to all those people who have helped in the past year. To those who have trudged round the village pushing a copy through letter boxes; to Mrs. Talbot who organises delivery; to Mr. and Mrs. Heppell [the printers] for their kind forbearance; to Miss Kemp who looks after the £ s. d. and posts copies to "many parts of the world"; to the advertisers who help us *nearly* to pay our way; the contributors who write to me; and, finally, you who purchase the magazine – thank you.'

January 1968

Vicar's Notes: 'Some regular Communicants at the early service have asked that we should revert, for the time being, to the 1662 Service at 8am – and this will be done. When a Parish Communion is held at 11am or 6.30pm the New Form of Service will be used.

Many of you will have seen on television the "Z car" episode filmed at Sonning Bridge and shown on BBC1. But did you see the bottom half of a rather bedraggled pair of clerical trousers on the far bank? Easily mistaken for weeping-willow stumps. I was visiting near the Mill at the time!'

Sonning Women's Institute: 'The December meeting was held in the newly decorated Pearson Hall. The Displaced Persons Adoption Committee has advised us that the Polish family are really no longer in need of our assistance. The children are almost beyond school age and are earning, which very much eases the burden on the parents. The Institute was thanked for its considerable efforts on their behalf over the last nine years.'

February 1968

Vicar's Notes: 'Throughout the year, a group of kind people give their time and their money (plus their talent!) to make our Church look beautiful with flowers. My wife and I feel especially grateful for all that is being done to maintain in our Church a very high standard of floral decoration. On behalf of us all a very sincere – thank you, to all the helpers.'

Sonning Scouts and Cubs: 'We are short of fathers on our Committee and would welcome their co-operation, especially if they were once in the Scouts. There will also be a rummage Sale in the Scout Hut on Wednesday, February 28, to help our funds.'

Sonning Football Club: 'The first Saturday of 1968 was a red letter day for Sonning football, on that day all three Sonning teams gained victories. Our first eleven visited Finchampstead and won 3-2; our second eleven entertained Argyle Athletic Reserves and won 5-1 and the third team defeated Checkendon in the away fixture 4-2.'

March 1968

St Patrick's Notes: 'The annual party of St Patrick's Sunday School was held on Saturday, February 3, at Charvil. Over seventy children sat down to a delicious tea in the decorated hall. After tea, games were played until the arrival of the puppet-show which the children enjoyed.'

The Sonning Floral Arrangement Society: 'The demonstrator at the February meeting was Dr. M. Vickery, Secretary of the Thames Valley Flower Arrangement Club. Dr. Vickery gave an extremely interesting display of simple spring arrangements with the use of very few flowers.'

1st Sonning Brownies: 'Jane Hiles and Carole Horne have just been awarded their Golden Hand badges and we congratulate them both. Pat Malkin is now a Second of the Imps, and Camilla Coldwell is a Second of the Sprites.'

April 1968

The "Top Ten" Hymns: In the September 1966 issue of the magazine a list of the ten most popular hymns appeared [*page 161*]. The following list was now selected by the Sonning Sunday congregation:
1 Now thank we all our God (New Tune) – 2 Abide with Me
3 The day Thou gavest – 4 Onward Christian Soldiers
5 The King of love my Shepherd is – 6 Praise my soul the King of Heaven
7 Jerusalem – 8 He who would valiant be
9 Heavenly Father send Thy blessing (New Tune)
10 Love divine all loves excelling

Sonning Parochial Church Council – Report for 1967
The Report of the Vicar and P.C.C. to the Annual General Meeting 1968 included the following items:
'Applications have been made for the use of St Patrick's Hall as a Nursery School. A great many formalities and official approvals have been necessary but it is hoped that all obstacles will be overcome and the school will be running by the autumn.
The Council's grateful thanks are once again due to our organist and choir, bell-ringers, our verger and Mrs, Field, church cleaners, flower arrangers and all the many people who have helped during the year; not forgetting Mr. Hugh Grainger who was instituted as a Lay Reader on July 1.'

May 1968
St Patrick's Charvil: 'It has been suggested that one communion should be held each month at 7.30pm for the benefit of those who are unable to manage the morning time.'

Sonning Whitsun Festival: 'An exhibition of Religious Art is to take place in Sonning for the three days over Whit-weekend. The exhibits have been staged in four different places:
Lady Chapel in the Parish Church: A display showing the latest ideas in altars, lecterns, seating, etc.,
The Deanery: Embroidery will be on display together with an embroidery demonstration in the setting of this lovely house and garden.
The Vicarage: Religious pictures will be on view (including a selection by Gilbert Spencer), cartoons for a stained glass window by John Piper and other collections of great interest.
The Pearson Hall: An exhibition of "Sonning through the Ages" going back no less than three hundred thousand years. This will include various models.
There will also be a Concert in Church on Whit-monday evening.'

June 1968
Sonning Glebe Women's Institute: 'At the April meeting there was a very attractive fashion display by Dorothy Perkins, and two models showed a good variety of clothes which members could purchase later.
Lady Young was invited to say a few words on the W.R.V.S. scheme. "Helping in Emergencies," and at least thirty members said that they would be interested.'

Two extensive and thought provoking articles appeared in this issue: "Christianity and Islam" and "Student Power."

[*June 6. US Senator, Robert Kennedy, a brother of the assassinated President John F. Kennedy, is assassinated in Los Angeles by Sirhan Sirhan an Arab immigrant.*]

July 1968
Sonning Exhibition: 'The Sonning Parish Council wish to express thanks to everyone who assisted with the organisation of this Exhibition of Fine Art which was held during the Whitsun weekend. The Exhibition was a great success.'

Altar and Pulpit: 'Lady Hamilton Fairley has made and embroidered the beautiful Laudian Altar Frontal which was dedicated on Whitsunday. She has also given the new curtain at the back of the pulpit. This has a distinctly regal air about it, which, however, is partially dispelled when the resident preacher mounts the pulpit steps!'

Charvil Mothers' Club: 'The monthly meeting was held in St Patrick's Hall on June 18, when Mrs. Sandra Odhams gave a demonstration of Wigs and Hair Pieces. It was an enjoyable evening and latecomers had difficulty in recognising various members in their "Brigitte Bardot" disguises!'

August 1968

Sonning Young Wives: 'The meeting on July 17, consisted of a barbecue in the garden of "Wild Wood", Warren Road, Woodley. About twenty members and friends enjoyed a pleasant evening and were pleased to have a dry night for the occasion.'

Sonning C. of E. Primary School: 'The prizegiving was held at the School on Wednesday, July 23. A great many parents and friends attended. This year's prizes were given to the fourth year leavers only. Miss Kemp gave away the prizes and Mr. Prismall, on behalf of the Managers, thanked her.
The small children's choir and percussion band entertained the parents with some of the songs they had sung at the Central Berkshire Musical Festival.'

September 1968

Sonning Parish Council: A meeting of the Council was held on Tuesday, August 6. The following items were included in the report:
'A Public Enquiry has been arranged by the County Council to consider the following proposals:
1. The formation of a separate Parish for Charvil.
2. To transfer part of Coronation Ward from Woodley to Sonning Parish, which would include West Drive, Holmemoor Drive and the Old Bath Road.
Pound Lane – the County Council have formed a new footpath in Pound Lane connecting with Little Glebe. A new path is badly needed at the lower end of the Lane and it is hoped this will be put in hand soon.

The Village has again been awarded first place in the "Best Kept Village" competition. Many thanks to everyone who assisted to keep the Village tidy. Sonning Lock has been awarded First Prize also for the "Best Kept Lock" on this section of the Thames. Congratulations to Mr. Schofield for keeping the Lock so beautifully and for the success again.'

Advertisements: 'It's time that we said another "thank you" to all those firms who take up space in this magazine. They help us, and I hope we help them.'

Reading Blue Coat School: 'The new Headmaster, Mr. Richardson, takes over at the School at the start of this winter term and we all wish him well in his new work.'

October 1968
Vicar's Notes: 'Congratulations to Mr. "Roly" Hunt on winning the major award at the Produce Show. My onions, I regret to say, looked sorry for themselves alongside the champions – but they *taste* jolly good all the same and next year . . .
Congratulations again to Mr. Hunt – this time on being chosen to lead the Sonning Fire Brigade in place of Mr. T. Edwards who is retiring. Together, with his father the late Mr. A. F. Edwards (skipper), he served with distinction for a great many years and we offer him our thanks for all the considerable contribution he has made in the service of the Sonning Fire Brigade.'

1968 Sonning Produce Show: 'The Show was again held this year at the Pearson Hall on September 7. Fears that the wet summer would cause the reduction of entries in the fruit, flower and vegetable sections was unfounded and although entries were fewer in the handicraft section and in children's art the total number of entries at 504 was much the same as last year.'

British Legion–Women's Section: 'The monthly meeting of the Section was held in the Pearson Hall on September 19. Mr. Lyall and Mr. Matthews of the Typhoo Tea Co., came and gave an interesting talk and showed films of tea from the planting, and its progress until it reaches the teapot.'

November 1968

St Patrick's Sunday School: 'We seem to be growing and growing and have welcomed several new children recently and what a lot of little ones we now have! Two of our older girls are now helping with the little ones and we are so pleased to keep them with us. It is our great joy to present seven boys and girls for Confirmation this December, they will be particularly in our thoughts and prayers.'

Sonning C. of E. Primary School: The headmaster, Thomas Feak, reported upon the commencement of the new school year: 'We had rather more entrants than usual and they settled down very quickly. We welcome a new teacher, Miss Barbara Evans, who is from Bulmershe College and is taking the place of Mrs. Gaynor, who will continue to teach on a part-time basis until half-term.'

Sonning Parish Council: An item was included in this issue which again addressed the need for the further bridge over the Thames in order to alleviate increasing traffic congestion in Sonning Village: 'The County Council has again been approached regarding the building of a new bridge over the Thames at a suitable point between Sonning and Reading. This was originally proposed as far back as 1926. A relief road should connect with the bridge from Suttons roundabout, also from the A4 near to Sonning Lane junction.'

December 1968

Vicar's Notes: 'We are in urgent need to recruit another bass and another tenor. Names please to Mr. Lusty. We also need more people to "lead" the congregation – the singing is good but it could be better!
Mrs. Merton has given to our Church a very beautiful Alms Dish and I want to say thank you on behalf of us all.
Congratulations to the Sonning Youth Club Football team on their excellent start to the soccer season. They may yet emerge top of their league.'

St Patrick's Notes: 'Evensong will be held on Sunday, December 8 and a very warm welcome is extended to everyone; we would like to see the little church filled to capacity.'

January 1969

Vicar's Notes: The parish magazine, first published in January 1869, celebrated its centenary this year. The vicar acknowledged this milestone by initially repeating the three objectives that the Rev. Hugh Pearson had laid down as the "guiding principles" of the magazine. 'Whilst enjoying the fascinating glimpse into the past, we must ensure that the current magazines are bound and preserved. So much for the old, now for the new - *long live the Sonning Magazine!*

The Christmas Services were as beautiful as ever and the singing was outstanding. The "Group Singers" again gave great pleasure, also Mrs. Beach, the Hand-bell ringers and, last but not least, our own choir . . . the Christmas message will never lose its appeal - we do so desperately need more love in the world.'

Sonning Men's Group: 'We may see Air Commodore Sir Bernard Chackfield again at some of our meetings; after his very instructive, and almost unbelievable talk, about "space" he thought that he might like to attend some of our other meetings - as a guest.'

February 1969

Vicar's Notes: 'The new "old" cover to our 1969 magazine has been well received (the poor old knight was never very popular). I wonder how many people actually examined the picture and detected differences as compared with the Church today. The position of the flagpole has been changed. Iron railings no longer exist at the west end of the Church, and what a pity it is that the seat has gone (or is it a tomb?). The artist obviously disliked gutters - no down-pipes are included in his drawing. The trees as one might expect after one hundred years, are very different - is that a notice board on the extreme left?' [*see: page 178*]

1st *Sonning Girl Guides:* 'The Guides had a very busy Christmas programme including carol singing at Borocourt Hospital. Then, despite Arctic conditions and with the help of three Rangers we were able to entertain members of the Darby and Joan Club at the Pearson Hall. Because of an increase in numbers the Company is now "full" and we, therefore, have a waiting list.'

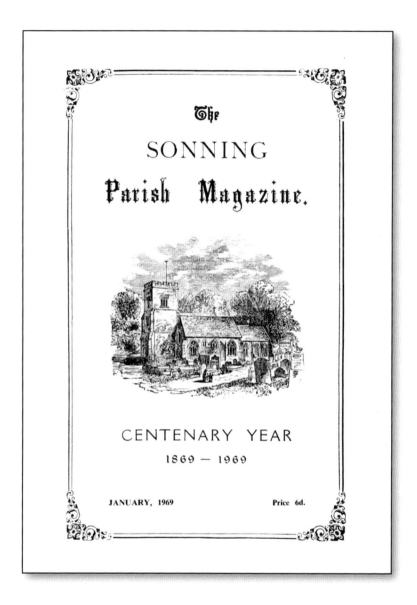

Cover page: January 1969 (23.5 x 17.5cm)

March 1969

Vicar's Notes: 'Lent is actually an old English word for becoming longer, *eg* LEN(g)Thening, and can be described as the Church's "Spring". At the time of writing it is snowing hard but in spite of the hard weather the days are lengthening and spring is on the way! Spring is a time of growth in the sphere of nature, and Lent should be a time of growth in the spiritual sphere of our own lives. Now is the time to correct bad habits and to find time for regular prayer, worship and devotional reading. We have got a soul as well as a body!'

The Charvil Coach: 'On several occasions recently the Church Coach has been usually full in the morning and evening. If this does mean that some people have come to St Andrew's for the first time, I would like to say *WELCOME*, and please forgive me if I did not welcome you at the Church door – I am incapable of spotting new faces!'

April 1969

The Witness Group: 'This group of young people, who meet for Bible study and prayer, on Wednesday evenings and again after Evensong on Sunday evenings, are going to add a monthly contribution to the parish magazine. The witness by the group, in various forms, is seen and heard throughout this Parish and also far beyond our own boundaries.'

Sonning Scouts and Cubs: 'The Scout camp at Bridport had been a tonic, a welcome from the farmer and lots of good scouting. Congratulations to our two Queen Scouts, Paul Smith and George Natriss.'

May 1969

Vicar's Notes: 'What a beautiful month May can be – especially here in Sonning. The daffodils have been better than ever. The cuckoo was heard in the Churchyard on April 15 and as I write the first Chiff Chaff can be heard announcing his or her arrival from the copper beech tree by the Tower.
Rogation Sunday on May 11, is the day on which we ask God's blessing on the "fruits of the earth", and I am glad to confirm that Mr. Malcolm Stansfield from the University Farm will be giving a talk at 11am and again at 6.30pm.'

Nature Notes: 'The Lock Keeper reports seeing six (yes six!) Kingfishers in a row sitting on the edge of his lock – one dived in and got a fish!'

June 1969

[*The pagination of the monthly issues were now varying considerably from six to sixteen pages of text matter. Interest articles were being included together with a wider range of reports from clubs and societies.*]

Sonning Parish Council: A report was published providing information upon various matters relating to the parish:
'Sonning Mill will shortly be closing down. Your Council will do all that is possible to preserve the mill building and amenities and hope that a suitable future use can be found.
Your Council has considered the problem of indiscriminate waiting by cars in the Village. We are informed that if we wish to have "No Waiting" it will be necessary to paint double yellow lines on either side of the roads throughout the Village. There is one advantage to leaving matters as at present in that waiting cars help to steady the through traffic.
The Trolley bus which has recently been stationed in the School playground has caused concern to residents. However, arrangements are being made to build a high wall as a screen which can also be used for a Fives Court.'

Darby and Joan Club: 'On May 12, a coach load of members were taken to the National Trust property Greys Court, Henley-on-Thames, to see the house and gardens.'

July 1969

Vicar's Notes: 'Some have justifiably complained that our Corporate Communion Services, to the New Order of Service, are too few and far between. Let's fix two dates now – July 6 (11am) and July 27 (6.30pm). The "New" Communion Service seems to have caught on in the country and will almost certainly be adopted after the trial period.'

Sonning Floral Arrangement Society: 'The Flower Club met as usual on the second Thursday of the month and had a most enjoyable afternoon. Mrs. Treweeke, from Witney, a well-known and thoroughly experienced demonstrator, entertained the Club members and visitors to "Summer Simplicity" – her flower arrangements were indeed beautiful.'

[At 3.56am (BST) July 31 man first set foot on the moon. Astronaut Neil Armstrong, commander of Apollo 11, stepped off the ladder of the lunar module and uttered these memorable words to millions of television viewers watching live pictures of this historic happening "That's one small step for a man, one giant leap for mankind".]

August 1969

Altar Frontal: 'The beautiful green Altar Frontal which is now in use has been kindly presented by Mr. and Mrs. Wallace in commemoration of their Golden Wedding.

Sonning Parish Council: A report of a meeting held on July 11 included the following items:

'Sonning Mill has now closed down and the milling machinery is being removed, and this property will shortly be offered for sale. The old mill is scheduled for preservation and dates back to about the 10th century and is mentioned in the Domesday Book.

An inquiry was held on July 10 at Wokingham regarding the owners appeal against the enforcement notice issued against them prohibiting the use of buildings and land at Inglewood for a "joinery works, stores and the dumping of old cars." Members of the Parish attended the meeting which took the whole day and the inquiry was adjourned until September 16.'

September 1969

Pearson Hall: A meeting of the advisory committee was convened on August 1, the following items were included in the report:

'Over the last two years improvements costing over £1,700 had transformed the Hall. This had been made possible by three generous donations – £600 from the Sonning Parochial Church Council, £497 from the Sonning Spring Festival and £375 from the Flower Arrangement Exhibition. The Hall had also been presented with a washing-up machine by an anonymous donor.

Seating facilities had been greatly improved and it was decided to improve the catering equipment and heating of the Hall and to replace the unsightly fence in front of the Hall by posts and chains.

Although the income of the Hall had shown a great improvement, the income from lettings did not cover running costs and some increase will be required.'

Table Tennis: 'The group will meet for the first time this "season" during the evening of Wednesday, September 10. We hope to see all our regular members on this occasion in order to get a good start.'

October 1969

Sonning Mill: The Mill was soon to be offered for sale at public auction and the Sonning Parish Council had expressed the sincere hope that the general character and appearance of the old building might be retained and converted for some other use. It was suggested that some of Sonning's wealthy residents might combine and convert the building into a dwelling house or flats. There had been a further suggestion to convert the Mill into a museum, but it was noted that this might be difficult to finance and maintain.

Sonning Produce Show: '545 entries this year – a record! The Hillier Cup was won for the second year running by Mr. R. Hunt. The White Hart Cup was won by Katherine Bodley Scott for her excellent cake.'

November 1969

Vicar's Notes: 'This Magazine – it gets bigger and better as it reflects more and more the activities of the village *as a whole*, this must surely be right; but we are far from paying our way! With this in mind a meeting has been called (to include the editor, distributors and all contributors) to consider how best to cut our losses without distracting from the general character of the magazine. I would like to say how grateful we are to the advertisers for their continued support.
At the beginning of the new Church Year I would like to pay tribute to all the Sonning and Charvil organisations who give us, whatever our age, something to look forward to every week.'

The Working Men's Club: 'The new bar and billiards room have been in use for six months. The old clubroom has hidden its old "Gothic" roof trusses above a new acoustic ceiling and lightened its darkness with a large picture window. Slowly the physical image of the club is changing and becoming rejuvenated.'

December 1969

The Magazine: 'At the recent meeting of contributors, distributors and others closely connected with the magazine, it was agreed that in order to reduce the considerable losses sustained in publication, the price should be increased to nine pence as from January 1, 1970. The

contents would continue to cover the activities of the parish as a whole. Thanks were expressed to the editor and to all those connected with the magazine which would continue to be excellent value for money.'
[*The new price represented a fifty per cent increase from six pence.*]

Holme Park Farm: 'Application has been made by the owners for permission to develop 8.5 acres of land to the north of South Drive. Your Council consider that this land should be retained for agriculture and as a green belt between Sonning and Reading.'

January 1970
Vicar's Notes: 'Canon Groves died at his home in Goring on December 17 after a long and distressing illness borne with great courage and patience. His death felt deeply by his many friends in this parish.
On the rare occasions I met Canon Groves I was struck by his quality of holiness and have found that his influence in the parish is as wide as it is strong. I must leave it to others, who have the privilege of being his close friends, to write, from long personal experience, of a man who will be remembered as one of Sonning's most devoted vicars. Our sympathy and our love go out to Mrs. Groves and her family.'

Sonning Parish Council: At their monthly meeting held on December 12, the parish council agreed to support the Ministry of Transport's proposal regarding the alteration to the A4 which included deviation at the eastern end of Charvil Lane to connect with Milestone Avenue.

February 1970
Vicar's Notes: 'Readings from Pilgrim's Progress – the idea is to meet regularly in the Vicarage and for some people to take the various parts as for a play reading, and to include the relevant references to the Bible. If you are at all interested to give it a trial, and if you don't find it a help, just drift away! I read the book again on holiday and found it of absorbing interest. Please bring your own copy if you have one – I will have a few spare copies for those who can't get hold of one.'

Charvil: 'The inhabitants of Charvil have been awarded Parish Status and the Sonning Parish Council send to them best wishes.'

West Drive, Coronation Ward: 'The transfer of this area into Sonning Parish has been agreed, to take effect from April 1, 1970. It has always been considered a part of Sonning and the Parish Council wish to extend a warm welcome.'

March 1970

Sonning Men's Group: 'The meeting in January coincided with a heavy snow fall and reduced the number, but the few who managed to reach the Vicarage enjoyed the Vicar's hospitality and each other's holiday slides. Perhaps it was well that we left out the February meeting, for the snow returned on the date we would have met.'

Sonning Youth Club: 'Tuesday nights in the Pearson Hall are as popular as ever. The average attendance being just over forty. Our thanks to the village residents for their encouragement and understanding over the past three years or so. Football-wise, the club has grown in stature. The youth team , although not winning many matches, has continued to have a keen and friendly team spirit.'

April 1970

Vicar's Notes: 'We have recently had our first Annual Parochial Church Meeting under the new system of synodical government. There are only minor changes at P.C.C. level, but the general hierarchy in the Church has been simplified with a greater share of "government" given to laity. Decisions relating to the Church will be made by Clergy (including Bishops) and laity meeting together in the National Synod (at the "highest" level) in the Diocesan Synod, in the Ruri-decanal Synod and (at the "lowest" level) in the Parochial Church Council. The Electoral Roll will remain for us the basis for representation on the Ruri-decanal Synod, but the Roll itself will be completely revised during this coming year, qualification for inclusion on the Roll remains virtually as before.'

May 1970

Vicar's Notes: 'Our best wishes to the newly formed Charvil Parish Council – Charvil was formerly attached to Woodley Parish. The historic first meeting took place at St Patrick's Hall on April 15, press reporters and photographers turned up in force.'

Bach's Passion: 'Congratulations to all those who took part in the wonderful performance on Good Friday evening. I believe it is eight years since we last heard it in our church and there must have been tremendous practice done to produce such a balanced effect. No doubt Mr. Lusty was the driving force behind it all and we thank him most sincerely for all his effort.'

June 1970

Vicar's Notes: 'The young people will conduct the evening service on Sunday, June 14. A former member of the group, who is now at a Theological College training for the ministry, will preach the sermon. This will be a rather different sort of service to our usual Evensong, and I am looking forward to it very much.

There are many in this parish who would like to wish Canon Robinson, Rector of Earley, all happiness in his well deserved retirement.

A good congregation turned out to watch the launch of our Ascension Balloon, later seen high over Henley at about one thousand feet!'

[*The general election held on June 18 results in the Conservatives led by Edward Heath replacing the Labour government with an overall majority of thirty seats.*]

Sonning Football Club: 'With the 1969-70 season now behind us, our feelings are somewhat mixed. The First XI have finished runners-up in Division I and gained promotion to the Premier League for the first time in the history of the club. Alas, the Second XI failed to make the grade and will be relegated to Division 4.'

July 1970

Sonning Women's Institute: 'The Pearson Hall presented a charming picture upon entering – the members in gay [*merry, joyful*] summery dresses and the usual lovely pedestal of flowers on the stage. Our speaker for the meeting was Mr. Rollinson, who showed slides of National Trust houses and gardens. This was most interesting as he described the places and where they were located.'

Charvil Parish Council: 'At a meeting of the parish council on May 21, Mr. J. A. Thomas of Woodley was appointed as Clerk.'

August 1970

Sonning Parish Council: The council met on July 10 and further discussed the traffic problems in Sonning:
'As an interim measure and economical solution, while long term planning proceeds, the council is to propose to the County Surveyors that the Ministry of Defence be invited to build a Bailey Bridge over the Thames between Reading and Sonning as a useful Army training exercise.'

Sonning Glebe Women's Institute: 'On June 15, Mrs. Davies gave a talk to Sonning Glebe W. I. on antiques. She specialised in Victorian glass. She told us how, at the end of the 18th century, George III taxed glass, and it became very expensive. At the beginning of the 19th century a tax was put on coloured glass, and when this tax was taken off in the middle of that century the Victorians went "mad" and produced great quantities of it.'

September 1970

Rev. Brutton's announcement that he was now intending to retire as Sonning's vicar had been met with strong encouragement for him to change his mind and continue his ministry. Two letters were included in this issue – from Sidney Paddick and with a response from Robin Brutton. The following are extracts from those letters:

My Dear Friends,
You will be pleased to see by the Vicar's letter below that we have been able to persuade him to continue his ministry in Sonning. He would of course have been terribly missed; in fact neither the Church nor Sonning would be quite the same without his presence here.
Your sincere friend Sidney Paddick

My Dear Friends,
Mr. Paddick has kindly let me see a copy of the letter which appears above. It is typical of the wonderful kindness and understanding which has been shown to me and my family particularly after my recent thoughts about "retirement". We have been deeply moved by the various expressions of goodwill and, if you are prepared to put up with my omissions, failings and irregularities, I would love to carry on a little longer.
My wife and I are terribly grateful to you all (we could never have a happier home than Sonning).
May God bless you all, Robin Brutton.

October 1970

Canon Robinson: The death on September 20, of Stanley Charles Robinson was included in this issue. He had been the popular vicar of Earley St Peter's Church for twenty-seven years and chaplain to the Lord Bishop of Oxford. He was a governor on the boards of St Peter's C. of E. Primary School, Earley and the Reading Blue Coat School, also a representative of many charities and other organisations.

Institution at Earley: As patron of the Living of Earley, Rev Brutton was to take part in the Institution by the Bishop of Oxford, of the Rev. J. C. Hutton as vicar of Earley St Peters, on October 22.

Sonning Mill: The Sonning Parish Council expressed concern that the Mill may be converted into a restaurant as this would result in a considerable increase in road traffic, especially over the bridge.

Sonning Produce Show: A very successful show was held on September 5, with a record number of 658 entries. The Brutton Cup, a new cup presented by Robin Brutton for excellence in the culinary arts, was awarded to Mrs. Gardiner who won both the preserves and cookery sections.

November 1970

Vicar's Notes: 'If all goes according to plan a "pageant" at our Patronal Festival on Sunday, 29 November, will take the place of the normal service. This will portray some aspects of the church and village life in Elizabethan times. The morning presentation will last for half an hour only and have the children especially in mind. The evening will be for "children of all ages".'

B.C.C. Sports Club: 'Proposals by the Berkshire County Council to extend their recreational facilities at their Sports Club in Sonning have been discussed with the County Architect and the Rural District Council. The Sonning Parish Council have been assured that their wish to retain the character of the approach to the village, as well as surrounding land, will be carefully considered in the overall plan with regard to landscaping and architectural design.'

December 1970

Sonning Parish Council Office: 'The new office in the Pearson Hall is turning out to be a very useful facility and it is hoped that it will be used as a means of communication between the Parish Council and the parishioners. The office hours are from 10am until noon.'

Sonning Voluntary Committee for the Elderly: Details of services which were available for older Sonning residents were mentioned:
'Hair Cutting and Dressing – Margaret has now been replaced by another hairdresser and O.A.P's may avail themselves of this service as before.
Meals on Wheels – These have now been started through the kind efforts of the W.R.V.S. after a long period of frustration. It is regretted that the service is at present rather limited but efforts are being made to extend the availability.'

Charvil Parish Council: At a council meeting held on November 2, it was reported that the council's intention was to publish an official guide for the Parish of Charvil and would welcome any articles or photographs relating to the area for inclusion in the first publication.'

CHAPTER SIX

1971 - 1975

Harry Chapman who had edited the parish magazine for a number of years confirmed his wish to retire from that role in 1971. The editorial responsibility was taken up by two local parishioners, Mrs. Forrest and Mrs. Perkins, who were to jointly take on the editorship. The pagination of the magazine had increased and now consisted of sixteen pages of which nine pages were given over to advertisements. The cover illustration used continued to replicate the first cover design from 1869. The January 1971 magazine included an eight page centenary issue of the inset *Home Words*; the inset carried a message from the Queen and the Archbishop of Canterbury offering congratulations on the insets one-hundredth birthday.

Robin Brutton at the age of sixty-two had chosen to retire from the St Andrew's ministry in early 1975. The new vicar to take the living at Sonning was Rev. George Stokes, the vicar of Amport Church in Hampshire, who had earlier served as a chaplain in the armed services. Churchwardens who served Sonning at this time were Sidney Paddick a long time member of numerous Sonning committees, Thomas Feak, who had succeeded Harry Chapman as headmaster of Sonning school, Thomas Cowley and Malcolm Stansfield director of the Reading University farm at Sonning.

January 1971

Village Christmas Tree Lights: 'Many of the Sonning village organisations
have contributed towards the cost of these lights which have, power cuts
permitted, decorated the Christmas tree in the churchyard.   After
Christmas the lights will be stored in the church and any organisation
wishing to borrow them may do so.   It has been suggested that next year
these lights decorate a tree in front of the Pearson Hall and that the tree
is provided by the Working Men's Club.'

[*Electricity cuts were now occurring regularly and most residents resorted to candle light
and oil lamps during the power cut periods.*]

Vandalism in Sonning: At the Sonning Parish Council meeting on
December 10, it was reported that a number of street lights had been
damaged by vandals and dumping of refuse was causing problems in
Sonning Lane.   It was also reported that the strongest possible objection
had been lodged to a proposal to build forty-five houses on Reading
University land to the west of Milestone Avenue.

February 1971

Vicar's Notes: 'The change-over to decimalisation is going to require a
lot of patience and understanding on the part of everyone.   Many of us
will put complete trust in the shop assistant to help us with our
difficulties, but the shop staff will themselves will need help . . .
Thank goodness my wife will do the shopping ! '

[*The "D Day" for decimal currency in Britain was February 15, 1971.*]

Sonning Mill: The Parish Council regretted that approval had been
granted for the ground and first floor of the Mill to be used as a
restaurant and tea rooms.   It was noted effort should be made to ensure
this does not lead to approval for "entertainment and late hours".

The Motorway and You: Concern was raised regarding the construction
of the M4 motorway.   'With the M4 sprawling and spreading across
Berkshire in close proximity to our village, the Sonning Association
have arranged for a motorway construction engineer to address a
meeting at the Pearson Hall on February 8.   No one should miss this
opportunity to learn more about this monster on our doorstep.'

March 1971

Magazine Records: The vicar raised the matter of missing copies of past parish magazines: 'The vicarage possesses bound volumes of our Parish Magazine dating from 1869 to 1925 inclusive, and from 1936 to 1956 inclusive. One volume (at least it appears to be one volume) is missing, namely the years 1926-1935 inclusive. Can anyone help to trace this book which is probably bound in green cloth?'

[*Despite extensive enquiries copies from the "missing years" have not been traced. see: volume one – pages 239 to 246*]

The Home and Family Group: 'At our February meeting our guest speaker was Mrs. Gayder, who spoke about "Making ends Meet", which applies to both limited money and time. This led to considerable enthusiastic discussion since everyone of us has been short of at least one of these essentials , or both, many times!'

Charvil Parish Guide: It was noted that the publishing company had withdrawn their interest in the guide and the Charvil parish council had decided to suspend further action in this publishing venture.

April 1971

Magazine Records: In response to an appeal in the March issue, Mrs. Pitman the daughter of a well known Sonning resident, Mr. F. J. Hoyle, made the following comment: 'As far as I can recall, the "missing" volume for the years 1926-1935 never in fact existed. My father, who came to Sonning in 1936, was concerned that the historical record represented by the magazine had been allowed to lapse.'

Sonning Glebe Women's Institute: 'It was most encouraging to see the Pearson Hall so crowded for the AGM on March 15. Over sixty people attended the meeting.'

May 1971

Vicar's Notes: 'I shall not forget this most memorable Palm Sunday, Good Friday and Easter Day – Our Church, thank God, is strong, and I am terribly lucky to have such a loyal regular congregation. Thank you all for making it such a wonderful climax to the Church Year.'

Sonning Scouts and Cubs: 'Easter was busy doing the time-honoured Bob-a-job. The summer camp this year will be in the Savernack Forest in Wiltshire from July 18 to 24, an ideal camping site has been booked far away from the busy crowds, where scouts can have all the fun that scouting gives.'

Darby and Joan Club: 'At the meeting on March 29, we were very pleased to welcome Mr. Chamberlain and his Labrador guide dog, Sally. He explained to us how Sally was trained, and told us how reliable and in many ways intelligent she is.'

June 1971

Vicar's Notes: 'Spring is always a wonderful experience but never has it been more beautiful that this year. Sonning Church and Churchyard provide a perfect setting for it all and the fine weather completed the picture. If only it would stay a little longer – already we are in summer, the carpet of snowdrops and crocus seem a long way back.'
'I was glad to be present at the licensing of Mr. Biddlestone (formerly curate at Woodley) by the Bishop of Oxford at our "daughter" church of All Saints', Dunsden on May 4. Our best wishes go to the Rev. and Mrs. Biddlestone and their family in their new home.'

Charvil Village Centre: The parish council confirmed that they were still pursuing the possibility of purchasing land for a future village centre and playing field. In the meantime the lease of the present playing field has been received for approval.

Sonning Youth Club: 'The Club continues to flourish and is extremely well attended at the Pearson Hall, the discotheques being the most popular evenings of all.'

July 1971

Vicar's Notes: 'The new circular stained glass window in the Sanctuary at St Patrick's, Charvil, has been enthusiastically received by all who have seen it. It is the work of Messrs, C. J. Earthy & Son, of Reading, who are also responsible for the design.'

Sonning Football Club: 'Our 75th Anniversary Dinner and Dance has come and gone, but what a delightful evening we had together. So now our thoughts turn to the coming season which is not too many weeks away. Training will commence in the latter part of July and practice games during August.'

Reading Samaritans: The Rev. Tony Fryer, Director of the Reading Samaritans, provided notes upon the organisation: 'The Reading branch has been established for nine years and in that time has encountered nearly five thousand clients and admitted 425 volunteers to membership. Our main aid is to provide support and friendship over a crisis period for those people who feel suicidal or are in despair. Regrettably, there were nine suicides recorded in Reading in 1970.'

August 1971
Church Bells: 'The P.C.C. has accepted the estimate from Messrs. Taylor's of Loughborough, for the pre-hanging of our church bells. The cost of pre-hanging the bells as about £600, and the P.C.C. hopes that friends of the tower will be given an opportunity to make donations to the cost of this work.'

Sonning Parish Council: The following item was reported from a meeting held on July 9:
'The Parish Council are dismayed to learn from a press report that the Sonning Conservation Area had now been agreed by the Berkshire County Council and that Holme Park and the University Farm had been excluded.'

Sonning Fire Station: 'The crew of Station 8, Sonning, are holding an open day at the Fire Station, Pound Lane, on Saturday, September 18. We hope the people of Sonning and district will come along and see the station, engines and equipment on show.'

September 1971
The Editor: The vicar announced in this issue that Harry C. Chapman had asked to be relieved of the editorship of the parish magazine. The new joint editors were to be Mrs. Perkins and Mrs. Forrest.

The Best Kept Village: 'Sonning has again been judged the Best Kept Village in Berkshire (Division 2).'

Royal British Legion: 'Sonning Branch will combine with the Women's Section in holding a Tramp supper on Friday, October 1, at Pearson Hall to celebrate the 50th anniversary. Proceeds will be given to the Earl Haig Poppy Fund.'

October 1971

Vicar's Notes: 'Under new management! This is the first magazine under the direction of the new editors. I would like to wish both Mrs. Perkins and Mrs. Forrest all success, and to assure them of our loyal backing.'

Editorial Policy: The new editors outlined changes and improvements which they would hope to make to the content of future issues of the magazine:
'We welcome contributions from people of all ages to make this a Magazine really representative of all ages.
We are starting, from now, a Correspondence Column, so think out a topic you would like to air your views on.
We have a few ideas up our sleeve, especially for younger readers – the Poetry Competition sets the ball rolling.
Increased circulation keeps the cost down, and means we can afford a fuller, more interesting magazine. If every family reading this could encourage other families to be regular readers, everyone would benefit!'

Sonning Produce Show: 'Although the number of entries was down this year by about twenty per cent, undoubtedly because of the weather, the quality of the exhibits was considerably higher. Profits this year, as well as donations from many kind people, exceeded those of last year by about fifty per cent and will make a most useful contribution to the cost of the Pearson Hall improvements.'

November 1971

The Vicar's Notes: 'It is good to have the bells ringing again and the ringers seem delighted with the new bearings. Plans are afoot for a Re-Dedication Service plus a Social and a "Hop".

What a good "first" magazine the new editors compiled for us - now it's up to us readers to produce really interesting material for all the new "features".'

Festival of Light: 'Our own beacon was lit in the grounds of St Patrick's Church on Thursday, September 23. It was wonderful to know that other beacons were being lit all over the country as a warning against the spread of evil and to demonstrate there are still a large majority of Christians who care enough to stand up for Jesus and the purity and love taught by him.'

December 1971
The Vicar's Notes: 'The foundation stone of St John the Evangelist Church, Woodley - one of our daughter churches - was laid during October 1871, and a special centenary celebration was held on Sunday, October 24, at which Mr. Cowley and I were present. It was an impressive occasion which lost nothing of its dignity being pleasantly informal - a number of parishioners turned up in Victorian dress - a number of churches of other denominations took an active part in the proceedings. The Vicar, the Rev. H. W. H. Wilkinson, paid a generous tribute to the various benefactors who, together with the then-vicar, the Rev. Hugh Pearson, made possible the building of this fine church. The centenary celebrations will continue for some months.'

Remembrance Sunday: 'The Service and Parade was held on Sunday, November 14, and was a great success. Thanks are due to the Vicar, Churchwardens, the Trumpeter from Kneller Hall, Reading Blue Coat School Band and Cadets, the Police and all others whose help made the occasion a memorable one.'

Help the Aged: 'A centre was held at Pearson Hall on November 3, for the collection of clothing, blankets and articles for sale in organisation's shops. Fourteen sacks of clothing and blankets were filled.'

[*The new editorial policy was clear to see. Articles reporting on local events were more prevalent, and a number of readers' letters and poems were now published in the magazine.* see: page 196 - Text page December 1971.]

Alastair Wright, promoted to the first XI, has settled in quite well and is proving a useful acquisition, while there is good news of Graham Allen who broke his leg during the first match of the season. He is back at work and talks of playing again early in the New Year. His return will be most welcome.

A new member in Sid Horne has been added to our Committee strength. Sid had several years as a Club Secretary behind him so should know what work is entailed off the field.

We were pleased to have Dave Norman with us recently when he was home. Naturally we found a job for him to do this time as stand-in team attendant. David appears to be enjoying his new life.

J.A.

Letter Competition

Since it seems that Sonning air is not conducive to very prolific letter-writing, we were all the more delighted with the three entries received for the competition. We thoroughly enjoyed reading them and we know others will too. Thank you for taking the trouble to enter.

As with the children's poetry competition, we were very torn between the varied qualities of your letters, but the originality of Mr. Horne's tipped the balance in his favour. We offer him our congratulations, to be followed shortly by a small prize.

We feel sure you will agree that these letters add greatly to the interest of the magazine. We hope they may encourage others of you to take up your pens, and have, therefore, decided to hold the competition open for another month. In case you may not have found any of the suggested topics inspiring, we are no longer restricting the subject —do send us a letter on any subject relevant to the life of the village (suggestions for improving the magazine, for instance ?).

Prize Letter

How a newcomer sees Sonning.

'June 1968 we moved in to Sonning, escapers from the metropolis where legend has it that one must reside in a village for 50 years before acceptance.

But no ! Within five minutes our immediate neighbour called, 'Welcome', she said simply, and meant it. A few minutes later a tall distinguished gentleman strode up the drive. 'Good morning', he boomed, 'How are you getting on ?' and 'I'm the Vicar'. You could have fooled me, no dog collar. "If I can be of any help the vicarage is through the churchyard, the gate of which is opposite the tap-room of 'The Bull' " — a very kindly thought.

From that day I have discovered a smile is rewarded with a smile, a cheerful 'Good morning', brings a similar greeting, and the reticence of villagers is a complete myth.

I was proposed and seconded, by eminent and respected elders, for membership of the village club, outside of which there stands a Banner with a strange device — "SONNING **WORKING** MEN'S CLUB'. You could have fooled me, again. Threading my way between E. Type Jaguars, Bentleys, Rovers and the odd bike, I received yet another welcome from the genial steward, and in no time at all I was making a fourth on the snooker table. It mattered not as to one's social status. Architects and plumbers, peasants and doctors, bricklayers and accountants — once over the threshold all are club members.

I think I'm in !'.

S. Horne,
Field Cottage.

Runners-Up
Memories of Sonning in the past.

The 18th century curate.

'This curate is said to have been very fond of spending his evenings playing cards with several old ladies of the village. In bad weather the members of the party were individually taken to the rendezvous in a sedan chair, which ran to and fro for the purpose.

One evening, in order to save time, the curate picked up one of the ladies on the way; but the combined weight of the two passengers being greater than usual, the floor of the chair fell out, and the spectacle was revealed of their lower limbs standing in the street, the upper parts of their bodies being hidden by the chair ! We can imagine the delight of the youth of Sonning at the sight ! It made so great an impression on their young minds that it was remembered and talked about for many years afterwards. Unluckily we cannot trace the cost of repairing the chair, or we might have been able to give some indication of the weight of this curate and his partner !'

A. South

Text page: December 1971 (25 x 18cm)

January 1972

New Electoral Roll: 'This year throughout the country the existing Electoral Rolls will be scrapped and new ones compiled. Only those who make a fresh application will be included on the Roll, which is the Church's register of electors, *eg.* those who are qualified to vote at the Annual Parochial Church Meeting.'

Sonning Glebe Women's Institute: 'Exciting news of the "Green and Pleasant Land" slides and tapes. The National Judging Panel awarded our entry the "Highly Commended" Certificate. Congratulations to Yvonne Cons and Nurse Papps and all who helped their efforts.'

[*"The Troubles", a period of prolonged conflict between Catholic and Protestant extremists in Northern Ireland, which required the deployment of the British Army, had commenced in the late sixties and continued until the early nineteen nineties. Many atrocities took place with the loss of many lives. On January 3, 1972 a bomb was detonated in a Belfast department store resulting in fifty five casualties.*]

February 1972

Sonning Roundabout: The parish council reported that the camber of the road at the north-east corner of the roundabout had been raised very considerably following a number of accidents that had occurred in that area.

Comment – from the Editors: 'We suspect that we may get into trouble over the increasing size of the magazine! Nevertheless, we are delighted that so many readers are contributing in various ways. Please keep it up; articles, poems, letters.'

[*This February issue comprised ten pages of editorial plus advertisements and cover.*]

Sonning Floral Arrangement Society: 'The Club spent a most enjoyable afternoon on January 13, when Mrs. Cundell from Newbury, gave her demonstration "making the most of what you have".

[*January 22 saw the signing by the Prime Minister, Edward Heath, of the Treaty of Brussels which was to commit Britain as a member of the European Community from January 1, 1973.*]

March 1972

Vicar's Notes: 'I hope that you managed to meet the new Bishop of Oxford the Right Reverend Kenneth John Woollcombe, either at St Patrick's or at St Andrew's. We enjoyed having him and he seems to have enjoyed his visit. We wish him health and happiness in his new work.'

Midsummer Madness!: 'Saturday, June 24, has been chosen as the date for our historic Village Cricket Match – The Vicar's XI v Sonning Working Men's Club. The Ground, with the co-operation of the Parish Council and the Sonning Cricket Club, has been booked, and the long-range weather forecasters bullied into promising a fine day!'

Comment – from the Editors: 'We are sad to have to report that we are running into trouble over the size of the magazine. Unfortunately, our efforts to broaden its content, in the hope of giving it a wider appeal, have not resulted in the hoped-for increase in readership which would have covered the cost of production.'

April 1972

Vicar's Notes: 'At present, I am the sole trustee of the Sonning Working Men's Club, and as such I would like to record my appreciation of all that is done to make this club so successful. It represents the village as a whole, and does a power of good in bringing people together in an atmosphere of friendliness and good fellowship.'

Sonning Parish Council: The Annual General Meeting preceded the monthly meeting on April 16. The report included the following item: 'The Charities Commission recommendation that the Ancient Village Charities should be amalgamated has now been approved and a new constitution is to be drawn up. The title is to be the Sonning and District Welfare Trust but the names of the original benefactors will be retained as well as the purpose for which the trusts were first founded.'

Sonning C. of E. Primary School: 'Children from the Sonning school joined with children from Woodley in a B.B.C. television production of a musical play "Golden Legend" which will be shown on B.B.C.1 on Sunday, May 28.'

Sonning Tennis Club: 'A holiday coaching course of ten tennis lessons for juniors will start on April 4, at the Sonning Tennis Club courts. Saturday morning coaching will continue as usual during this time.'

May 1972

Sonning Parish Council: At their April monthly meeting the council once again raised the matter of a new Thames bridge:

'The obvious need for a second bridge over the Thames off Shepherd's Lane was again brought up and the Parish Council will continue to press for it. In the meantime efforts are being made to arrange for discussions between the various local interested groups, on both sides of the river, to work out the best way of pursuing the matter.'

Drama at the Club: 'The Pearson Hall enjoys a wide variety of activities, music, dancing, jumble sales, produce shows and drama. But for real drama you must go next door to the Sonning Working Men's Club on Finals Night when the various tournaments have reached a climax. Billiards and snooker are battled out, the players emerging from the depths elated or sombre, the darts enthusiasts crowd around the board, the cribbage addicts sit in solemn concentration; but for sheer technical artistry the shove-halfpenny board is the crowd-puller.'

June 1972

Vicar's Notes: 'Please make a note that there will be a demonstration of Folk Dancing on the Churchyard "green" after the Family Service on June 18. Also "coming this month" yet another hymn card (we're running out of colours!) with some good new words and tunes.'

Sonning Football Club: 'Another season is now behind us and taking it as a whole it has been quite a satisfactory season. On June 9, we shall be holding a Social evening at the Sonning Working Men's Club and if past experience is anything to go by we shall have a most enjoyable time.'

Sonning Brownies and Cubs: 'The trip to Bristol Zoo on April 29, proved most successful and enjoyable, in spite of very dismal weather. With the lighter and better evenings the majority of our Brownies are now busy preparing for their Cycling Proficiency Certificates.'

July 1972

Vicar's Notes: 'We welcome Christians of all denominations to our church and hope that they feel at home here. On Sunday, July 23, we have been invited by the Rev. Dr. Ronald Ashman to join the Methodist Congregation of Wesley Church, Queen's Road, Reading, for a service starting at 6.30pm. Our coach will leave St Patrick's, Charvil, at 6pm sharp and will make the usual "stops" before continuing to Reading.

A friend has written to me as follows, concerning the Sonning Produce Show: "I'm told that marrows are big this year, so don't get them mixed up with your onions! This touched me on the raw, and I have been picking an assortment of brains to ensure that my seedlings are given every opportunity to develop to gigantic proportions. I'm told they like beer, and Guinness in particular!'

The Village Match: 'A cricket match took place on Saturday, June 24, at the Recreation Ground between an eleven captained by the Vicar and a motley assembly press-ganged from the Sonning Working Men's Club. The Vicar's team batted first and reached a formidable score of 156 for 5 when there was a short interval for beer. The innings closed at 229. After the tea interval the Club made a good opening stand, but were in dire straits at 70 for 6. The total was taken to a respectable 157.'

August 1972

Charvil Parish Council: The following items were reported from the July meeting of the council:

'The Clerk was instructed to pursue most rigorously the matter of car parking which was still being dealt with by the Rural Council. At the same time he was to pursue the matter of the derelict Walleys Cafe which had been referred to the R.D.C. Chief Public Health Inspector two months previously.

In view of the impending increase in population following the approval of the development off the Old Bath Road, it was agreed that the Council should write to the Clerk of the County Council requesting an increase in the number of Councillors on the Parish Council.'

Sonning Women's Institute: 'At our July meeting the salad competition did not attract many entries, but those that were entered looked very inviting. Mrs. Wauchope won first prize.'

September 1972

Vicar's Notes: 'The "Boat" Sunday Family Service has been fixed for Sunday, September 17. We look forward to welcoming members of the two Yacht Clubs who have their "base" within the Parish. We hope also to invite those whose boats are moored in "our" stretch of the river.'

Charvil Parish Council: The council reported on the subject of the number of parish councillors that Charvil has a right to appoint: 'The Berkshire County Council has informed the Council that the Parish is entitled to nine Parish Councillors, an increase of two.'

Royal British Legion–Men's Section: 'On July 10, a number of members attended the Annual Inspection and Passing-Out Parade of the Reading Blue Coat School Combined Cadet forces, held in the school grounds.'

Pigwig's Progeny: The following reader's letter appeared in this issue:
'*Three baby guinea-pigs, looking for a home,*
if they stay here much longer they'll just start to roam.
If you would like a guinea-pig – one, two or three,
please lift the phone and ring me up, or come to Appletree.
Carol Forres, Appletree Cottage.'

October 1972

Sonning Parish Council: The monthly meeting of the council was held on September 8 and the following matters were reported in this issue:
'The cork life-belt situated at the Wharf, an important piece of equipment, which was removed presumably by vandals, has now been replaced by the Rural District Council.
As to the oak gate at the entrance to the Wharf, for one reason or another the County Council is now finding it difficult to erect it as promised and so the Parish Council will now carry out the work with financial assistance from the District Surveyor.'

Pearson Hall: 'Mr Sidney Paddick has offered to provide the Hall with cloakroom facilities which would do much to improve the amenities. In view of this generous offer, the need to launch an appeal and pursue the registration of the Hall as a charity, which might make it eligible for a grant-in-aid, was felt to be unnecessary at this time.'

November 1972

Sonning Parish Council: The October meeting of the council reported upon the future proposed use of Sonning Mill:

'It is now proposed to convert the Mill into flats without affecting the character or appearance of the structure and also to build appropriately designed maisonettes on the island overlooking the mill stream.

These proposals were supported by the Parish Council and it was noted that it is the intention to build a new drainage scheme in Sonning Eye which will readily fit in with them.'

The Produce Show: 'The decrease in the number of exhibits at this year's Show was mainly caused by the cold spring and early summer and late holidays. There was no decrease in the enthusiasm of the exhibitors or in the number of visitors. The auction of produce went very well and tomatoes fetched ridiculously inflated prices. The small boy who bought the Vicar's onions was greatly upset to find that they were made of plastic, but was happier after selling them back to the original owner at a profit!'

December 1972

Vicar's Notes: 'There are many good friends who contribute time and money toward the Christmas decoration of our Church – the Christmas Tree, the Flowers, the Advent Wreath, the Candles and the Floodlights all combine to make St Andrew's a very beautiful setting for our Christmas Festival. We owe them our sincere thanks.'

Sonning Working Men's Club: 'The membership list still remains fully subscribed, and those who wish to join are required to await their turn. Thankfully both young and old are attracted to the Club, and each night sees a fair group of under 20's playing snooker and darts. These young members are essential to the Club, they give a balance to the membership, which rejuvenates the old 'uns and helps to bridge the generation gap.'

Help the Aged: 'Members of the Young Wives and Mothers' Union manned the Centre held at Pearson Hall on November 8, and collected good clothes, blankets, and several other items of bedding which filled as many as 23 sacks.'

January 1973

Sonning Bells: 'As our dear familiar church bells ring in the New Year of 1973, and the comforting sound echoes across the river and village, let us spare a thought for the indefatigable group of Ringers who, week by week, month by month, come wind and rain, give of their time and skill in this important part of church life. Our grateful thank you to all of them!'

1ˢᵗ Sonning Brownie Pack: 'Our Christmas venture was to make table decorations and Mrs. Feak kindly came along to show the Brownies how it should be done. The results were really quite attractive and imaginative. The finished table centres were then used at the Darby and Joan Christmas party and we hope they all liked them.'

[*January 1: Britain, Ireland and Denmark join the European Economic Community.*]

February 1973

[*The magazine had now grown rapidly in page extent, consisting of the cover page, ten pages of editorial, eleven pages of advertisements and the eight page "Home Words" inset. see: page 204.*]

Vicar's Notes: 'Signs of Spring! Snowdrops are out in the Churchyard, and the evenings are getting noticeably lighter – spring is just around the corner! And talking of "nature" the snipe is "drumming" in the water meadows between Sonning and Shiplake.'

Keep Fit in Charvil: 'Our first class on January 15, proved to be a great success, and twenty three people arrived at St Patrick's Hall and bared their feet ready for action. If we can attract as many people regularly, we will undoubtedly be able to continue. The fee is 20p per evening, squash and biscuits provided.'

March 1973

An Appreciation: The vicar contributed the following item in this issue: 'It is high time that we paid tribute to those Charvil "regulars" who Sunday after Sunday wait in all kinds of weather to catch the Church Coach and join in one or more of our Sunday Services.'

HOME WORDS

102 YEARS in the service of the Church   **JANUARY 1973**

The BISHOP of
STOCKPORT
asks...

WHAT ON EARTH IS THE M.U. UP TO?

NEW DIMENSIONS, a plan for the future of the Mothers' Union, suggests the founding of "Christian Family Groups" and sets out these alternatives for membership of the M.U.:

> A—that existing rules should remain unchanged, saving that women whose marriages have been legally terminated by divorce and who have not subsequently remarried shall be eligible;
>
> B—that ordinary membership shall be open to any baptised woman . . . but that officers down to branch level shall be required to be communicant members of the Church of England or of a Church in communion therewith.

MANY readers who are members of the Mothers' Union must be bewildered at all the debate and discussion which has been going on since the publication of *New Dimensions.*

Does it mean that the Mothers' Union is to be so changed that only the name will remain?

Will it be able to make up its mind what it is for and retain a vital witness in the life of the Church?

It would be a sad day if the Mothers' Union lost its identity and ceased its supporting role in the parishes.

The Commission responsible for *New Dimensions* has had to take a world view of the work and influence of the Mothers' Union and recognises that not every country can accept the same set of recommendations.

The two questions of membership and activity will be occupying the attention of members and their representatives and it would be improper for me to give advice on internal matters which do not affect the Church at large.

Nevertheless, where decisions of policy are likely to cause embarrassment to existing work or to enter a field already well served it is important to speak frankly.

The Commission has noted other forms of work among women in other parts of the Anglican Communion, but has been quite blind to the lively and important ☞ *to P. 8*

VITAL WITNESS NOW LOOKS TO BE IN DANGER

The Rt. Rev.
GORDON STRUTT, B.D.

Drought and heat consume the snow waters: so doth the grave those which have sinned. —Job 24.19

The Asians and US

IS the influx of Ugandan Asian refugees a racial matter?

It has been said that if they were so many thousand Europeans, there would be no outcry.

Wouldn't there? If these people, whatever their race, are to be found jobs and houses here it means someone else has to wait longer—homeless and unemployed. You cannot call him a racialist for feeling resentful.

The root fault is that there are too many people in this country. The whole world is overcrowded, and the solution will only be found when nations are prepared to work together to stabilise and redistribute population.

This may seem unlikely ever to come, but it is made even more unlikely while people think only of keeping their own country as they want it, and insisting that anyone who doesn't fit in is somebody else's responsibility.

That is the attitude of President Amin. It is also, I fear, the attitude of many people here.

Our ancestors were proud of the privilege of counting vast areas of Africa as part of the British Empire. We are now realising that privilege also involves responsibility.

But they may help us always to remember that the problem we face today is not a problem of law, or of race, or of money, but of people: human beings.

—*The Rev. BERVAL KELLY, Rector of St Barnabas, Openshaw, in his parish magazine.*

1

Home Words, an eight page inset included with each issue of the parish magazine.

The Royal British Legion Annual Dinner: 'On Friday, February 2, there was gathered at the White Hart Hotel a distinguished company of some 136 villagers, the occasion was the Annual Dinner. The Dinner was followed by enjoyable entertainment from Gloria Gay who, with piano accompaniment, sang ballads of Old Vienna, this led eventually to community singing in more or less close harmony.'

Personal Column: 'Want to sell or buy something? – looking for a helping hand in the garden or in the house? Here's your chance to make your needs known in our new personal column. There is a fixed charge of 25p for each advertisement, maximum twenty-five words. Sorry, no trade advertisements.'

April 1973

Sonning Parish Council: The following item was included in the parish council's monthly report:
'We are now waiting to hear what the District Valuer has to say about the value of the 1.3 acres which the Rural District Council wishes to buy from the Parish in order to extend the Little Glebe Group of houses.'

Nurse Papps: 'We wish Nurse Papps much happiness in her retirement, and we are thankful that she will be living on in her present home in Little Glebe. She is going to be missed very much because she has been such a good district nurse and such a true friend.'

May 1973

Sonning Parish Council: At this meeting held on April 13, it was confirmed that the Secretary of State for the Environment had over-ruled the inspector's recommendation and decided to allow residential development on Holme Park Farm.

Football: 'Mr. Prismall's team (it all started in the Youth Club) have emerged top of their league and now go up to Division 1. They also did well in the Cup and narrowly missed appearing in the final.'

The Choir: 'Mr. Lusty and the Choir are to be congratulated on the rendering of Stainer's Crucifixion in our Church on Good Friday.'

June 1973

Vicar's Notes: 'Our annual "Social" on June 24, will be held on the Vicarage Lawn, weather permitting, immediately after the Family Service. The P.C.C. hope that congregations representing the three Sunday Services will meet together, first for worship and then for "fellowship" – the idea being to get to know new faces, and to this end we move around at the blast of a trumpet! It sounds awful but in practise it does work! And there will be a glass of sherry!'

Sonning Glebe Women's Institute: 'May 4, drama hit Sonning – no, not a major catastrophe, but a drama evening of three plays, one by our own institute and two visiting plays from Maiden Erlegh W. I. and Woodley Towns-women's Guild. We were able to try out the new lighting, new staging and new curtains in the Pearson Hall, all of which are clearly a great asset.'

July 1973

Vicar's Notes: 'We have been invited to join the Quaker's in worship at the Friends Meeting House, Church Street, Reading at 6.30pm on Sunday, July 8. Our coach will leave St Patrick's punctually at 6pm stopping at the usual collection points.'

The "Ascension" Balloon: On a number of earlier occasions an aerial balloon, with a message attached, had been released from Sonning in the hope that on landing in some faraway place someone would make contact with the "sender" in Sonning. Another balloon ascent was mentioned in this issue with the following comment: 'Last recorded by London Radar 25,000 feet up above Daventry and still going strong – every delivery of the post is scanned eagerly for news of its ultimate destination!'

Sonning Parish Council: At the Annual General Meeting on June 8, the main business of the parish council was concerned with the sale of the 1.3 acres of land for use in extending Little Glebe:
'The District Valuer has recommended a sale price of £63,500. Although there was general agreement to sell the land it was agreed not to complete the sale until it was decided how the proceeds should be used to benefit the parish.'

August 1973

Vicar's Notes: 'We have invited the Quakers from the Friends Meeting House in Reading to join in our worship in St Andrew's Church on Sunday, August 19 – either at the Family Service or Evensong. We were glad of the opportunity to share in their worship last month and much appreciated their warm welcome.'

Charvil Parish Council: 'Whilst at the Council's monthly meeting [July] on Monday, current amenity problems were fully discussed, there was a strong emphasis on Charvil's future need, particularly bearing in mind the forthcoming increase in population due to the new housing development off the Old Bath Road. The Council will press that the District Council's budget for the forthcoming year should provide adequate financial assistance with the purchase of land for the planned recreational purposes.'

September 1973

Vicar's Notes: 'We have got some fine Elm trees in Sonning, and all of them are threatened by this wretched Dutch Elm Disease. The Parish Council, after consultation with the County Council experts, called for volunteers to give injection treatment to some fifty of our best Elms, and the response has been magnificent. Skilled operators with special equipment assisted by these willing helpers, have already treated many Sonning trees, and I, for one, feel terribly grateful for this effort to save a glorious part of our national heritage. Elm trees are so typical of the English scene.'

Charvil Summer Fair: 'What a success! The weather was perfect and the band marched through the village playing, the crowds came, and this year we managed to raise over £100 for "our" girls at the Andrew Duncan House.'

October 1973

Sonning Parish Council: The following item was included in the parish council's report from the meeting held on September 14:

'It is nice to see that the work of constructing the long-awaited foot-path on the western side of Sonning Lane has now started.'

Sonning Produce Show: 'An excellent attendance, much enthusiasm and good humour at the show this year delighted all those who had a hand in organising it. There were over five hundred entries – more than last year – covering a wide variety of classes, all of which were of a very high standard.'

1ˢᵗ Sonning Brownies: 'Our outing to Child Beale, Lower Basildon was very pleasant despite a few showers. With no trains to worry about even the Guiders were able to relax a little and admire the peacocks etc along with the Pack.'

November 1973
Vicar's Notes: 'You will probably have heard that my wife and I leave Sonning on February 8. We hate the idea of leaving you all and it has been a very difficult decision. Anyway we will have Christmas and the start of the New Year together.'

Sonning Parish Council: The council's report of their meeting held on October 5, included the following item:
'It was unanimously agreed to accept the Parish Council's recommendation to sell the allotment land to the Rural District Council, in order to extend Little Glebe, after all the queries which had been raised at the previous Parish Meeting had been explained.'

December 1973
Lighting: 'We hope to make good use of candles for the Christmas Services, our floodlighting has been prohibited. Christmas Tree lights will function as usual providing power cuts, during the present period of disputes, don't interfere!'

The Pearson Hall: 'The recently completed Men's Cloakroom is a gift to the Village from Sidney Paddick. It fits in remarkably well with the existing building and serves a most useful purpose!'

[*"Who rules the country?"* – *The government were now locked into a highly damaging nationwide industrial dispute with the trades unions. Industry and commerce were restricted to the use of electricity for only three days per week and a crisis budget was announced by the Chancellor of the Exchequer on December 17.*]

January 1974

'*Our Vicar's Retirement:* Robert (Robin) Brutton's announcement of his retirement was responded to with a warm and appreciative item in this issue: 'We are all very sorry that the Vicar's retirement will take place in early February. We would all wish to express our sincere thanks to him for his Ministry during the past eight years. Robin is blessed with a loving and generous personality and is held with love and affection by everyone.'

Sonning Branch Conservative Association: 'One hundred and twenty guests attended an enjoyable annual dinner dance at the White Hart Hotel on December 7, nearly £300 was raised for party funds. The raffle prizes were fabulous and there was dancing to "Sound of Music" an excellent band – a wonderful meal, controlled by "mine host", Michael Garner.'

February 1974

Vicar's Notes – A Farewell Message: An extensive message from Robin Brutton expressed his appreciation for the support and affection shown to him and his family during his Sonning ministry:
'There is so much to thank you for, and whatever I write will be hopelessly inadequate. What luck it was for me that in 1965 I was invited to come to Sonning – known to me and my wife as a beautiful river-side village with a frighteningly large Church and Vicarage! It has turned out to be a wonderful parish from every point of view; a beautiful home, interesting work, a lovely church and above all wonderful people.
Elizabeth joins me, together with Sue, Sarah and Tim in saying "thank you" for everything.'

Sonning Parish Council: The following item concerning the sale of land for the further development of Little Glebe, Sonning was reported from the council meeting held on October 5:
'The plan now is to exchange half an acre of our remaining allotment land for half an acre behind Pound Lane which will now be turned into allotments. This means we will still have around a third of an acre lying to the north of Little Glebe which will be serving no useful purpose. The RDC have agreed to purchase this also, for a sum to be assessed by the District Valuer as was the case with the 1.3 acres.'

March 1974

The Sonning lay reader Hugh Grainger had assumed responsibility for all pastoral matters during the interregnum period preceding the appointment of Sonning's new vicar. A "*Message for March*" from Hugh Grainger, which appeared in this March issue, included the following appreciation: 'How memorable and how inspiring were those services on our Vicar's final Sunday; an appropriate memory of a man greatly loved, an inspiration to us all to maintain the vitality of Sonning Church.'

Our Vicar's Presentation: The churchwardens contributed this item: 'The voluntary subscription towards the Vicar's presentation amounted to £375. 00. Robin always admired the small circular coloured window, which is in the gable end over the Chancel Archway. This has been repaired and restored and he would wish to adopt this window and defray the cost of the restoration out of the presentation fund.'

New Vicar of Sonning: It was announced by the churchwardens that: 'the Reverend George Stokes, the Vicarage, Amport, Andover, has accepted the appointment as Vicar of Sonning.'

[A *hung parliament resulted from the general election held on February 28. Labour eventually formed a minority government under Harold Wilson's premiership.*]

April 1974

A Message from Rev George Stokes: 'I want to say that I am looking forward eagerly to my ministry among you and that my wife and I are hoping to meet you all soon.'

The "Chain Gang": 'In the middle of Sonning there is a "Chain Gang". It meets every Monday morning and makes vestments for churches, and studies methods of embroidery with application to modern art. The Gang has just completed two wall hangings, a chasuble, burse, veil and stole, a tabernacle veil, an altar cloth and a credence cloth. The Gang are members of the Embroiderer's Guild. They are greatly indebted to many friends who contribute materials, cords and gifts of all kinds.'

May 1974

The Vicar's Notes: 'Greetings to you all! So far as the parish is concerned, I have much to learn and perhaps in due course much to say, but in the meantime (because I am not clairvoyant), I beg you to tell me please when there is sickness or other serious need among our parishioners. Your concern is now my concern, and this is one of the reasons why I am here. *Please!* This is important. The message of Jesus is always happy and joyful – "Be of good cheer! I have overcome the world".'

Captain Anthony Pollen: The "troubles" in Northern Ireland had continued and had involved the deployment of the British military in the conflict. Anthony Pollen who had lived at the Deanery for most of his life, was killed on active service in the Province on Easter Sunday, April 14.

[*A memorial wall plaque commemorating Captain Pollen, together with those who fell on active service during the two world wars, is displayed in St. Andrew's Church.*]

June 1974

The Vicar's Notes: 'What a truly memorable evening the institution was and, if I may say so, a considerable ordeal for a new Vicar. It will always live in my memory, and the tremendous reception afterwards. I would like to thank everyone who had anything to do with the arrangements. My wife and I have both been considerably encouraged by our reception all round and look forward to being able to sort out the many names, faces and voices, and so learn to know you all. But do be forbearing if we get you wrong!'

Charvil Parish Council: The Annual General Meeting was held on May 6 when the future development of Charvil Park Estate was discussed:
'The main business of the evening was the decision by Royco Homes to sell the larger part of the houses on the estate to the Greater London Council for local authority housing.
Details of a new planning application to include three storey flats was discussed, and it was resolved that the Council would oppose these new plans.'

[*Inflation in Britain had soared to 16%, a new post war record.*]

July 1974

Sonning Deanery Fellowship: 'The first meeting of the newly constituted Sonning Deanery Fellowship was held on June 11. The new Fellowship is now a sub-committee of the Deanery Synod, but otherwise will continue much the same functions as did the Lay Chapter. It studies topics referred to it by the Synod, or deals with other topics of a general interest which are not items of formal business of the Synod.'

1ˢᵗ Sonning Scout Group: 'Congratulations to Skipper Harris who, at the Loddon Vale A.G.M. on May 23, received a long service medal for fifteen years continuous service to Scouting.'

Sonning Women's Institute: 'We certainly had some excellent advice on speaking in public by Mrs. Mates, herself a very good speaker. Her talk was entitled "The Pleasures and Pitfalls of Public Speaking". The pitfalls could be numerous, but Mrs. Mates also helped us find many of the pleasures too.'

August 1974

Dutch Elm Disease: 'This disease is again with us and the Parish Council has decided to continue the injection treatment which certainly had considerable effect last year. Trees on public property will be treated by volunteers and the equipment, materials and advice are available to parishioners, who wish to treat trees on private land.'

Charvil Art Group: 'This group is just concluding its third year of existence and looking back over the year, it has been a progressive one. We have run several social events successfully, made visits to the Royal Academy and the Stanley Spencer paintings in the Burghclere Chapel, and continued with the outdoor weekend landscape painting in very pleasant local surroundings.'

September 1974

Horne's Corner: A regular article contributed by Sid Horne and having an amusing storyline were included in each issue. The topic for this month was the treating of elm trees for Dutch Elm Disease by two workmen who realised that they had been treating oak trees by mistake!

Table Tennis: 'The group open their new season on September 25, usual venue the Pearson Hall. Last year we saw the addition of several new members and newcomers would be welcome again this year. We are able to have use of three tables and this leaves little excuse for "standing around" Our main aim is to have an enjoyable and friendly evening.'

Sonning Football Club: 'Training sessions continue to be well attended and if enthusiasm is an indicator, the Club's prospects appear better than in the three previous seasons. Our new Team Manager, Bill Gill, is just getting to know the players (old and new), and is making his presence felt.'

October 1974

The Vicar's Notes: 'I think that our church has a wonderful dedication, St Andrewstide has always been connected with the Mission of the Church. He it was who brought Peter his brother to Jesus, engineering the first meeting between them, so St John tells us. This year we will keep our Patronal Festival on Sunday, December 1, the day after St Andrew's Day.

Harvest Thanksgiving is nearer, October 6. As a countryman by birth I have always loved this Festival. Gifts of flowers, fruit and vegetables for the decoration of the church will be welcomed.'

Sonning Produce Show: 'Considering the adverse weather conditions this summer which culminated in the exceptional gales and storms during August, the Produce Show was much better supported than one would have imagined possible. Exhibits were a bit down this year, but only by fifty and there were 455 entries, the standard was high, and the judges all said how much they enjoyed coming and were very complimentary.'

[*The second general election of 1974 was held on October 10, returning Harold Wilson's Labour party to government with a narrow majority of just three seats.*]

November 1974

St Patrick's Notes: 'The Church looked lovely for the Harvest Festival Service. Children of the Sunday School brought their gifts and with other gifts were taken to The Church of England Children's Home.'

Robert Palmer's Almshouse Charity: 'The Trustees of this Charity will shortly be filling a vacancy. Single men or women, or widows, or widowers, or married couples without children of good character, who have been living in Sonning, Woodley, Sandford, Eye, Dunsden or Sonning Common for at least two years, and who are wholly or in part unable to maintain themselves by their own exertions, may apply for the appointment.'

December 1974

Vicar's Notes: 'Christmas! What fun! All the exhausting preparations! Not so much fun! But at last the day comes. What excitement in the full stockings and gaily wrapped presents! What laughter and family parties! What a dinner! And the Church too! The Mystery of the Midnight Mass as we welcome the birth of Jesus! The Carol Service and Family services! Everything about Christmas is Merry!'

Sonning Glebe Women's Institute: 'The Fashion Show held in the Pearson Hall on October 18, was well received and enjoyed by all. The clothes were a selection from "Sirene" and the models were all members of the Institute. And a glamorous group they were too! Many thanks to them for stepping out along the catwalk!'

Charvil Parish Council: 'At a public meeting called by the Council at St Patrick's Church Hall on November 6, a Steering Committee was elected to investigate ways of raising money for the purpose of improving public amenities in Charvil. It was generally accepted that with a major new development taking place in the village, the present facilities would soon become inadequate and the Parish Council, with the voluntary organisations in the village, was looking ahead and planning for the future.'

January 1975

Vicar's Notes: 'Time flies! When we were young the time from one Christmas to the next Christmas, from birthday to birthday, seemed an eternity. As we get older the years shrink to almost nothing! It seems no time since I came to live in Sonning. Then the trees were bare. Now they are bare again. But in between they put on their summer green and their autumn gold. Jesus said that they who would become members of his kingdom must do so as a little child would. He illustrated this by telling of the men who were so pre-occupied with their various businesses that they could not attend the wedding party. The point in this context is that a child would surely have opted for the party without hesitation. And so it was with the Kingdom and the Messianic Banquet.'

An Apparition? George Stokes related the following account with a . . . 'After the service on December 1, my son Adrian was walking in the churchyard, when he saw the figure of a fine gentleman dressed in a blue frock-coat approaching him; Adrian was about to speak to the gentleman when he had almost reached him – then he vanished into thin air! Was this some visitor from the past?'

1ˢᵗ Sonning Brownies: 'Brownies have been practising for their Hostess and Entertainments Badge tests. We hope that the testers will enjoy their cakes and cups of tea and the little Nativity Play devised by two of our Brownies, Ruth Wild and Annette Cons.'

[*Serious concern for the British economy was confirmed with official sources now recording wage inflation at 28.5% and the price of coal to have risen by 30%.*]

February 1975
Church Fire: 'All of us share the sadness of a desecrated church, and the damage which has been done for no reason at all.' This comment by Rev. George Stokes referred to an apparent malicious fire that occurred in St Andrew's Church. Fortunately, a passer-by took instant action and averted a serious tragedy. The churchwardens also made comment about the fire: 'We express our sincere appreciation to the wonderful band of parishioners who offered their services to "clear up the mess" after the fire. The Police asked for the Church to be kept locked, and everything untouched, until they return on Monday morning to investigate the matter further.'

[*Edward Heath resigns as leader of the Conservative party and is replaced by forty-nine years old ex Education Secretary, Margaret Thatcher.*]

March 1975

Choir and Bellringers: 'The Annual Supper was held on February 10, at the Vicarage by kind permission of the Vicar and Mrs. Stokes. Forty-five persons attended and a first class meal was served. The usual toasts were proposed and honoured, followed by a musical evening.'

Sonning Flower Club: 'We enjoyed Mrs. Jill Smith's visit last month to give us information on Preserving and Drying, as well as creating some lovely arrangements using a few fresh flowers. We were all so busy taking notes. There's no knowing what'll come out of it all!'

[*The cost of electricity in Britain rises by a record 33 per cent.*]

April 1975

[*The magazine now consisted of sixteen pages including a cover. Seven pages were given over to editorial matter with eight pages comprising advertisements. The design for the front cover continued to feature the original line drawing of St Andrew's Church which appeared on the first issue in 1869.*
see: pages 218 and 220   Advertisement and text pages.]

The Royal British Legion: 'There is a very important event on Sunday, April 27, when new Standards are to be dedicated for both the men's and women's sections. A parade will be formed in the recreation ground and will march to St Andrew's for a 3.30pm service. It is requested that members will wear medals.'

Sonning Working Men's Club: 'The Annual General Meeting was held on March 7, some ninety or so attended including the sole trustee, the vicar. The meeting concluded with the chairman suggesting that the club was an integral part of the village, and hoped all those present would be there next year for the club's centenary.'

May 1975

Vicar's Notes: 'We had our annual meeting on April 3, in the Pearson Hall. I know that everyone will be sad that Mr. Sidney Paddick felt that the time had come for him not to seek re-election as Churchwarden. He has given so much time and money to this church and parish during almost fifty years, and by popular acclaim he was elected Churchwarden Emeritus. Mr. T. Cowley and Mr. M. Stansfield were then elected churchwardens for the year.'

The Mothers' Union: 'At the meeting last month Mrs. Cowley gave the notices and started a talk with us on "But what does the M.U. do?" It acted as a good basis for general discussion, and we downed a cup of tea with gratitude afterwards.'

Sonning Football Club: 'With their league programme finished, the record of our 1st XI makes dismal reading, it does appear that they will be relegated at the end of this season.
Our congratulations to club skipper Trevor Weston who has been selected as a reserve for the Reading & District League side in the final of the Inter-league tournament.'

June 1975
New Tennis Courts: 'Recently the Parish Council have had the two tennis courts used by Sonning Lawn Tennis Club re-surfaced. The work has been carried out by Gazes Hard Courts Ltd – the surface is known as Grey-Green courts. The new surface, in common with all bitumen bound surfaces, can soften during the early part of the court's life due to hot weather. If this happens, the surface will be damaged by continuing to use it. Therefore, play should be discontinued until the surface has cooled down and hardened again.'

The C. of E. Children's Society: 'The result of the recent house-to-house collection in this parish last month was £78. 05. The Society was very pleased and a letter of thanks to all helpers and donors has been posted in the Church porch.'

July 1975
Spring Cleaning the Church: 'The re-decoration has been done and a fine job has been made of it by Mr. Paddick's men. Since then the spring cleaning of the "ground floor" has been started. Our thanks are extended to all those who have worked hard to date, but we still need more volunteers please.'

1875 CENTENARY YEAR 1975

LANGSTONS
Telephone: **Reading 55134, 50721**

LANGSTON & SONS, LIMITED

OUTFITTING, TAILORING and FOOTWEAR FOR MEN AND BOYS

CAMPING SPECIALISTS

WEST STREET CORNER, READING

Riding Wear and Accessories — 6 YIELD HALL PLACE, READING

G. SLEEP LTD.

HANDICRAFT
MODEL MAKER'S SUPPLIES
AIRCRAFT KITS
MODEL RAILWAYS
DO-IT-YOURSELF SUPPLIES

WOODWORKS' SUPPLIES A SPECIALITY

22/24 KING'S ROAD, READING

Telephone 50074

Telephone : Reading 692110

A. E. HUGGINS
Family Butcher

SONNING - ON - THAMES

Purveyor of Best Quality

MEAT & POULTRY

at Lowest Possible Prices

Frozen Foods

All Orders receive Prompt and Personal Attention

GREEN SHIELD STAMPS GIVEN

FUNERAL DIRECTORS

TOMALIN & SON

48 New Street, Henley-on-Thames

Telephone Henley 3370

A. H. WHITE

(incorporating J. E. HOPE)

15 Boult Street, Reading

Telephone 54334, 53988 or Night 63921

Private Chapels: Henley and Reading

MEMORIALS — EMBALMING — CREMATIONS

Advertisement page: April 1975

Charvil Parish Council: 'At the Annual General Meeting of the Council, discussion took place concerning the housing development being carried out on the Charvil Park Estate: The Council are still very concerned about the continued abuse of the conditions of the planning consent by Royco Homes on this Estate recently purchased by the G.L.C, and the following resolution was sent to Wokingham District Council:

"This Council is most disturbed by the work being carried out by Royco Homes Ltd on the Charvil Park Estate as it is not in accord with the plans finally approved by the District Council's Plans Committee. The plans show some 50 three-bedroom houses but four-bedroom houses are being built".'

[*The referendum to decide whether Britain should continue membership of the European Common Market returned a "Yes" vote with two-thirds of votes cast in favour.*]

August 1975

Charvil Summer Fair: 'The Fair was held at St Patrick's on July 12 and there was a good attendance to this annual event. The Fair is in aid of Andrew Duncan House, Shiplake for disabled ladies, several were present at the Fair. The Woodley Girls' Brigade Band provided the music and paraded from the Wee Waif. We wish to thank the members of the Charvil Women's Club and all helpers for their efforts in raising £110 towards the fund.'

Dancing School: 'The School gave a demonstration of work at the local school fete on June 28. The dancing opened with a modern dance to the well known tune Fancy Pants, followed by the Babies class in a Fairy Dance. The autumn term commences September 18, with the Feet Fit class.'

September 1975

Charvil Art Group: 'The group closed its season with some landscape painting during the wonderful spell of weather in June and July. During the winter months the group met fortnightly in St Patrick's Hall when an interesting range of subjects was dealt with, such as flowers, still life, portraits etc., in oils watercolour, pastel and pencil.'

There are one or two **"Parish Practicalities"**:

1. A chéche exists at the Vicarage during the Morning Service for babies and tinies.
2. A Sunday School is held in the Vicarage during part of the Morning Service where young children go to have their own lesson.
3. The Thursday Club for Young People has got off to a good start. Varied things to do. 7.30-9.30 p.m. Ages 12-16. Any of our Church young people are most welcome. Average attendance has been about twenty.
4. The Tuesday Youth Club in the Pearson Hall has suffered the loss of Miss Anne Yeates through ill health and of Mr. David Old through removal from the district. Thanks to them both for what they have done. It is not intended that the club shall "fold up". But is there some one, or two or three or four, who would like to serve the youth of this parish and therefore the parish itself by undertaking to give this club fresh light and life?

Yours very sincerely,

George Stokes

From the Registers

Baptisms

Jan. 19   James Edward Hortop
Feb.   8   Nicholas Martin Steele
              Sarah Katheryn Walker
              Richard John Walker
Mar.   2   Gail Bernadette Atkins
              Kirsty Fiona Richards

Burials and Cremations

Jan. 30   John Doughty
Feb. 13   Harriet Roper
Feb. 26   Cecily McKenna

"In sure and certain hope of the Resurrection to Eternal Life".

St. Patrick's Notes

Holy Comunion will be celebrated on:
Thursday, 10th April at 10.15 a.m.
Thursday, 24th April at 10.15 a.m.
Evensong Sunday, 13th April at 6.30 p.m.

A Letter from the Bishop of Oxford

Dear Children,

Paul and Mary may be neighbours of yours or you may see them around. They look just like you and your school friends, but if you speak to them they won't answer, because they can't hear what you say. For the same reason they can't talk properly.

What is it like to be deaf? Try turning on your favourite T.V. programme—then switch off the sound. Or, try to understand somebody who is speaking under his breath whilst a very loud programme is going on.

Paul and Mary have to have special teachers and complicated electronic aids to help them begin to understand even simple things said to them. They may be just as clever as you are, perhaps even more clever, but being deaf they need very much more help than you do. Learning to speak when you can't hear is extremely difficult, and they also have to learn the very difficult art of lip reading. So, if you meet somebody who is deaf, speak clearly and slowly and don't hide your face. They will never be able to hear properly, but with the best teaching and the best equipment and very hard work, they may learn to speak and lip-read well in the end. But they need real friends to help them. and that's where you come in. If you meet any of them, and there are about 300 in our diocese. please try and help them all you can, and make friends with them. Your friendship is the best thing you can give them, and theirs may be wonderful for you.

A few of them have other handicaps as well as deafness. Some of them are blind. They need extra special help and very expensive gadgets if they are to have any chance in life at all. There are about twenty-four of these very handicapped children in a wing of the Borough Court Hospital near Reading. I would like you to help to buy some special teaching and play equipment for them. They need all the help we can give.

I shall look forward to seeing you at the Cathedral on Saturday, 31st May, to receive your gifts and introduce you, I hope, to one or two deaf children.

Your sincere friend and Bishop,

Kenneth Oxon

The Mothers' Union

At the quiet afternoon last month only 6 members managed to attend; this was rather sad.

At the usual meeting, Mrs. Cowley gave news of Mrs. Egglestone—she had had a letter telling her that our gift had gone towards buying roses for the new—and empty—garden!

Our speaker was Mrs. Benyon, who gave us a beautiful talk entitled "Does it matter what we believe?". A good discussion ensued because of this.

Don't forget there is a Bring-and-Buy this month when we meet on April 3rd at 2.30 p.m. in the Vicarage.

F.B.

Text page: April 1975

Sonning Glebe Women's Institute: 'Do you realised just how unobservant we all are? This was proved at our July meeting when Mr. Gold gave us an illustrated talk on "Old Houses of Reading" which was most interesting. He showed us a large number of slides of many impressive buildings in Reading, which we all regularly pass and just take for granted.'

October 1975

Vicar's Notes: 'Autumn has arrived this year after a wonderful summer. One of the consequences of the drought has been the shedding of a large limb by the beech tree between the vicarage and the church. It brought many other branches with it. We had watched the leaves turn from purple to green during the last few weeks, and the tree men say that there is very little sap in it. It reminds me of the fact that if we are to be alive and efficient as Christians we must be always taking in power from the source of our being – God; always returning to drink at the fountain of life – Jesus.'

Sonning Women's Institute: 'With the winter evenings in view what better subject could we have had at our meeting on September 9 than making wool rugs. Mrs. D. Malvern came to tell us about them and showed some beauties she had made and gave many useful tips on making them and buying wool etc.'

November 1975

Vicar's Notes: 'A tourist came into the church one day in August, I happened to be there and spoke to her. She said, "Is this a Scotch church, then?" I replied "No". "But, it's called St Andrew's and he's Scotch, isn't he?" she said and sailed out!
St Andrew was as Jewish as they come – a Galilean fisherman. We are privileged to have a church dedicated to St Andrew. We keep his day on November 30, the very first day of the Church's Year.'

Sonning Parish Council: An experimental one-way traffic system had been introduced for the full length of the High Street and a public meeting was convened on October 10 to discuss and recommend a permanent scheme that would help to reduce Sonning's serious traffic problem.

Forty-eight parishioners attended the meeting and it was shown that while the residents of the High Street and others living nearby were well pleased with the system, a few others were dissatisfied. A suggestion that the one-way system should stop at the Thrift Shop and thereafter revert to a two-way flow was considered. The feeling of the meeting was that the more complicated one-way/two-way system had much to commend it and, even though difficult to achieve, thought might well be given to trying it experimentally on the basis that virtually everyone would be satisfied.'

Festival of Sonning: 'One very important feature of the Festival in June next year will be the Flower Festival in the Church and this will undoubtedly be a great attraction. In order to keep the costs down to an absolute minimum, it has been suggested that flower lovers might like to contribute to the Festival by thinking now about growing flowers in their own gardens and greenhouses which they would present to the Festival Committee in June.'

December 1975

Vicar's Notes: 'When we wish you "A Merry Christmas" from our Church of St Andrew in Sonning, we are reminding you and ourselves that we are celebrating a really stupendous event in the world – God's interference in human affairs at a particular time and place. A new era in history was begun, and we count our time from that event.'

Cost of the Magazine: 'We regret to announce that, owing to the ever rising cost of producing this magazine, we have been forced to take the following action:
Price: As from January 1976 the cost of an individual magazine will be 10p. For those who have a copy regularly delivered to them the price will be 50p for six months and £1 for a year.
Inset: To further reduce costs it has been decided to discontinue inclusion of the "Inset". We are sorry if this is a disappointment.
[*The new "cover price" to be charged from the January 1976 issue represented one hundred per cent increase.*]

CHAPTER SEVEN

1976 - 1980

The extent and appearance of the magazine had been unaltered in recent years and the printing continued to be undertaken by the Woodley printer J. Heppell.   A change in the editorship of the magazine had taken place with Mrs. Drake joining Mrs. Perkins to form the new editorial partnership.

A change in the Sonning church 'team' occurred in 1977 when the organist and choirmaster Harold Lusty retired and the role was taken up by David Duvall, the appointment proved to be most successful and remained so for many years.

Those who lived at anytime during history would no doubt have considered that they were living in challenging times, it was clear that this period was no exception.   At home the economy was causing extreme concern with raging inflation and constant national trades union disputes.   Northern Irish extremists were continuing to cause devastating outrages resulting in many deaths, not only in Northern Ireland but also on the mainland of Britain.   In the midst of all these troubles a general election was called; for the first time in the history of British politics a woman was elected as prime minister, would she, Margaret Thatcher, be the inspirational leader Britain so badly needed?

January 1976

Vicar's Notes: 'A New Year's resolution would be to examine ourselves to see if our standards are the right ones; is our spirituality equal to our temptations? How are our ways of living agreeable to Christian profession?

New Year Resolutions are good – if we keep them. Whether we do this, or don't do that, is important – if we keep it up. But I believe our best resolution would be to be on the side of God's Light – the Light of Christ – and to fight against everything that makes for darkness. Best wishes for 1976.'

Wanted –Voices!: 'Many of you will have heard by now of the proposed Son-et-Lumière which is to take place in St Andrew's Church as part of the Festival of Sonning next June. For this we need a number of voices – men, women and some children. This is an appeal for anyone who would like to take part in this venture, to come forward and offer their services.'

Sonning C. of E. Primary School P.T.A.: 'The Christmas Fayre held on November 22, raised £195 thanks to the generosity of so many people in the village. On February 28, there will be an auction in the Pearson Hall. Gifts of surplus household and sports equipment urgently needed please.'

February 1976

Charvil Youth Club: 'The Dads v Boys football match resulted in a draw, 3 all. Seems ages ago now, and after such a long Christmas break, no doubt some of the Dads will have forgotten the score – just thought I'd mention it in passing!

We really do hope to hold a Disco during the winter months, subject to the Hall complying with the fire regulations.'

Sonning Cricket Club: 'The Club has a strong membership and is highly regarded in the area, including a fine fixture list with several formidable sides. We run a second team and a colts eleven, and besides playing ordinary fixtures on Saturdays and Sundays we have mid-week games and we enter cup and league competitions.'

March 1976

Vicar's Notes: 'I am writing this at a time when very many of you are down with "flu". Our wish to you all is "get well quickly".

Arthur Smith keeps telling me that he has known eight vicars of Sonning, he has pneumonia but is getting better. There are many good people around who give great help when sickness strikes, and the community is richer for their presence. But you don't need me to tell you that.'

[*The Sonning vicars referred to by Arthur Smith would have been: The Reverends Pott, Barter, Holmes, Crawfurd, Wick-Legg, Groves, Brutton and Stokes.*]

Church Flower Arrangers: 'All Church flower arrangers are warmly invited to attend the Sonning Floral Arrangement Society Meeting in the Pearson Hall on March 11, when Mrs. Moody will demonstrate the making of swags etc., which are to be used for the Festival of Sonning in June.'

April 1976

Vicar's Notes: 'I imagine that we have all spent some time looking through the introductory pages of "The Book of Common Prayer", and been bewildered by such things as "A Table to find Easter Day". The date of Easter is determined by the Lunar Calendar in the same way as the Jewish people calculate Passover. The Jews kept their yearly cycle by the moon, and not the sun. So there were thirteen months to their year. We fix Easter by the moon also. Easter is the first Sunday after calendar full moon on or after March 21; Easter Day therefore can be on any date from March 22 to April 25 - a bit complicated.'

Care of the Churchyard: 'The major tasks such as grass cutting and leaf collection are carried out by hired help, but assistance is required from a small group of willing helpers. More volunteers are required please, so that if your own garden is rather small, and you are looking for a few extra weeds to pull please give your name to the Vicar. You are welcome to select your own "plot" to tend and work at your own convenience.

Volunteers usually have just one problem - constant interruption from visitors admiring our beautiful church and churchyard.'

May 1976

Vicar's Notes: 'The secularisation of our lives goes on apace in a materialistic society in which money and its pursuit seems to be the only way of measuring good. Here is a little medieval wisdom from St Bonaventure (I think):

Let a man play till twenty, labour till forty and rest till the end of his days.
Let him drink when thirsty, eat when hungry, and rest when tired.
Let him have one wife and a clear conscience.
Let him be meditative in the morning, industrious at noon, social in the evening.
Let his disposition be affectionate, his genius lively and his friends numerous.
Let him keep his rule of his calling, law of his country, commands of his God.
Thereby his body will be healthy, his mind easy and his soul pure, his end bliss and his God will love him.'

Royal National Lifeboat Institution – Sonning Branch: 'We are extremely grateful to everyone who contributed so generously to the collection in our Sonning Parish which raised £80. Everywhere was heard said "It's a very good cause".'

[*James Callaghan is appointed prime minister following Harold Wilson's resignation.*]

June 1976

Sonning Festival – Antiques and Victoriana Stall: 'We aim to sell "Your Items" for you, and to take 15% commission for the Festival Funds. Please let us have details of items you wish to sell – with prices, as soon as possible. If you are in any doubt as to price or whether an article is suitable please contact us.'

Sonning Glebe Women's Institute: 'Our recent Jumble Sale was extremely successful with "buyers" literally banging on the door. Something of the "Sales" fever seemed to pervade the premises and gallant sales ladies strove to deal with the onslaught. However, the £30 profit made the bargaining etc., well worthwhile.'

The Mothers' Union: 'The Centenary Service held last month in Reading was a most uplifting experience, and all of the Sonning members who were present readily agreed that we felt thoroughly proud to be part of such an organisation.'

July 1976

1ˢᵗ Sonning Scout Group: 'May was a very busy and successful month for us. Six Scouts received instruction at the Fire Station. Fourteen were taught Water Safety - rescue by non-swimmers from the bank. Spring Bank Holiday Camp was very much a training camp and many tests were passed during the three days.'

Darby and Joan Club: 'The meeting on May 25, was a bit depleted. However, it was with pleasure that we welcomed our own Nurse Papps who spoke to us about so many of the interesting experiences in her busy life.'

1ˢᵗ Sonning Brownies: 'After the half-term break the Sonning Brownies concentrated on work for various Interest Badges. Badges gained this month were for Needlework and Road - well done those Brownies!'

August 1976

Vicar's Notes: 'I have only one thing to write about this month, and that is the Festival of Sonning. As I sit and think back over it all, the more I can see how splendid everything was. The exhibitions - of course! I went around marvelling at the range and quality of what was displayed. The Flower Festival - some of the arrangements brought astonished gasps from those who saw them. The Reading Phoenix Choir and Horatia Raphael's recital - splendid. The Saturday night barbecued pork and trimmings were pretty easy to negotiate too - in a different vein! And what can I say about the Victorian Fayre in the High Street? everything about it was just fantastic. I saw the "Son et Lumière" each night. Altogether a wonderful week which brought large numbers of people into the village to enjoy it and all that was going on.'

Annual Cricket Match: 'For the fifth year the Vicar' XI and the Sonning Working Men's Club XI met at the Recreation Ground to demonstrate some of the lesser known aspects of what could be vaguely described as cricket. Every year it is intriguing to witness the selectors' choice of candidates, it would seem there is indiscriminate poaching as well as scraping the bottom of the barrel. The result was of course immaterial but this year the Club won by 58 runs.'

September 1976

Lay Reader: 'Mr. Hugh Grainger has been associated with this Parish for a long time at St Patrick's Sunday School and as a Reader on the Parish generally, also during the interregnum. His work is in Slough and he has decided that some years of commuting is enough. So sadly we must lose him when he moves to a new home nearer to his work.'

Dancing School: 'On the afternoon of July 19, the school, as an end of term activity, gave a demonstration of their class work for the benefit of parents and friends, with all the pupils taking part. Members of the Ladies Keep Fit Class also joined in and showed us how much they enjoyed their activity with some lively movements.'

Charvil Art Group: 'Painters could not ask for more accommodating weather for landscape painting than we have had during this summer. Members of the group have again had a successful year exhibiting. Several members were among the winners of various classes at the Tilehurst Eisteddfod, one of whom, was awarded the "Edith Barkus" cup for the best painting in the show.'

October 1976

Vicar's Notes: 'The Harvest Thanksgiving Services will be on October 3. Someone said the other day – "you won't be having Harvest Festival this year will you? Because of the drought I mean". Well, some parts of this country have suffered terribly, some people's gardens have not produced what they usually do. But we still have much to be thankful for. I read a review of the national grain harvest for the year and it seems that yields are somewhat better than last year's. Garden produce for the Church may be short – but packaged and tinned goods are equally welcome, even more welcome to those who receive the gifts.'

Royal British Legion–Men's Section: 'On Sunday, September 5, in fine weather, 36 members travelled by coach to the Legion's Convalescent Home at Weston-super-Mare. One double bedroom is dedicated to the memory of Major-General and Mrs. Price Davies and the Sonning branch of the Legion undertakes the maintenance and furnishing of the room.'

November 1976

Queen's Silver Jubilee: Preparations were being made to celebrate the jubilee next year and a meeting was arranged for Friday, November 12 to consider what form the celebrations might take. Prior to the meeting photographs of the Sonning Festival taken by Mr. Glasscock and Mr. van Went were to be exhibited and copies of the photographs would be made available for purchase.

Sonning Parish Council: 'At the last monthly meeting of the Council it was decided that a new landing stage at the wharf is needed as a village amenity and the work will be put in hand very soon.'

December 1976

Vicar's Notes: 'I believe that Christmas is a challenge. We live in a time when the Festival of the birth of Jesus is completely commercialised. Very well – I suppose that we have to live with it. We cannot divide Christian doctrine.
Jesus Lives! That is the message of Easter. It is also the message of Christmas. That is what separates Christians from the frenetic world that is searching for it knows not what.'

Sonning Volunteer Fire Brigade Trust: 'The Trust was established by the Charity Commission in 1952 to administer funds which had been received through renting the Fire Station to Reading Fire Brigade. For the guidance of the Trustees, the conditions governing the allocation of these funds are:
"The Trustees shall apply the yearly income of the Charity and if they think fit the capital endowment thereof for any public purposes for the benefit of inhabitants of the Parish of Sonning and not provided out of rates or other public funds"
In cases of doubt, the advice of the Commissioners is sought.'

1st Sonning Brownies: 'At the Hallowe'en Party, six Brownies completed and passed their Entertainment Badges and seven Brownies passed their Hostess Badges. Games at the party included a very colourful and sometimes horrific collection of Hallowe'en masks the "Green Witch" was voted as the best .'

January 1977

Harold Lusty: 'Mr. Lusty has been organist and Choir Master at St Andrew's Sonning for the past 25 years. During this time he has given devoted service to three vicars. He has also composed several items of sacred music and his Wedding March is very popular.

At Matins on Sunday, December 5, a presentation was made to Mr. Lusty on his retirement at the Chancel Step by the Vicar supported by the Wardens.'

Dutch Elm Disease: 'Dutch elm disease has sadly taken its toll in the churchyard, necessitating the felling of further trees. All brushwood has been burnt but there is a considerable quantity of timber suitable for sawing into logs for sale to help church funds.'

February 1977

In Aid of Church Funds: Details of a Victorian Evening to be held in the Pearson Hall on February 5, were given in this issue. The event, organised by Thomas Feak, headmaster of Sonning school, was to feature "Barber Shop" singing, solos, acts and melodramas. In addition to the entertainment, bread, cheese and pickles were to be available all for an inclusive cost of 75p.

St Patrick's Sunday School: 'Mrs. Eileen Brown announced to the Sunday School children that she had decided that the time had arrived when she should hand over the running of the Sunday School to someone else. Mrs. Brown has given seventeen years devoted service to St Patrick's. Apart from the Sunday School she tends the Sanctuary with loving care.'

March 1977

Royal National Lifeboat Institution: 'Our new branch is holding its first Coffee Morning and sale of nearly new clothes, mainly supplied by the Thrift Shop, on March 9, in the Pearson Hall. There will also be a cake stall and a stall selling useful and attractive items made by the RNLI.'

Victorian Evening: 'The event raised at least £110 for church funds. Our thanks to Mr. Feak, and all those who made the evening successful.'

Darby and Joan Club: 'Two very good Sonning friends entertained us on January 24 and February 7. At the first it was our pleasure to welcome Miss Libby Stokes who sang and played to us and encouraged all to join in. At the next meeting we had a second treat with Mr. Malcolm Stansfield who showed some lovely slides of places and friends very dear to him.'

April 1977

Vicar's Notes: 'About the Magazine, I feel that I must say as gently as I can that it is the Church Magazine of the Parish of St Andrew, Sonning (Sonning, Charvil and Sonning Eye) and that we invite all of the contributors that make it a real parish symposium. But it is at a cost. I see that in the accounts for 1976 the loss on the Magazine is £430 and that in spite of increasing the price by 100%. This means that the worshippers in St Andrew's have subsidised it by 7p a copy, and in the last five years by £1,816 – a lot of money.'

Sonning Lawn Tennis Club: 'The A.G.M. of the Club was held in the Pearson Hall on March 8. The Chairman, Mr. Peter Holland, reported that the Club had had a good season in 1976 with a membership of eighty-one. Play had been possible on the new court surfaces throughout the summer in spite of the hot weather and play had continued this winter. He was pleased that the course of fourteen coaching sessions on Saturday mornings had been attended by sixteen juniors.'

May 1977

Vicar's Notes: 'The celebration of the Queen's Silver Jubilee in the churches of the land will be on June 5. There has been some heart-searching about the celebrations, not because of the cost at a time of national bankruptcy, although voices have been raised on this account, but because June is not the anniversary of the Queen's Accession – which was February 1952. However, being a Queen's man, I propose to go along with the special service for June 5. The Archbishop of Canterbury and his associates have conferred with the Cardinal Archbishop of Westminster, and others, who have also authorised the service.'

Jesus of Nazareth: 'It is estimated that around twenty-eight million viewers watched I.T.V's much publicised film "Jesus of Nazareth" on Palm Sunday and Easter Sunday. The film has been widely reviewed by leading critics both favourably and unfavourably, stimulating strong reaction so that one is tempted to write a criticism of the critics!'

Sonning Flower Club: 'What a change we had last month, when we watched Mrs. Townson messing around with Polyfilla and water and bits of sheeting, which were then added to wire-netting and cotton wool; the result was superb cloth sculptures!' – we all appreciated that her undoubted skill and artistry made most of it possible.'

June 1977

Vicar's Notes: 'I have appointed Mr. David Duvall as Organist and Choirmaster.   He is young and enthusiastic and we very much appreciate his expressed wish to give his services to the Church. In this connection, we all owe a considerable debt of gratitude to Mr. Thomas Feak who for six months has freely put his considerable talents at our disposal, to the great benefit of choir and congregation.

I want to say a word about the Altar Cloths made for the Church by Mrs. J. Brown. Some time ago Mrs. Brown made an Altar Cloth for the High Altar. Now she has made a cloth for the Lady Chapel Altar from linen given by Mrs. Watson.   In addition to these she has made a number of cloths for the Credence Tables over the past two years. We are very grateful to her for her hard and loving work.'

The Queen's Silver Jubilee Celebrations: 'Final arrangements for Sonning's Jubilee Day are almost complete. Thanks to Nigel Broakes and Chris Rowbotham at least two shipping lines are without their Code Flags, and the High Street must be the best decorated village street in all of England. Mugs with the Queen's Head and inscribed "Sonning-on-Thames" are to be given to all Sonning School Children.'

New Editor: One of the two editors of this magazine, Mrs. Ann Forrest, had decided to live overseas for a period of time. Her role was taken over by Mrs. Shirley Drake who joined Mrs. Angela Perkins as joint editors.

July 1977

Vicar's Notes: 'What a splendid day Sonning's Jubilee Festivity was! The week began with the Silver Jubilee Service in St Andrew's where there was a large congregation and St Patrick's which was packed out. The whole nation became festive and co-operative in all kinds of projects.
Grand-daughters are wonderful – Our Grand-daughter is 100 years old in July! Formed out of the Parish of Earley, which is a daughter Church of Sonning, Earley St Bartholomew was inaugurated on July 11, 1877. So it is their centenary!'

Mothers' Union: 'Mrs. Hales from Crowthorne gave us a very thought provoking talk on "Time" last month. She said that with all our labour saving devices in this modern world we should, in theory, all have very much more time – when in fact, the pace of life is much faster and we begin to wonder whether we are any better off.'

August 1977

Vicar's Notes: 'The Confirmation on July 3, was a good and well attended service. There were well over three hundred people in church and two hundred and twenty Communicants. But I marvel that in the ordinary run of things the older churchpeople are so little aware of their responsibilities in encouraging the young people. What is a young communicant to think if he or she comes to our 8 o'clock service, or to the service at 11 o'clock on the first Sunday in the month, for that matter? Clearly we are lacking in a sense of Christian Community, and the words *duty* and *responsibility* in relation to worship are sadly not in fashion.'

Sonning Scouts: '1ˢᵗ Sonning Scouts Group held their A.G.M. on July 21, in their Headquarters. Reports given all emphasised the growth of the whole Scouts Group in the past year. We now have a total of 69 boys, with seven uniformed leaders and in addition several helpers. This is really marvellous news.'

Help the Aged: 'The annual collection of blankets, bedding and clothing was held at the Pearson Hall on July 13, when we filled sixteen bags of very good things. Grateful thanks to all donors and helpers.'

September 1977

Vicar's Notes: 'The Bishop of Reading is coming to St Patrick's, Charvil on Sunday, September 4. He is our own area Bishop and has not been to Charvil before. I hope that there will be a good turnout of Charvil people, and of course all parishioners are invited. The Service will be a Families' Communion, and I hope that it will be the first of a monthly series, but not on the first Sunday of the month. In future this service will be on the third Sunday in the month at 9.30am and will be, I hope, a Families Communion properly sung.'

Sonning Church Youth Club: 'This will start its autumn session on September 8, at the Vicarage. It caters for a twelve to sixteen years age group and is open to children who live in the village or who attend Church regularly. We would like to hear from anyone who feels that they can talk or entertain the young on any subject of interest, such as their own profession, holidays abroad, and interesting hobby, or whatever.'

October 1977

Vicar's Notes: The country Festivals were in older days a special feature of English Church life – Plough Sunday in January, Rogationtide in Spring, Lammas (Loaf-Mass) the bringing of the first fruits in early August, and Harvest Thanksgiving in October. All of these nearly died in the dead days of the 18th and 19th centuries. Some have been revived, I would like to see an old-fashion shining plough in Church on Plough Sunday – or perhaps a tractor and its accessories, or both? Rogationtide and Harvest we keep. But what about loaves made from the first ripe wheat in August? Simple Festivals that show that Religion and Life are not things apart.'

November 1977

Vicar's Notes: 'I need hardly remind you that everything costs more. This year the Diocese did not increase Parish Shares so our amount remained at something under £3,000. Next year the increase will be about 30%, at least £900 more, most of it for the Clergy Stipends Account. So if our social activities can raise a little money so much the better. I hope you will support these events.'

Sponsored Sing by the Choir: 'On November 12, the Choir will sing from 10am to 5pm – seven hours which will be divided into quarter-hour units. Sponsoring is by the unit – so 1p a unit will bring 28p, £1 a unit £28, and pro rate. The Choir is doing this to defray the cost of a new (second hand) stop in the organ. It is a generous gesture and should be well supported.'

December 1977
Rural Deanery: 'The division of the Rural Deanery of Sonning has now been accomplished. From January the Deanery of Sonning will comprise the parishes of Sonning, Wargrave, Ruscombe with Twyford, Hurst, Arborfield and the three Wokingham parishes. The new Rural Dean will be the Reverend Kenneth Martin, Rector of Wokingham, All Saints.'

1ˢᵗ Sonning Brownies: 'At the District Brownie Revels on November 12, we think that the football spectators must have wondered what had happened as girls came dressed in crowns, capes and even a really splendid jester! As you may have gathered the theme for the afternoon was "Royalty" and after playing various games we were very pleased that our Pack won the District Competition Shield for the best decorated regalia. Well done all of you!'

January 1978
Vicar's Notes: 'A New Year is often a time for making personal "good intentions". But we also approach it with hope that national and world problems may be solved and a better life emerge for everyone. We are carrying into 1978 a fine crop of problems. At home – industrial relationships, race relations, which are not only about colour but about devolution of government which many people fear will lead to the break-up of the United Kingdom, and of course Northern Ireland. As if this were not enough, there is the growing pollution of earth's land and water, and the warnings that earth's resources of some essential commodities are now running out. Perhaps the most terrible of our problems is the threat of atomic warfare under which we all live. If ever there was a time when the wisest statesmanship on a world-wide scale was needed it is now.'

[Mrs. Thatcher says Britons fear is being "swamped by people with a different culture". Edward Heath slams Thatcher's remarks for causing an "unnecessary national row".]

The Parish Magazine: George Stokes addressed the readership with the following item: 'I fear, that the magazine price is to go up again. We print 500 copies. If we sell all of these each month at 10p the income is £50 per month. The printers bill is around £100. Loss therefore, taking advertisements into account, about £500 a year. Another way of saying this is that you pay 10p for something that costs your Church 20p! By charging 15p we hope to halve our loss. Many parishes are giving up magazines altogether, or having duplicated papers. We do not want to do that, but one day we may have to consider the whole business very seriously.'

[On a number of occasions in the past a Sonning vicar had brought to the attention of readers the possibility that the magazine's future was in jeopardy.]

Choir News: The recently appointed organist and choirmaster, David Duvall, had taken responsibility for organising and conducting the choirs sponsored "Sing". He announced in this issue that £225 had been raised towards the £500 required for the organ improvements.

February 1978

Vicar's Notes: 'I have been saddened to hear that some people are giving up the magazine because of the increased price – this means wanting something for nothing; half the magazine for no price at all. What do we get in the commercial world for 15 pence? One parish I know – Tilehurst – have acquired a printing press for £2,000, and produce a top class magazine and can sell it for 15 pence. I am not suggesting that we should do something similar because we have not the expertise. But something will have to be done. The people who put money into the collection do not expect it to be used to subsidise an ailing magazine that should be paying for itself. What do we do?

Editorial Comment: In addition to the vicar's remarks concerning the magazine, one of the joint editors, Angela Perkins, added further comment: 'Surely three and a half pence per week – the cost of half a second-class stamp or half a small Kitkat – is not overmuch to pay for a monthly record of parish activities and prior information about Church and village fixtures. A parish magazine is an invaluable printed record of church and social affairs and the general outlook of the age. It would be tragic if, because of lack of support, Sonning's magazine had to be scrapped.'

Mr. H. C. Chapman: The death was reported of Harry Chapman at the age of eighty. He had made a considerable contribution to Sonning over many past years, including his eighteen years as a popular Sonning school-master, also, for several years his role as editor of the parish magazine.
[Harry Charles Chapman (1897-1978) is interred in the Sonning churchyard.
see: Record of Burials etc. Church of St Andrew 2012.]

March 1978
Vicar's Notes: 'It is very difficult to think about Easter during this very long cold spell although up to now we have missed the worst of the weather, and have much to be thankful for. However, we can look forward to Easter and its message of Resurrection and Life.'

The Mothers' Union: 'How nice it was to have a Corporate Communion Service last month, even though it was a bitterly cold day. However, when we adjourned to the Vicarage we were met with the sight and comfort of a lovely fire; and a most welcome cup of tea that put everything right.'

The Parish Magazine: Sid Horne a regular contributor to the magazine, commented in this issue that due to money constraints many of the local subscribers, particularly pensioners, were unwilling to pay the recent increase in the cost of the magazine. He suggested that a less expensive production might be considered such as "typed sheets".

1st Sonning Guides: 'Once again we have been selling sunny smiles for N.C.H. This year we have raised £16. 60 and four girls, Helen Taylor, Debbie Kemp, Hilary Nutbrown and Shona Campbell were presented to the Mayors of Reading, Newbury and Henley when they took the money to Reading Town Hall on February 8.'

April 1978

Sonning Parochial Church Council: The annual accounts were included in this issue for the year ended December 31, 1977. It was noted that although the last two years had resulted in a surplus, there would be actual and potential additional expenditure to be met in the ensuing year. Examples were listed included: an increase in the parish share of diocesan expenses, church roof repairs and renovations to the organ.

Choir News: David Duvall's regular column concerning choir and organ matters included the following "appeal": 'We still have vacancies in the Choir for men's voices; maybe I should fit some of the prettiest choirgirls out with badges saying "Men Desired!" Ideally, I should like at least one more tenor and two more basses.'

May 1978

The Parish Magazine: Robin Garstone, a business manager, contributed an article in this issue which addressed the concern for the future of the magazine. 'You will have seen from the accounts that the Parochial Church Council subsidised the magazine last year to the extent of £466 – which is something like six pence per copy. But, like everyone else, the P.C.C. is having to tighten its belt in view of steadily rising costs, and the subsidy can no longer continue. So it is obvious that we have got to do something to save the magazine.
The Vicar and Editors have asked me to assist them in arriving at a solution to the problem. A small working party is looking into the various ways that costs could be reduced or income increased, but what you can do is to let us know what you want from your magazine.'
[*No further mention was made of the working party's deliberations.*]

St Patrick's Church: 'The Jumble Sale held on April 1, raised over £82 for the Curtain Fund. With this contribution we are confident that we shall be in a position to provide new curtains for both hall and annexe.'

1st Sonning Scouts: 'It was the Sonning Group who organised the St George's Day Parade and Service for Loddon District, 1978. Nearly 600 Cub Scouts and Scouts plus the Girls' Brigade Band paraded through the village to the Church where an inspiring service was held.'

June 1978

Pearson Hall Improvements: A fund raising group was formed to raise a substantial amount of money to fund improvements to the hall. The eventual cost incurred was some £14,000 for the enlargement of the caretaker's cottage and the redecoration of the hall, both internally and externally. The fund raising campaign included a series of charity events commencing with a "Gigantic Jumble Sale" on June 14.

Glebe Players: 'A successful Drama evening was held on May 5. We were pleased to welcome Caversham Heights T.W.G. who performed a poignant play entitled "The Trial", and Earley W. I. who were our light relief with their hilarious comedy "Blush Pink". The Glebe Players concluded the evening with an unusual play about four female tramps entitled "Pearls of the Poor".'

Going for a Song: 'An unusual event took place in the Pearson Hall on May 17, when the populace were invited to bring along household treasures for valuation by John Beauchamp, F.S.V.A. There was an astonishing response and almost 200 items were on display. On the stage also were Dr. Hughes and Graham Ravenhall, who were invited to examine and place values and dates on selected items.'

July 1978

Vicar's Notes: 'Many people are mystified about the assessment of Parish Shares. Briefly, it is the amount due each year to the Diocese for the maintenance of the Church's work at Diocesan and National level. It does not include Missionary Societies and other voluntary bodies. Its Heads are Parochial Ministry, Diocesan Administration, General Synod, Education and Training, Social Responsibility, Church Buildings and Publications and Publicity.

There was no increase in Shares last year when we paid £2,898 as in 1976. This year all Parish Shares have been increased by one-third, so our share is £3,864. There are not many Parishes in the Diocese who pay more than we do here in Sonning and almost all of those have much larger populations.'

[A list of parishes in the diocese who paid more than Sonning for the year 1977 was included. The highest rated parish was Caversham at £8,903.]

Pearson Hall Improvements: An extensive item explained in some detail the funding requirement of the hall improvement scheme. Moreover, it was noted that George Stokes had arranged to have delivered to every house in the parish a letter from him explaining the need for the improvements and how each parishioner might assist with the appeal.

August 1978
Vicar's Notes: 'The curtains which we decided to place behind the screen in the Lady Chapel to go with the beautiful Altar Frontal are now in place. They match the gold of the Cross beautifully. Mrs. Shirley Drake has made them and given her work to the "Greater Glory of God". Our gratitude goes deep and we say thank you to her most sincerely.'

The Annual Cricket Match: 'The match between the Working Men's Club v Vicar's XI – referred to as the "Peasants" verses "The Holy Lot" was played at the Recreation Ground on June 17. After some indifferent batting, bowling, fielding and umpiring! the Vicar's XI scored 184 runs whilst the Working Men were bowled out for 142 runs. Several interruptions of play took place due to the somewhat frequent distribution of tankards of ale.'

September 1978
Pearson Hall Improvements: 'Money is still being made by events run by hard working people in the village. Mrs. Allaway and the Spinners and Weavers had a super coffee morning in July at the home of Mrs. Bodley Scott, which was a great success and added over £80 to the fund. In August several children descended for a "Paint-in" – a great time was had by all, painting feet, hands and even the lawn.'

1st Sonning Guides: 'Our district of Loddon has recently been transferred to the division of Bulmershe and for our first competition in this new division Sonning's Kingfisher Patrol represented the district. Under the leadership of Sarah Stansfield our girls won the Division Cup. We were very proud that Saturday afternoon and so pleased that Sonning managed to get their name printed on the Trophy the very first year we competed.'

October 1978

Vicar's Notes: 'The Produce Show, Fete, Barbecue and Dance were great village events. We had fine weather, record entries and a wonderful turn-out. As Chairman of the Organising Committee I was intending to mention the names of those responsible for the whole effort, but it would be a long list and I fancy that they will be happy to accept a general word of thanks. The result has been most satisfactory, whilst we haven't got a final figure yet, we think that there will be a profit of something like £170.'

Sonning Cricket Club: 'At the finish of a highly successful season, it is pleasing to record that the first XI are champions of the Berkshire Mercury League; the second XI finished top of the third division; the under 17's won the Morris Cup, and the under 15's won the Jubilee Cup. This is a remarkable achievement for a small village, and our congratulations to Peter Kay the club captain, to the respective skippers, to the players and officials, and a special word of thanks to all the ladies who supplied and served the teas.'

[*1978 proved to be the year of the "three Popes". Paul VI died on August 6 and was succeeded by John Paul I who died just 33 days after taking office. The third Pontiff was the Polish born John Paul II.*]

November 1978

Vicar's Notes: 'For the past four years we have had a coffee and bring and buy fair at the Vicarage in the late autumn which has raised about £120 each time for Church Funds. We want to repeat this effort this year and the date will be Saturday, December 9. Christmas gifts, cakes and produce will be welcome – also raffle prizes.'

Sonning Girls' Choir: 'On Saturday, September 23, the inaugural concert of the choir took place at the Pearson Hall. The programme was varied and appealed to all tastes, finishing with a touch of humour – an original rendering of "Tripping Higher" from Iolanthe, after which the audience called for an encore. The pieces chosen were of a technically high standard and impressively performed – the choir would appear to have a great potential.'

Moses–a variation: George Stokes included the following story of Moses in this issue:

'An eight year old boy was asked by his mother what he had learnt at Sunday School. "Well", he said, "our teacher told us about when God sent Moses behind enemy lines to rescue the Israelites from the Egyptians. When they came to the Red Sea Moses called for the engineers to build a pontoon bridge. After they had crossed they saw the Egyptians. Then Moses radioed H.Q. to blow up the bridge and so he saved all of the Israelites". "Surely that isn't what your teacher actual said to you?" "not exactly," said Bobby, "but if I told it her way you'd never believe it".'

December 1978

Fostering Care in Berkshire: 'Children come into care for a variety of reasons. Their parents may temporarily need help over a family crisis; their problems may be more long term; or they simply may not be able to care for their children at all.

More and more, Social Services Departments prefer to place children in care with foster parents rather than in a Local Authority Home. The advantages to the child are obvious.

If you have the time to be a foster parent, and space at home for one or more additions to your family, contact your local fostering advisor and find out more about it,'

Rotary in Your Parish: An extensive article supplied by the Rotary Club of Loddon Vale explained the origins of the Rotary Movement and its aims and objects. The article emphasised the charitable contributions that the club undertakes and the support that they receive from local parishioners was emphasised with the following comment: 'Rotary has identified the need, but you, the people of the Parish within the Club's boundaries, have given generously to our various charity efforts and enabled help to be given and the particular needs to be satisfied. This Christmas our Charity Shop will once again be located in the Shopping Centre at Woodley to sell for charity anything that may be given and, of course, there will be our Christmas float, with carols and Father Christmas, for the children, coming round many streets in the Woodley and surrounding area during the week before Christmas.'

January 1979

Vicar's Notes: 'The sad thing is that today Christmas Day seems to be the end of the Festive Season instead of the first day of it. And yet people will sing the Carol "The Twelve Days of Christmas" which lead up to the Feast of the Epiphany. In ancient times January 6 was in fact Christmas Day and is still so observed in the Eastern Orthodox churches.'

Darby and Joan Christmas Lunch: 'Again, the happy familiar gathering in the festive Pearson Hall. Guests present included the Vicar and his wife and Mr. Sidney Paddick. After a lovely meal, the Magician, who had us all enthralled, ended his entertainment by inviting us to take part with him in music-making with various instruments brought along by him, tambourines, etc.'

Scripture Union 1879–1979: 'This important centenary is to be marked by, amongst other things, a "workshop" on Saturday, March 24, for leaders of various bodies to learn more about passing on the Bible to others, and Reading has been chosen as one of the centres. It is hoped that every church will send its leaders along – the Sunday school, the schools, guides, brownies, scouts, youth clubs, etc.'

February 1979

Vicar's Note: 'At the last meeting of the P.C.C. we discussed our Services and attendance at them. We felt that some variety might be introduced at the Evening Service and a monthly "Songs of Praise" was suggested. This is not quite the same as Community Hymn-singing, although similar. People like Hymns and in such a way we can explore the Hymn-Book and introduce some new Hymns and thus widen our repertoire.'

Pearson Hall Improvements: 'Hopefully, some of you will have been able to experience the great change in the kitchen at the Pearson Hall. It is a vast improvement and when it is finished it will look super! The ladies cloakroom is also taking shape and will soon be well worth a visit! We have raised just on £1,000 to improve these two amenities and buy the new tables.'

St Patrick's Hall: 'Our grateful thanks to all those individuals and organisations involved in the raising of over £200 for the material which was required when making the new curtains for the hall. The groups using the hall all made contributions, as did the Hall Users Association and Charvil Residents Association. Our thanks to those who worked on the curtains and also those who helped to hang them.'

Sonning Handicraft Evenings: 'It has been suggested that some handicraft evenings would be a good thing in the village. Several ideas have been put forward – crochet, macramé, cake icing, dressmaking and more! The easiest of these to arrange has been dressmaking. If you are fourteen years of age or more, male or female, we will be pleased to see you. twenty-five people is maximum, so don't think about it too long!'

March 1979

Vicar's Notes: 'The audited Church Accounts for 1978 show that it has been a fairly good year in which we have kept our heads somewhat above water, and indeed increased our giving to Missions and Charities – thanks to your support in collections and other ways. But we must keep it up, for we have to spend some money on repairs to the church, and our Diocesan Share or quota is to be £4,521 this year. Quite a rise!'

Quinquennial Inspection: The churchwardens reported the results of the five yearly inspection of the church fabric by the diocese architect: 'It is pleasing to have the report and to find that no major items of expenditure are envisaged in the foreseeable future. Items of routine maintenance are listed, including external painting, and some pointing of the tower.' The report concluded with the following statement by the diocese architect:
"This church, together with its landscape setting, now comprise a treasure which could not have survived without devoted and informed care over recent generations. The Victorian setting in the interior has been enhanced with great skill, and has achieved a rare harmony of form and colour, which could so easily have been dissipated by spurious efforts to move with the times. If the same vigilance can be continued it should be practicable to maintain this fine church at reasonable cost, indefinitely."

Sonning Volunteer Fire Brigade Trust: 'At the Annual General Meeting of the Trust, Mr. Sidney Paddick was re-elected Chairman for the ensuing year – for the sixteenth successive time. The other Trustees, who are appointed for a period of five years, are Mr. Mark Bodley Scott, in his capacity as Chairman of the Parish Council, the Rev. George Stokes, Mr. Roly Hunt and Mr. Tom Edwards.'

April 1979

Vicar's Notes: 'As I write this the northern parts of our country are again in the grip of snow and ice – the worst of the winter it seems. It has been a long winter and signs of spring are slow to appear. However, we look forward to spring days soon, and the Easter Festival – which means so much to Christian people. We live in Jesus, we die in Him, and we come to our own Resurrection in Him. There is no sad word in our Church of England order for burials, I no longer wear a black stole at funeral services, but white, because of our "sure and certain hope of the Resurrection to Eternal Life".

The Clergy of the Deanery meet monthly for prayer and discussion about theology and pastoral issues. One of the concerns to village clergy is the scattering, or burying of cremated remains at the Crematoria instead of the village churchyards. We feel, that before too long, the practice will cause a separation between the villages and their intimate burying places. Parishioners, throughout the ages, have always regarded the Churchyard as a family centre where the dead of every generation are laid to rest. The large town cemeteries are impersonal places which do not tie the community together; but in a village the Churchyard is a place to which families and the whole parish community can look with remembrance and affection. Here in Sonning, we make provision for the burial of ashes, and I commend to you the keeping of the Churchyard as a focus of parish remembrance.'

Another "Help the Hall" Success: 'Once again Doris Woodward and her splendid team have pulled off a resounding success with the sale of books, magazines and pictures for the Pearson Hall Improvement Fund. The sale, which included a wide range of books on so many topics from westerns to window-cleaning and "Beano" comics to Bertrand Russell raised £126 profit.'

May 1979

Vicar's Notes: 'You will receive this issue of the magazine either on the day of polling in the General Election or a day or two later. I don't think that anyone would expect me to advise you how to vote. I have not done so; some clergy do. But there are certain considerations. Christians are concerned with the value of the individual as a child of God. Any political theory that seeks to denigrate this or put it aside is not for us.'

[*The General Election held on May 3 was a resounding victory for the Conservatives resulting in the first woman, Margaret Thatcher, to serve as prime minister. The Tories won 339 seats and Labour 269 seats. The new government held an overall majority of 43 seats.*]

Sonning Working Men's Club: 'Friday, April 6, was the evening of the tournament finals. The snooker contest between Stan Robinson and his son John provided an excellent finish and an extremely youthful champion. The billiards was won by Andrew Feak, holding off a strong challenge by Bill Murdock. Mike Forward beat Monty Raphael in the bar billiards final, Nicky Baker won at darts and Bert Walsh became champion at shove-halfpenny.'

1ˢᵗ Sonning (Swordfish) Cub Scouts: 'Celebrations for St David's Day included making four dragons. On March 22, each Cub made a table mat as a present for his Mother on Mothering Sunday. The following week all skills and games were based on the use of ropes.'

June 1979

Sonning Girls' Choir: 'There was a very pleasing musical evening in the Pearson Hall on May 5, when the glamorous Girls' Choir with their equally glamorous conductor, Helen Clarke, entertained an audience of about one hundred with a wide and varied programme. We had excerpts from Arthur Sullivan, Mozart, Strauss, Lehar and Lionel Bart.'

Pearson Hall Fund Raising: 'The Edwardian Soirée held in the Hall on May 12, provided everyone with an evening of splendid entertainment, and a contribution of £75 towards the cost of the Hall improvements.'

July 1979

Vicar's Notes: 'Our Church of St Andrew was at some time during the Middle Ages a centre of pilgrimage for healing, particularly for the "disease of madness". I feel that we ought to be exploring how we can again channel God's healing power to his people through our Church. There seems to me to be no doubt that its atmosphere is not only welcoming but restorative.'

In Memoriam: The death of two men who had made a considerable contribution to the welfare of parishioners was announced in this issue: Captain L. O. C. Langridge (Church Army) came to Charvil with his wife and children in 1955 and was in charge of St Patrick's Church under Canon Groves until 1965. Dr. Alfred George Hammond was a well respected local doctor, known as "Uncle Alfred" to many local children. He was a senior partner in a local medical practice which had its largest surgery in Woodley, and smaller surgeries in Reading and Sonning's High Street.

Darby and Joan Club: 'We hardly expected a fine day for our meeting at the Vicarage – but we did have one, and we had a very nice meeting in the garden. We thank our Vicar and Mrs Stokes for having us there again, and an extra thank you to Mrs. Stokes for allowing us the use of the kitchen in which we prepared tea. Mrs. Johnston had thought of a good competition for us – searching out flower names, which was good fun.'

August 1979

Sonning Church and Churchyard: An extensive article referred to the recent work that had been carried out by parish volunteers under the expert hand of one of the churchwardens, Mr. Malcolm Stansfield. It was noted that the churchyard had been thoroughly tidied and was very satisfying to look at. The article also mentioned that a retired local resident, Mr. Crook of Glebe Lane, who had many years experience in the building trade and was also a one-time Sonning chorister, was undertaking masonry repairs to the outer walls of the church. He was also intending to offer his free services to carry out further masonry repair work to the church in the future.

1st Sonning Scouts Group: 'Breaking new ground for Berkshire is the major County Scout Expedition this year when eighty-four Scouts and Leaders, lead by Cyril Harris from Sonning Troop, will be travelling to an International Camp and expedition at Zellhoff, near Salzburg. It is hoped this will lead to a permanent Austria - Berkshire link.'

Sonning Women's Institute: 'At our July meeting, Mrs. Ball introduced Mrs. Sparrow who enthralled us all with her talk and pictures on "Painting for Beginners". Her varied paintings had been done in oils, charcoal, felt tip pens and pencil. These were much admired by all, and Lady Fairley thanked Mrs. Sparrow on behalf of us all.'

September 1979

Vicar's Notes: 'I have recently written in this magazine about the importance of a family having a place in the Churchyard for the bodies of their loved ones or for their cremated ashes. Now I cannot believe that the commemoration of the dead is of no importance to families. Of course it is; and the Church has a day set aside for this purpose – All Souls' Day, November 2. We have here in St Andrew's Church a Service of Commemoration at 7 o'clock in the evening – a Eucharist at which the names of the departed are read out – and remembered. Do please join us in the service.'

Platinum Wedding Anniversary: George Stokes offered the following congratulations to a couple who had both made notable contributions to the parish over many past years: 'We all send our love to Sidney and Elizabeth Paddick on the occasion of the 70th anniversary of their marriage. We wish them a happy and quiet day on September 8. For those wishing to offering their congratulations in person there will be a "calling book" available for signing at their home.'

Our Own Burning Bush: 'I wonder how many people who walk through our tranquil churchyard at this time of the year realise how close they may be to God. There beside the church is a real live burning bush – just like the one Moses saw so long ago. The name of our burning bush is Rhus Cotinus, *cotinus coggygria* – the one Moses saw is thought to be the thorne bush Acacia *nilotica*.'

Royal British Legion: 'On August 15, the coveted Gold Badge of the Royal British Legion was presented to Harry Edgington for outstanding services over many years. Harry is a veteran of Dunkirk where he was severely injured and since the war he has been an active member of the Legion serving in many capacities.'

Help the Aged: 'The annual collection of blankets, clothing etc., was held at the Pearson Hall on July 18, when we filled thirty bags with very good clothing. The collecting tin for donations produced a most generous response - £108. 05.'

October 1979

Sonning Produce Show: 'The Show was held in the Vicarage grounds on September 1, and was a triumph of organisation, with all sections of the people of the parish taking a part in some direction or other – on a remarkably lovely sunny early autumn day.'

Pearson Hall Fund Raising: 'We are pleased to say that the Hall now owns one hundred dinner plates to match the existing cups, saucers etc., This is due to the support at the Jumble Sale in June, and the Clothing Sale in July. We have a social function arranged during October, a Tramps Supper, dress is optional!'

George Preston: Dear "Old George" as he was known, who died in August, worked hard for many years keeping the Village neat and tidy and was always kind and helpful. Only recently the *Reading Mercury* published his photograph paying tribute to his services to Sonning.'

1ˢᵗ Sonning Guides: 'On September 14, we invited all of our friends to the Primary School to join with us in celebrating the Queen's Guide Award presented to Sarah Stansfield. The Stansfields baked and decorated a lovely celebration cake for the evening, and the Patrols displayed some of the things we get up to at Guides.'

Choir News: 'Last month we had to say goodbye to both Alex Crouch and Bernadette Bowman, who have now joined the Girl Guides; this unfortunately means that they are committed on Fridays.'

November 1979

Soft Furnishings in the Church: 'It has been suggested that a working party should be formed to make and care for the soft furnishings in St Andrew's Church. The first pressing need is kneelers for the sanctuary.'

Sonning Cricket Club: 'Following the Club's successful 1978, much had to be lived up to in 1979. Shall we say it was good and bad in parts. The 1st XI retained the championship of the Premier Division, but how close it was! We finished level on points with Kidmore End, but as we had won one more match than Kidmore End the rule covering such an eventuality gave Sonning the title once again. Unfortunately, the 2nd XI was relegated from Division 2.'

Charvil Brownies: We have a number of Brownies who will want to become Guides in the near future so there is an urgent need for a Guide Company to be formed in Charvil now. The Sonning Company is very full, being served by Sonning and Charvil Brownies, so it is inevitable that there is a long wait before our Brownies can join.'

Sonning Lawn Tennis Club: 'Now a thriving club 150 members strong, we had our first ever social event this month, according to our Chairman, Jim Ballard, who has been a member for thirty years. The Tennis Club Dance, held on October 13 in the Pearson Hall was extremely well supported and incredibly successful.'

December 1979

Sonning Women's Institute: 'Fifty-eight members and guests gathered in the Pearson Hall on November 3, to enjoy the Diamond Jubilee Dinner of the Institute. The following day in church we sang "Jerusalem" with even more feeling, as it was on November 4, 1919 that Sonning W. I. under the care of Mrs. May was actually founded.'

Choir News: As many members of the Choir as possible, took part in a Choirs Festival on October 6, arranged by the Berkshire Organists' Association in All Saints' Church, Downshire Square, Reading. A good time was had by all, although some of us felt that perhaps the conductor could have been a little more dynamic and instructive.'

January 1980

Vicar's Notes: 'When wishing people a Happy New Year, one can conscientiously mean it, especially at times like these when the future is uncertain and very hard to look forward to. All that is certain is that there are troubles of all kinds ahead. It would seem from the press, radio and television that fighting, murder and violence are the favourite occupations of the human race. If people aim in life for happiness, then it follows that millions and millions of people are pursuing it and finding it this way –through war and violence.

A Happy New Year? ultimately happiness is only achieved by being true to oneself, whatever the circumstances that confront each of us, so be that. A Happy New Year to you all!'

1ˢᵗ Sonning (Swordfish) Cub Scouts: 'Pack meetings continue to be very well attended. Two have been based on Lord Baden-Powell's book, and devoted to early Scouting. Examples of the uniform and other items were supplied by dads who have been "Wolf Cubs". The name was changed in 1966 when the Scout Movement was "modernised". Traffic signals were learnt, and the Green Cross Code revised in preparation for the Road Safety Quiz on November 22.'

Sponsored Church Cleaning: 'During the afternoon of December 8, a dozen members of the Church Youth Club worked extremely hard for a period of three hours in the Church. Many areas of the building that cannot be dealt with during the routine cleaning received attention, including windows, reredos, pulpit and font canopies etc., Some extremely tired, dusty and dirty young people went home to their parents, proud that they had earned their sponsor money for Blue Peter and the Church had undoubtedly profited by their labours.'

February 1980

British Red Cross Society–Junior Branch: 'It has been suggested that a Junior Branch might be formed in Sonning, if enough people are interested. It would be open to boys and girls from 10-18 years of age, and could be a worthwhile and exciting project. Members would promise "to serve God, Queen and Country, and to join with others all over the world to help the sick and suffering".

Sponsored Church Cleaning: 'The magnificent sum of £100 approx. was raised with three hours hard work for the Blue Peter Oxfam Appeal. We warmly congratulate the members of St Andrew's Church Youth Club on their achievement.'

March 1980

Vicar's Notes: 'Holy Week, that is the week from Palm Sunday to Easter Day, has for 1,500 years been familiar for its apparent celebration of single events in the Passion of Our Lord, which somehow have been seen as together making a united whole. But in fact there was no such thing as Holy Week before the fourth century. There are other surprises for someone who looks into Christian observance during those early centuries. There was no Christmas, no Epiphany in the West, no Ascension Day, and neither Lent not Advent. Instead there was only the weekly celebration of Sunday and the annual feasts of Easter and Pentecost.'

Annual Parochial Meeting: 'It is sad that after four years of surplus we must this year report a small deficit, due mainly to three factors; the vast increase in the cost of oil for heating, the necessary expense of controlling the honey fungus which appeared in the churchyard and the cost of repairs to the Church which included the damage caused by the violet storm in January 1979. And we already know that the Diocesan Quota for 1980 will be increased from £4,400 to £6,600.'

The Mothers' Union: 'This month sees a wonderful celebration, as it was 80 years ago that the Mothers' Union came into being here in the village. There will be a service in the church at 3pm on March 6, when the address will be given by the Archdeacon. We hope about 100 members and friends will be present, and then we will enjoy tea and a chat in the Pearson Hall.'

April 1980

Sonning Working Men's Club: 'The Annual General Meeting was held in the Clubroom on March 7 at 8pm. Fifty-one members were present. The Club staff were thanked for the very good service given to members and for the way they managed ever increasing sales which over the year had amounted to the record sum of £46,271. The Chairman warned members that they must expect fairly sharp increases in the bar prices during the forthcoming weeks, as the year's excess of income over expenditure was too low at £796, this fall in profitability was due mainly to the increased costs of staff, rates and fuel together with the holding of prices at a level rather lower than normal.

The Club membership still remained at its maximum level and no applicants from outside the Parish were being accepted onto the waiting list.'

Sonning Girls' Choir: 'The Woodley Festival was held at the Bulmershe College of Education at the beginning of March and on the Saturday and Sunday the Choir and individual members took part in various classes. The event proved very successful for all those who took part as well as being good experience for less practised performers, and a very enjoyable occasion for everyone.'

The Sanctuary Kneelers: 'This project is well underway; it is hoped that the workers will bring their efforts in, whatever stage of progression, to the Annual Church Meeting on April 15. As the total cost of these, *i.e.* materials and professional completion is understandably high (and our Church deserves the best), contributions however small would be gratefully received either by Lady Fairley or Mrs. Ball.'

May 1980
Vicar's Notes: 'Just now the world is in a very sad and uncertain state and the relationship between East and West in Europe and the Middle East has deteriorated. It could not be otherwise after the events in Iran and Afghanistan. Some commentators on the news have it that we are drifting towards war. I do not think that it can be so – too much is at stake for the future of all mankind. We must do some hard and dedicated praying for the nations and their rulers that they will return to rationality.'

[*Widespread unrest in the Middle East region was causing great concern to the Western Powers. January 1979 saw the pro-western Shah of Iran deposed by a regime headed by Ayatollah Khomeini, and in December 1979 Soviet troops had entered Afghanistan.*]

Choir News: 'First, a big "thank you" to Tina Guppy who "retired" as Head Choirgirl on her 17th birthday in March. Secondly, a warm welcome back to Roly and June Hunt , who had never really left. One of the chants for the *Nunc Dimittis* has been waiting for him, with his splendid bottom E flat!'

Sonning C. of E. School: The headmaster, Thomas Feak, announced in this article that there was to be a service in St Andrew's to celebrate the fifteenth anniversary of the opening of the new Sonning School. 'For those too young to remember and for those who have moved into the area in recent years, the former school was on two sites, one in Thames Street (now converted into houses) and one in Pearson Road. The latter served as a school canteen, an infants' department and a library. This was completely demolished and a new house built on the site. It was marvellous to have the new school on one site in Pound Lane, to have central heating instead of coke boilers and, blessed relief, to have indoor toilet facilities!'

June 1980

British Red Cross Society–Junior Branch: 'our grateful thanks to all those who supported our meeting at the Pearson Hall on May 6. Although numbers were fewer than we might have wished, it was a successful evening, ten young people were keen enough to ask to join the new Branch. Now it is up to us to show that we are worthy of all this help, and to work at forming an efficient and useful Junior Branch, which will not fall short of the proud tradition of the Red Cross Society.'

Charvil Women's Club: 'This year's Summer Fair will be held at St Patrick's Church Hall on July 5. During the year we reached our target of £1,000 to train a Guide Dog for the blind and a cheque will be handed to the Blind Association at the Fair. We are now fund raising for our second £1,000 and the proceeds of the Summer Fair will be given to this fund and to our permanent charity, Andrew Duncan House, Shiplake.'

[*Britain's pressure to have its financial contribution to the Common Market reduced, resulted in a massive reduction from £1,100 million to some £250 million by 1981.*]

Sonning Football Club: 'After last season's disastrous ending, with both teams relegated to lower divisions, we have had one of our best seasons ever. The first team have won the championship of Division 2 East, losing just one match throughout the season, and so return to the First Division. Sonning Reserves finished third in Division 4 East, but bring honours to the club by winning the Jubilee Cup.'

July 1980
R.N.L.I. Sonning branch: 'We should like to thank Mr. and Mrs. Richard Cooksey for lending their house this year for our Wine and Cheese Party. The party was a great success and, due to all of your generous support, it made a profit of approximately £250.'

Alice Elizabeth Paddick: 'Everyone who knew Mrs. Paddick was saddened to receive the news of her death on June 17. She was a charming and gracious lady, of wise counsel and sound judgment, deeply devoted to her husband and family.
[*Alice Elizabeth Paddick (1883-1980) is interred in the Sonning Churchyard. see: Record of Burials etc. Church of St Andrew 2012.*]

Christian Aid Report: 'What a grand effort was made by Sonning for Christian Aid Week. A total of £132.76 was taken from house-to-house collecting, and an additional £100 was donated by the Parish Council.'

St Andrew's Church Youth Club: 'Congratulations to the Youth Club for winning "three trophies in three weeks" in their sections of the three Drama Festivals which they entered (Tilehurst, Woodley and Shinfield). Their production of "What Next" by Peter English was warmly received by audiences as well as adjudicators.'

August 1980
Sonning Flower Club: 'Once more we welcomed popular Mrs. Rowton-Lee from Henley who on her frequent visits never fails to delight us, both with her artistry and witty commentary. Summer's Joy was the subject chosen for demonstration, but as the afternoon's weather was anything but joyful, we were pleased that Mrs. Rowton-Lee had, with summer blooms and bright foliage, made the day a Summer's Joy!'

Ken Thomas Body Scanner Appeal: 'I wish to thank all the ladies who took part in a two hour sponsored keep fit evening at the Pearson Hall, and also their friends who kindly supported us. I am very happy to say that we raised the grand sum of £170.'

1ˢᵗ Sonning Brownies: 'Practically the whole Pack went along to Ascot at the beginning of July for the Festival of Guiding. We had a truly wonderful day and the weather kept fine. The celebrations took place in the presence of Princess Margaret, who is President of the Girl Guides Association. She arrived in time to watch an impressive Colour Ceremony, and an international dancing display by the Brownies.'

September 1980

Charvil Art Group: 'To say that this has not been a painter's dream summer is perhaps understating the case a little. At the time of writing we have had six outings, one was totally rained off, several were dull or cold, but we have had some glimpses of the sun between rainy periods. This year the club arranged a visit to the Royal Academy by coach, which is the most comfortable and enjoyable way to see this exhibition. The winter sessions in St Patrick's Hall, Charvil, commence on September 17 at 7.30pm. A professional tutor is available for many of our meetings, and there is always help available for those in the early stages of painting and for beginners.'

Loddon District Scouts 1980: '1ˢᵗ Sonning are part of the Loddon Scouts District which altogether embraces an area covering Woodley, Twyford, Hurst, Sonning, Wargrave and Knowl Hill. Loddon District was formed in 1930 to cater for all the needs of the Scouts' expansion, in the area as a whole, and has gone from strength to strength. At present we total 365 Cub Scouts, 252 Scouts, 55 Venturers and 93 Leaders, who this year celebrate the Golden Jubilee of Scouting in Loddon. The emblem of the Loddon District is the Loddon Lily which grows only in the Loddon Valley; this we wear with pride, and in the same way look forward to a further fifty years of Loddon Scouting.'

Darby and Joan Club: 'On July 28 we entertained ourselves and had lots of fun and laughter. Something we can all do with a little more often.'

October 1980

Live Television Transmission: 'The Remembrance Service which is to be held on Sunday, November 9, will be televised live by I.T.V. from our own St Andrew's Church. The Service which will commence at 10.30am is to follow the usual pattern of recent years. As space will be required for the cameras and other essential equipment, it will be necessary to restrict the size of the congregation. Blocks of seats will be allocated to representative members of the Royal British Legion branches, Fire Brigade, Guide and Scout movement and Reading Blue Coat School. Other seats will be by ticket only.

T.V. monitors will be installed in the Vicarage for the overflow congregation, but no doubt many people will prefer to watch the Service from the comfort of their homes. The Producer has indicated that the cameras will show the real beauty of the Church that is not possible in normal light.'

Sonning Produce Show: 'The weather was kind for the Sonning Produce Show, Fete and Barbecue 1980. The entries poured in during the morning and the marquee looked most attractive by 11 o'clock when the judging began. We were pleased to welcome Waltham St Lawrence Silver Band who played during the afternoon. The Cups were won by Mrs. Gardiner (Cookery), Mr. R. Williams (Vegetables), Mr. S. Clarke (Onions), Mrs. A. Perkins (Art), Deborah Butler and Gillian Murdoch (Under 16).'

Sonning R.N.L.I. – Free Film and Coffee: To thank our many supporters we have arranged to show the film "Storm Force 10" at the Pearson Hall on Saturday, October 25, at 7pm. There will also be a short talk on R.N.L.I. activities. There is *no charge* for the film or coffee which will be provided. All are welcome, including children.'

November 1980

We Will Remember Them . . . 'When you have been walking through our churchyard, I wonder if you ever contemplate how the gravestones of servicemen who were buried there during World War I are kept in such immaculate condition. This is carried out by the staff of the Imperial War Graves Commission annually.'

Choir News: 'First, welcome to Denise Fortune, Sarah Millard and Matthew Hunt who have recently joined us. Secondly, I'd like to say a heartfelt thank you to everyone who helped in any way at the R.S.C.M. Choirs Festival, not least the members of our own choir.'

1ˢᵗ Sonning (Swordfish) Cub Scouts: 'Recently the Pack has had to say goodbye to Simon Nutbrown, who has gone away to school, and Gordon Roberts who has joined the Scouts. Congratulations Simon and Gordon on being awarded Gold Arrows.'

Sonning Glebe Women's Institute: 'Our speaker at our monthly meeting was Mrs. Wheeler who demonstrated the art of Cake Icing. I think that most of us present were fired with enthusiasm and will endeavour not to produce a snow scene on our Christmas cakes again this year!'

December 1980
Remembrance Sunday: 'The members of the Royal British Legion assembled in Pearson Road and, headed by the Central Band of the Salvation Army and with our own village policeman in the lead, marched to St Andrew's Church followed by representatives of the Ladies Section, Fire Brigade, Scouts, Guides, Cadets, Brownies and Cubs. They filed into their allotted places under the glare of television lights, for the Service to be seen throughout England and Wales. A solitary member of the Legion gave the Exhortation "They shall not grow old as we that are left grow old", and whilst two trumpeters of the Royal Engineers sounded the Last Post the outside camera focussed on the flag of St Andrew high above the tower and came slowly down to take in the Church, the giant yew and the trees in their autumn cloak, and finally a single poppy in front of a gravestone.'

Comment: Mrs. Shirley Drake, the joint editor of the parish magazine, included the following appreciation: 'I feel the opportunity has presented itself to say "congratulations and thank you" to Mr. Stokes for the Remembrance Service. It was beautifully done and I felt very proud to be a member of St Andrew's Church. Mr. Stokes said that Robin Brutton had rung him to offer congratulations, and to send his good wishes to us all, which Mr. Stokes reciprocated on our behalf.'

CHAPTER EIGHT

1981 - 1985

The extent of the magazine now varied between sixteen and twenty-four pages with the page size and appearance remaining constant. A further change in the editorial appointment took place in 1982 when Mrs. Edmonds joined Mrs. Perkins in succession to Mrs. Drake who had occupied the joint editorial role for five years.

A change in the ministry of St Andrew's was to take place in 1985 when Rev. George Stokes announced his retirement and was succeeded as the vicar of Sonning by Rev. Christopher Morgan.   During the early eighties the churchwarden responsibility was taken mainly by Malcolm Stansfield and Thomas Feak.   Sidney Paddick, who had been awarded emeritus churchwarden status in recognition of half a centenary service to Sonning church and the local community, died in 1981.

The British economy and Britain's relationship with the European Community were the two major factors preoccupying the Thatcher government at this time.   However, in the spring of 1982 the attention of the government and people throughout Britain was immediately focused upon an international incident in the far away Falkland Islands. The territory was invaded and occupied by Argentina and a British battle fleet was launched to confront the aggressor.   The conflict was short in duration and the Argentine forces were quickly repelled.

W. R. BOURTON & Son, N.A.F.D

Funeral Directors and Monumental Masons

(D. J. BOURTON DIP.F.D.)

1 PRINCES STREET, READING

Tel: 53825/595828/9

Out of business hours:

Tel. Reading 694283, 663917, 82945.

97 BUTTS HILL ROAD, WOODLEY, READING

THERE IS A WARM WELCOME AT THE

FRENCH HORN HOTEL

SONNING-ON-THAMES

Telephone: READING (0734) 692204

E. C. J. THOMPSON

EXPERT UPHOLSTERY at Reasonable Prices

LET ME GIVE YOU A FREE ESTIMATE

Phone TWYFORD 345598 or write:

9 WARGRAVE ROAD   TWYFORD

Advertisement page: January 1981

January 1981

Vicar's Notes: 'The Epiphany is little regarded as a Christian Festival nowadays. I think this is because it has become chiefly associated with the visit of the Wise Men and we have attached that to the Christmas Story. But – the Epiphany – the showing of Christ to the world, has a much wider field of thought and celebration than the visit of the Wise Men. It is about Christ in the Temple Catechism, about his Baptism in Jordan by St John the Baptist and about his first miracle at the Wedding in Cana of Galilee.'

Trees: 'The last of the dead elms in the spinney in the recreation ground, which were fast becoming a serious menace to life and limb, have now been felled and the problem besetting the parish council is how best to replace them.

When a call went out for volunteers to help in the job of injecting the elms, in the unavailing attempt to save them from Dutch Elm disease, the response with excellent. The idea now is to invite a few parishioners, a couple of dozen or so, to enter into a scheme whereby they would each provide a tree, plant it in the spinney themselves and then tend it, by watering for instance, until it became established. They would then be able to watch their own personal tree take shape.'

Charvil Brownies: A report concerning recent local Brownie activities was included in this issue: 'Under a threatening stormy sky, our first meeting of last term was taken up with running our heats to select our team for the District Brownies Sports, for which, for the second year running, we were surprised and pleased to win the Cup. We were pleased to be able to take part in the Remembrance Service; it was a very nice service and we were sorry that some Brownies were disappointed that they could not be with us, but only a certain number could be accommodated. In November we held a very successful bazaar in aid of our fund; £64 was raised, and £35 was sent to the Ken Thomas Appeal.'

February 1981

St Andrew's Church Finance: The Treasurer, Alan Smith, had prepared a brief statement of the church financial situation which was causing concern to the vicar and the P.C.C. George Stokes used this issue of the magazine to make an appeal for more funding to be provided by parishioners. 'I would like to appeal to everyone to increase their giving both by Covenant and in the collections. Our parish share for 1981 is £11,109, an increase of 68% on the 1980 share. I make it my business not to know who contributes by covenant, but I know that only sixty people make a covenant at all, Sad! The increase in the Diocesan Share means that our income for 1981 must rise to £20,000 if we are to break even.'

Crèche and Sunday School: The vicar made the following "thought provoking" comments. 'When children are baptised their parents give an assurance that they will be brought up in Christian ways of belief, worship and morals. Most parents disregard their obligations. By and large God-parents are of no help whatsoever. In this parish of St Andrew we try to make it possible for parents to carry out their obligations. During Morning Service there is a Crèche at the Vicarage where toddlers may be left safely. Also there is a Sunday School for young children who leave the Service for an instruction of their own. Please use these facilities.'

Choir News: David Duvall thanked the members of the choir for their support at recent memorable events. 'We've had the R.S.C.M. choirs festival, then the televised Remembrance Service, and finally, of course, Christmas. A warm welcome to the choir, if I haven't already welcomed them, to Gordon and Matthew Hunt, father and son; what with Roly and June (no relation) the Hunts are taking over!'

March 1981

Vicar's Notes: 'The season we call Lent begins on Wednesday March 4. The Church has always had a genius for teaching by symbolic acts. Centuries ago the universal custom was for the people to bring last year's Palm Crosses back to Church. They were burned and reduced to ashes and then imprinted on the foreheads of the Parishioners with the words "Remember O Man that dust thou art and unto dust shalt thou return". So, that is the reason why the first day of Lent came to be known as Ash Wednesday.'

Sonning Produce Show: 'After much deliberation it has been decided to give the £350 from Show funds to the Pearson Hall, so that the electrics may be improved. Heating in the Hall was also a priority but with this help from the Show for electrics it is hoped that Hall users will organise a project to raise the heating money.'

Junior Red Cross: 'In May of last year a Sonning Branch of the Junior Red Cross was started by Winifred Way, and initially the response was meagre. A meeting was held in the Pearson Hall on January 27, more in hope than in optimism, but lo! the hall was packed to capacity, and standing room only for late-comers. There were many young people to enrol and to give their promises to succour those in need.'

April 1981

Vicar's Notes: 'During Holy Week a play "The Circle" by Peter English is to be presented in the Church on Palm Sunday evening at 6.30pm and on Tuesday, April 14, at 8pm. I strongly commend this to you as part of our observance for Holy Week and Easter. The following members of the congregation will be in the cast of the play –
Sheila Bowman, John Edmunds, Kate Garstone, Catherine Maskell, Leslie Moss, Betty Stokes.'

The Pearson Hall: 'The opening meeting of the Management Committee held on February 24, unanimously agreed that a new hall heating system was needed. To achieve this a fund will be started and all users of the hall asked to contribute by their own fund raising activities.'

Sonning C. of E. School: 'The P.T.A. would like to thank everyone who contributed so generously to the Auction Sale held on March 14, and helped to make it such a successful event. We are pleased to say that a profit of £360 was raised for the School funds.'

May 1981

Vicar's Notes: 'You may have seen the item in the Evening Post or the Church Times about the Candle-extinguisher invented by Mr. James Brown, a member of the P.C.C. It is a great improvement on the traditional snuffer.'

Thank You–Len Crook: 'Few apart from those actively involved in running the church, can know of the enormous tasks undertaken by Len Crook in repairing the roof, damp and crumbling walls etc., all this in addition to being a regular member of the choir, reserve organist and server. Our gratitude and thanks to Leonard for his kind attention to the fabric of the church and churchyard to which he gives so generously of his skill and time.'

John Heppell: The small printing business based in Woodley and owned by Mr. Heppell was responsible for producing this parish magazine for many past years: 'It is with the greatest sadness that we have learned, immediately before going to press, of the sudden death of Mr, Heppell.'

June 1981
The Vicar's Note: 'It was with great horror and sadness that we learned of the shooting of the Pope. Let us hope and pray that he will recover quickly. The world has gone mad. Millions of people of all religions pray for peace, but it seems that the chief pre-occupation and pleasure of the human race is in fighting and killing each other. Not only in organised warfare, but in tribal and racial feuding.'
[*May 13: Pope John Paul II was shot by a Turkish gunman, Mehmet Ali Agea, but thankfully recovered from his wounds.*]

University Farm–Villager Evening: 'A cordial invitation is extended to local residents and their friends to visit the University Farm in Sonning on Wednesday, June 3, at 7pm. This will be an opportunity to see the developments with the dairy herd as well as some of the research projects in crop production.'

Sonning Football Club: 'The 1980-81 season ended with mixed feelings in the Club. After one season in the Reading and District League Division I, the first XI are relegated to Division 2 for next season. However, the Reserves side won Division 4 East, dropping five points out of a possible forty. We are very sorry to lose our President, Mr. Sid Morris, who has resigned the post due to ill health. We wish to thank him for his considerable support in the past and very much hope that his health improves.'

July 1981

Sidney Paddick: The death of Sidney Paddick, at the age of 94, was announced in this issue. 'His love and devotion to St Andrew's Church during his fifty odd years as Churchwarden, and before, can never be surpassed. When Sidney first came to Sonning in 1920 the interior of the Church was very begrimed and damaged in many parts. Being a perfectionist when it came to buildings, Sidney soon set to work to repair and re-decorate the whole interior. As a Parish Councillor, from 1923 until just before he died, his contribution is outstanding. He was Vice-Chairman from 1947 until 1961 at which time he took over the Chair, reverting to Vice-Chairman again in 1976 to make way, as he so delightfully put it, for younger blood. He will never be forgotten by the people of Sonning but it is nice to know that we shall always have "Paddick Close" to remind us of him.'

[*Sidney Paddick 1887-1981 is interred in the Sonning churchyard,*
see: Record of Burials etc. Church of St Andrew's 2012.]

Sonning Working Men's Club: 'On Saturday, June 13, the Club held its annual Supper Dance and we were fortunate enough to have chosen the finest and warmest weekend of the year. Many chose to dine outside on the terrace or at tables on the lawn. The garden was adorned with coloured lights and flags.'

Pearson Hall Fund Raising: 'With over £600 already received towards the Heating Fund, a Book Sale was successfully held on June 18, raising £25 towards the £3,000 needed. There are other "happenings" in the village towards this cause – please support them or even think about organising them.'

August 1981

1ˢᵗ Sonning Brownies: 'District Revels were held this year in Ruscombe, a lovely setting for our theme of "Robin Hood". There were around 100 assorted Robin Hoods, Maid Marions and Friar Tucks, and eighteen of them came from Sonning. We had a lovely afternoon playing games, entering competitions and the usual picnic. How excited we were when it was announced that 1ˢᵗ Sonning had won the District Cup with our competition entries.'

Sonning Bell Ringers: 'We recently rang a sponsored quarter peal of Plain Bob Major in response to a nationwide appeal ("Peal a Peal") to mark the centenary of the Church of England's Children's Society. This raised £109 for this worthy cause.'

Sonning 8120 Red Cross Youth Group: 'We extend a warm welcome to those members who have joined recently and also to those who have transferred to us from Woodley, whilst their own Group is temporarily closed down. No examinations have been taken by the older cadets this term, the emphasis having been on further training and taking part in "events". Early next term at least ten cadets will make an attempt for their ordinary First Aid Certificate and six further cadets will try for the advanced First Aid Certificate.'

September 1981
Vicar's Notes: 'The Royal Wedding was watched by the whole nation and much of the world. I was reminded of a comment made by the then Archbishop of Canterbury in a radio broadcast at the time of the Queen's marriage – that every bride and bridegroom had the same service that the Princess Elizabeth and her consort were having – even in the simplest village church. Basically this is true. Take away the "extras" and what did we see? We saw a young man and a young woman giving themselves to each other for life.'
[*July 29: Charles, Prince of Wales married Lady Diana Spencer at St Paul's Cathedral.*]

Parish Outing to Oxford Cathedral: The Vicar had arranged a visit to Oxford for Friday, October 12. 'We should learn to know more about Christchurch for it is our Cathedral. Mrs. Welsh is kindly organising it and it should be a most interesting outing. There will be a conducted tour of the Cathedral, then time for us to do our own thing in Oxford, ending with Evensong in the Cathedral.'

Charvil Art Group: 'The art group has recently completed its summer programme and only one session was rained off which is remarkable bearing in mind the earlier months of this so called summer. The locations have been very pleasant and included a day in a bluebell wood and an evening on the banks of the Thames.'

October 1981

Sonning Produce Show: 'We were once again blessed with a hot, sunny day on the first Saturday in September. The marquee was standing on the Vicarage lawn and between nine o'clock and eleven o'clock the entries arrived. Vegetable marrows, knitted jackets, oil paintings, cakes, marmalade etc., etc., By one o'clock the judges had made their choices. At two o'clock Waltham St Lawrence Band struck up and the Fete was in full swing.'

Best Kept Village 1981: 'Sonning should be very happy with the judges' comments on this year's competition. They found it a delightful village, the allotments a model of efficiency, the playground well equipped, a satisfactory absence of litter and they considered that a great deal of co-operation must have gone into our effort. We achieved 88.8% in the first round, coming second to Bray who were the eventual winners of our group.'

Sonning Flower Club: 'Our thanks go to Mr. and Mrs. Cheyney for affording the club members the use of their naturally lovely and charming garden as the venue for this year's outdoor meeting on August 13. Lucky 13, as this time the sun smiled down so warmly.'

November 1981

Sonning Vicarage: The following article from the P.C.C. Treasurer, Alan Smith appeared in the issue: 'We all realise that the Church, the Churchyard and the Vicarage comprise the heart of our village, and that the house and large garden of the Vicarage complement the ministry of the Church.

The Vicarage is vested in the Diocesan Parsonages Board and should its maintenance prove excessive the Board have the power to sell it, and replace it with a smaller residence on a different site – possibly remote from the Church.

Towards the end of his life Sidney Paddick was well aware of this possibility and was prompting the formation of a Trust Fund which could meet such part of the maintenance costs of the Vicarage as the Diocesan Parsonages Board deem excessive, so that the Church precincts can be retained.

Sidney and others gave generously to this end and the P.C.C. have added the legacy of just over £4,000 which Mr. Rapley gave to the Parish.

The legal formalities necessary to create the fund have been completed and, almost simultaneously, A Paddick legacy of £5,000 has been received, so that the P.C.C. can announce that the Vicarage Maintenance Fund amounting to some £20,000 is here.

This Capital Sum should bring in, say, £2,000 a year, but inflation being what it is , more will be needed to make the project really viable over the years. We are therefore appealing to all parishioners to make a contribution to the Capital Sum.'

Sonning Village Day to Help the Disabled: 'Like Topsy this idea has "grown" and plans are well in hand for our Sonning Village Weekend of fund-raising for the Year of the Disabled.   Without the generous offers of venues for the various events, this December 5 and 6 weekend of fun and fund-raising just wouldn't be possible.   Events will include a Photographic Exhibition and Competition, a Fun Run, a Teddy Bear's Picnic, a Concert etc.,'

December 1981

Vicar's Notes: 'The P.C.C. decided that we would try for one year "Rite B" of the Alternative Service Book for the Parish Eucharist. We have used "Rite A" for one year. "Rite B" is in large measure a return to the language of the Book of Common Prayer with the Traditional Texts. You will recall that our organist, David Duvall, composed music for the new texts. He has also composed a setting for the Traditional Texts for "Rite B" and would like everyone to come before 10.45am on December 6, for a short Congregational singing practice of the new tunes.'

A Midsummer Night's Dream: 'Your response to the projected production of this play to be presented by the village of Sonning in the garden of "Sonningdene" in early July 1982 in aid of the Pearson Hall Fund, has been most encouraging. In consequence, auditions will be held at the Vicarage on January 5, 1982 at 7.30pm. Please contact Dawne Vincent or Betty Stokes if interested in an acting or non-acting capacity.'

January 1982

Vicar's Notes: 'I am writing this during the severe cold spell we are having. It is not often that we have such snow and ice in December. It causes a great deal of chaos, but I think I am in agreement with the authorities who contend that, in view of its relative infrequence, it would be too expensive to be prepared all the time.

I was talking to one of our very senior citizens who has suffered much, but she told me how much she had to be *thankful* for - "I have a nice little cottage and it's warm; I can see and hear well; I have good food and I can still get my own meals ready; I have friends who come to see me sometimes, though they are getting fewer; I have a nice little dog and, above all, I have a good son who comes to look after me regularly. What a fine example to us all!'

Travel Feature: A monthly interest article commenced in this issue. The articles were supplied by a local travel agent, James Bird Travel, who paid an advertising contribution for the commercial benefit they received from having their name attached to the features. This issue carried an account of a fly-cruise holiday in the Caribbean.

February 1982

Choir News: 'Many thanks to all who gave so much support over the Christmas period, and especially to those who sang solo - Bernadette Bowman, Sheila Bowman, Viki Davey, Ann Duvall and Rodney Huggins. Thanks also to those who came and sang at the White Hart on Christmas Eve - we made £30 in aid of Madge Loader's fund for the Year of the Disabled.'

Pearson Hall - Memory Lane: A number of short articles taken from past issues of this magazine and featuring the Pearson Hall were included in this issue. The articles originally appeared during the period between 1894 and 1910.

[*A number of such articles appear in Volume One of this work.*]

Pearson Hall Fund Raising: 'We are pleased to say that £1,300 has been raised towards the Heating Fund. However, we still need over £1,500 to cover the cost of a desperately needed new heating system for the Hall.'

March 1982

Volunteer Centre: 'A new Centre was opened on February 1 to cater for Charvil, Wargrave, Twyford and Ruscombe. The Volunteer Centre is a clearing-house, matching up offers of help with calls for assistance. This can involve visiting the elderly, shopping for the house-bound, driving people to hospital and many other tasks. If anyone in Charvil needs help of any kind or can offer a little of their time please contact the co-organisers. Woodley is planning to start a centre soon which is intended to include Sonning.'

Churchyard Working Party: 'What a splendid response there was to the recent request for help with the clearing of snow-damaged trees and shrubs. Thanks are due to the parishioners of all ages who arrived in force to prune, saw, rake or burn. All agreed how much they enjoyed the morning and especially the fellowship, so that by popular request another "party" has been arranged for Saturday, March 13.'

April 1982

St Andrew's Church Window: 'In 1966 vandals broke into the church by breaking a panel in a stained glass window in the South Wall. In memory of his late wife, Mrs. Stella Anne Poulton, Mr. Walter Poulton commissioned the restoration of the window by G. Maille & Son, Ecclesiastical Art Craftsmen in Cambridge. There is a small copper plate beneath the window in memory of Mrs. Poulton.'

Sonning Flower Club: 'Mrs. J. Hancock showed us just how impressive the use of a small number of flowers, carefully placed, can be and how important "line" is in Ikebana, the Japanese art of flower arranging.'

1ˢᵗ Sonning Scouts: 'Sunday, March 14, proved to be most important for the Troop. We have become proud owners of the new Troop Colours, and on this Sunday we met in Church to witness the dedication and blessing of these. The Rev. George Stokes took a simple but moving service, reminding us all what our Colours are for.'

[*April 2: Argentina invades and captures the Falkland Islands, overwhelming the single company of Royal Marines guarding the capital, Port Stanley.*]

May 1982

Vicar's Notes: 'At the end of April, Mr. Thomas Feak, Headmaster of our Parish Church School, formally retires. He has been in the post for eighteen years during which time the new school was built. But it was not only in the school that Mr. Feak's personality and enthusiasm impressed all of us. He has been a major contributor to the life of the parish and church in many ways. In everything Thomas has been supported by his wife Zoe and we are glad that they will be continuing to live in the parish.

We welcome the new Head – Mrs. Stella Beardmore who takes up her duties with the summer term. We hope that she will enjoy her work and association with the parish. Mrs. Beardmore and her husband live in Wokingham.'

Easter at St Patrick's: Les Hudson, Charvil's lay reader, reported on a lively and well attended service on Easter Day: 'I do thank all those who helped to prepare St Patrick's for the service. Mrs. Zordan and the Guides for the lovely flower arrangements, Mrs. Stewart for her flower gift, the whole of the Sunday School which was organised by Mrs. Easton, Victoria Davey for her Easter cakes and of course Mr. Davey who played the piano.'

June 1982

Vicar's Notes: 'I am writing this at a time of great anxiety over the Falkland Islands. Our forces are deployed and we pray that the casualties will not be heavy. It is very sad when Christian peoples have to oppose each other. All Christians are members of the Body of Christ by reason of their Baptism and therefore members of one another. Our thoughts and prayers are with our forces and their families - especially members of our congregation and their young people with the Task Force. Pray also for the Argentine forces and their families – a son or husband killed or wounded is an equal grief no matter what the nationality.'

[*June 14: The Argentine invaders fly the white flag over Port Stanley and British forces are again in control of the Falkland Islands. During the conflict 255 British and 652 Argentine deaths were recorded.*]

July 1982

Retirements and Appointments: ' Mr. Cowley has been a Churchwarden of St Andrew's for eleven years. His interest and devotion to St Andrew's has been exceptional. He has thought that the time has come for him to give up that office and he did so at our Annual Parochial Meeting on April 21. We all say "thank you" Tom for being such a dedicated servant of St Andrew's. We warmly welcome Mr. Thomas Feak as Churchwarden in his place, together with Mrs. Welsh and Mrs. Bowman on the Church Council, while thanking Lady Hamilton Fairley, Mrs. F. Smith and Mr. Lyne who retire after three years service.'

Bishop of Reading: 'The new Bishop, Canon R. G. G. Foley is to live in the Parish of Sonning – in the Old Bath Road. We welcome him and hope that he and Mrs. Foley will be happy among us.'

New Life for Sonning Mill: 'How fortunate we are to have such an exciting venture as the new Theatre-Restaurant starting up on our very doorstep. Our thanks to Tim and Eileen, Frank and Patricia Richards for rescuing our beloved old Mill from oblivion.'

A Midsummer Night's Dream: 'The performance will be remembered by many of us for a long time. The players, production and lighting were pure magic in a perfect setting on a lovely summer evening.'

August 1982

Church Cleaning: Mrs. Betty Stokes provided this item of appreciation: 'A very big "thank you" to the fourteen people who arrived at the Church with all manner of cleaning aids for the second of our special cleaning days. A lot of hard work was done with de-cobwebbing windows, shining marble, gleaming brass and polishing wood – not to mention kneelers and pew cushions.'

A Midsummer Night's Dream: 'Some 460 villagers and friends attended the three performances which brought us an income of £1,007.
Many people have suggested that we should build on the success of the production by re-establishing the Sonning Village Players. Anyone who is interested please contact John Edmonds at North Lodge, Sonning.'

September 1982

Vicar's Notes: 'Mrs. Shirley Drake feels that she must now give up being one of the editors of the Parish Magazine. For five years she has given up her time and talents in serving you, the Readers, in what is a rushed and exacting job. Thank you Shirley, for what you have done. Her place is being taken by Mrs. Armine Edmonds, whom we welcome to the staff. Her long connection with the Parish is well known.'

Darby and Joan Club: 'The highlight of the July meeting was the arrival of Joanna Davey and Shirley Fry, and it was great pleasure they gave us by singing to piano and guitar accompaniment – all so ably and cheerfully performed by these cheery young ladies.'

Sonning Glebe Women's Institute: 'The August meeting which was entitled "A Summer Evening in the Garden" was held in Mrs. Patricia Richard's garden at Cedar Cottage. Thirty-three members braved a chilly, and far from summery evening to hear gardening tips and advice from Mrs. Lyn Lush. Walking around the garden, members learnt a great deal from Mrs. Lush and were able to seek help on particular plant problems in their own gardens.'

October 1982

Pearson Hall Fund Raising: 'The Chairman and Committee would like to thank everyone concerned for the magnificent Fund Raising efforts, from Coffee Mornings to "A Midsummer Night's Dream". There is scarcely an organisation in the Village which has not made a contribution. The work of installing the new heating system is now in hand and should be completed before the cold weather is with us. Prices continue to rise, so we have gone ahead and put the work in hand, but another £600 is still needed.'

Sonning Produce Show 1982: 'Once again we were lucky with the weather and the sun shone all day on September 4. Entries were slightly down on last year, but as usual the judges found their task difficult with standards being high. The day ended with a Barbecue and Dance at which 300 people danced 'til midnight – an extremely successful and enjoyable village day.'

November 1982

Sonning C. of E. School: 'Mrs. S. Beardmore, the new Head teacher, joined the School at the beginning of the Summer term. We also welcomed Mr. J. Stubbs to teach the older children.

This term has seen the introduction of a School magazine, edited and produced by Ms. Liz Dickinson. It will be called "100 Lines" named by Elizabeth Hall in the magazine's first competition.

Money raised by the P.T.A. has paid for a Paper Photo-copier machine and two SRA Reading Laboratories.'

1ˢᵗ Sonning Scout Group: 'The year 1982 marks seventy-five years of Scouting. In the eyes of many people in Sonning and beyond it is also important because it marks twenty-five years of service by our Group Leader, Cyril Harris, to the Scout movement. In order to celebrate these twenty-five years, some sixty former Group members were invited, without Cyril's knowledge, to attend the Loddon District seventy-fifth Anniversary Social on September 25. When Cyril arrived he was confronted by 180 people who burst into the song *"Nice One, Cyril".'*

December 1982

Sonning Village Players: 'It was very encouraging that nearly one-hundred people attended the party held on November 9, to launch the "Players". Over seventy adults and sixteen student members have been enrolled so far, and more members will be most welcome. It is hoped to stage a Production in late March, possibly at the Mill Theatre. Casting for this will take place soon, with rehearsals starting early in the New Year.'

Sonning C. of E. School: 'The School is now buzzing with activity, preparing for the annual Christmas concert. This year the children will be performing "Aladdin", which promises to be a feast of colour and song.

Mrs. Beardmore would like to start a Chess Club for the children at the School and would be pleased to hear from anyone in the village, who could spare a little time and run one on a regular basis.'

Pearson Hall Heating: 'The new heating arrangements are complete, it is hoped that the improvements will be enjoyed and appreciated by all.'

January 1983

Police Force and the Community: The Home Office had invited parish councils to suggest ways in which there might be closer liaison between the police and the community. The following comments were made by the parish clerk: 'We in Sonning are fortunate in having our own "Beat Bobby" in the person of P.C. Stan Robinson to whom we always look to help and advice, and everyone knows how splendidly the system works. It has become known that Stan had declined promotion to Police Sergeant, which would have meant leaving the beat, because he wished to continue serving as our own "Beat Bobby".'

Music at St Andrew's: 'Music lovers were richly rewarded with the concert evening on December 4. The programme began with a Bach choral. The main work was a really ambitious choice; Handel's magnificent "Messiah", Part 1 with the addition of the Hallelujah Chorus. There were memorable performances including that of the augmented choir under the rousing direction of David Duvall.'

February 1983

St Patrick's Charvil: 'The number of people who came to support the Charvil children in their Nativity Play on December 18 was very gratifying. We are very proud of our children who did so well and the parents who gave so much encouragement to them. Our thanks go to Dudley Perring and Chris Easton for erecting and operating lights and scenery.'

Sonning Hand Bell Ringers: 'We would like to thank all those who welcomed us and showed their enjoyment of the ringing when we were out again during Christmas time. We raised £100 for local hospital charities.'

Sonning C. of E. School: 'This term the Juniors have started a County Council run swimming course at the Arthur Hill, Reading indoor pool. This will give a chance for the children to either learn to swim or improve their strokes.
The Spring Term commenced with a visit, for many of the children, to the Hexagon, Reading to see "Paddington Bear's Magical Musical".'

March 1983

Parish Council–Finances: The parish clerk provided a financial report which explained the source of income which was required to fund the parish expenditure: 'The cost of running the parish is covered mainly by the following; the interest from our invested capital, which came from the sale of land to the District Council in 1974 to enable Glebe Gardens to be built, the ground rentals from the sports clubs and the refund of value added tax. If it is anticipated that such an income will not be sufficient for our needs, we then precept on the District Council. This latter means that a small amount of the rates paid to the District Council, by parishioners, is returned for us to run the parish. Obviously, if a precept is called for, the rates paid by parishioners will be slightly higher than they otherwise would have been.

After much thought, the Parish Council has decided that for the coming year we need to precept at a two-penny rate, this will mean that any emergencies can be attended to and, more importantly, any balance can replace some of the capital spent in 1980.

Sonning Parish Magazine: The magazine losses incurred annually had now increased to £527 and a meeting had been called to discussed what measures might be taken to improve the unsatisfactory situation. It was reluctantly agreed that a price increase from January 1984 was probably inevitable but other ways of increasing revenue should be considered, this included trying to increase the distribution by approaching newcomers to the area.

April 1983

Absurd Person Singular at The Mill: 'This was the Sonning Village Players' second production under the sure direction of Betty Stokes. It was so well supported, not only by very large audiences but also by many people who greatly helped to make the undertaking a success. We are especially grateful to the management of The Mill Theatre for their generous co-operation.'

1ˢᵗ Sonning Brownies: 'Mrs. Feak came to see us in the middle of March and she helped us make Easter table decorations for the Darby and Joan Easter Dinner Party. We really enjoyed making them.'

May 1983

Vicar's Notes: 'We all are grateful to the people who made our Church so beautiful for Easter Day. The beauty of springtime reminds us each year of life restored after the winter of apparent deadness. Easter tells us that our faith is a Resurrection Faith. I try to remind people of this at every funeral I conduct.'

Sonning C. of E. School: 'Mrs, Beardmore would like to start a Table Tennis Club for the children at the School and would be pleased to hear of anyone in the area, who has a table tennis table that they no longer require and would like to offer it to the School.'

Sonning Women's Institute: 'Our new President Mrs. Gwen Cheyney opened our meeting. Warm congratulations were given to Mrs. Thelma Richards upon being elected as County Chairman. Our speaker, Mrs. Critchley, gave us a most interesting and hilarious talk on "Antiques for the Beginner", giving us helpful hints on what to look for or to avoid.'

June 1983

An Evening at The Mill: 'There was a very pleasant entertainment on May 8, presented by the Sonning Girls' Choir. Among a varied programme we had the excellent singing of Helen Clarke and Caroline Oliver, dramatic soliloquies from Catherine Hall, a piano solo from Joanna Davey and some fine music by the harpist Jane Carr.'

Sonning Football Club: 'At the end of the 1982-83 season there was more success for the Club as both teams have won promotion. We would like to thank the people who have come to see us play and give their support during the season, alas, very few village folk.'

Sonning Glebe Women's Institute: 'For the first time ever we held our own Mini Produce Show which proved to be a great success with over 120 entries. We hope it will now become an annual event.'

[*June 9: The General Election proved to be a landslide victory for the Conservatives returning Margaret Thatcher to 10 Downing Street. The Tories won 397 seats with Michael Foot's Labour party winning just 209.*]

July 1983

Royal British Legion–Women's Section: 'During May forty-five members of
the Women's Section and the Men's Branch paid a long-awaited visit to
the Legion's Poppy Factory at Richmond. We were made most welcome
and were all astonished at the cheerfulness and independence of the
disabled workers.'

Sonning C. of E. School: 'on June 14, the fourth year children visited
Ascot School, where they were fortunate to view the Queen and
members of the Royal Family in their carriages en route for the start of
this year's Royal Ascot race meeting.
This term the first and second year Juniors have been learning about
London and on June 21, an outing was arranged to visit the Museum of
London which included a coach tour of some special London sights.'

R.N.L.I. Sonning Branch: 'We should like to thank Dr. and Mrs. Grenfell
Bailey for lending their garden at The Thatched Cottage for this year's
Wine and Cheese Party. It was a lovely venue for a party and they must
have worked hard to have the garden look so beautiful. The party was a
great success, we were able to send £500 to the R.N.L.I. which is a
record for this event,'

August 1983

Vicar's Notes: 'I am writing this during the Festival of Flowers. I have
been very impressed and moved this week to see so many people busied
at interpreting the allotted items of the Christian Year and, of course,
with the final accomplishment of the aim. The Christian Faith has
been communicated through the beauty of the flowers and the skill and
love of the arrangers. "Thank you" to all who have contributed to the
Festival, especially to Mrs. Eileen Brown who co-ordinated its setting-
up.'

Sonning Parish Council: 'After several years without a contested election
for seats on the Parish Council, there were two bye-elections this
summer, to fill the vacancies due to the death of Mrs. Frances Ball and
the resignation of Mrs. Angela Perkins. The successful candidates were
Mr. Peter van Went and Mr. Nigel Rose.'

September 1983

Vicar's Notes: 'You probably know that our alms box has recently been broken and rifled. We installed a new one but that also has been broken open. The police have been active in trying to find the thief. But on the morning of August 17, we were informed by a parishioner who had been walking her dog that a window had been broken in the south side of the Church. The thief has destroyed one part of the stained glass memorial window to Lt. Seymour Ingleby, R.A.F., and broken open the new alms box again. I do not intend to keep the Church locked as this defeats all that a church stands for.'

Sonning Flower Club: 'On a perfect Summer's day, a gracious stately old house near the Thames was a lovely setting for our Garden Party. We must thank our host and hostess, Mr. and Mrs. Barlow for inviting us to The Mill House. It was indeed a charming English scene with the ladies in their beautiful hats, somewhat reminiscent of years ago, with tables set out on the lawn and terrace for tea.'

October 1983

Vicar's Notes: 'The first Sunday in October is always our Harvest Thanksgiving. There is a dearth of produce this year it seems but please bring what you can. If you have nothing, please bring packaged or tinned food instead. Our offerings all go to Dr. Barnardo's Home in Wokingham.'

Best Kept Village: 'Sonning did very well in this year's competition, but not quite well enough to win, coming second out of five with 85.5%. Donnington was the winner with 87.4%. Congratulations to those responsible for the School surrounds and for the Playing Fields, both of which were given full marks. In their notes the judges commented that they were disappointed with the surrounds of the Village Hall.'

The Parish Clerk: The retirement of the parish clerk, Frank Smith, after serving in that capacity for fifteen years, was to be effective at the end of the financial year in March 1984. Candidates were invited to fill the position and it was noted that the current remuneration was £1,000 per annum, reviewed annually.

November 1983

Sonning Churchyard: 'Visitors to the Church and village frequently pass compliments on the general care and tidiness of the Churchyard. For over twelve years the job had been ably carried out by Brian Mooney of Woodley, who is now unable to continue with the task. We are pleased to welcome local gardener and parishioner Stuart Clarke to take over and we congratulate him on such a splendid start.'

Sonning Women's Institute: 'Our September meeting was also our Harvest Lunch, with Malcolm and Mary Stansfield as our special guests. Thirty-six members and guests were present. Our President asked us to raise our glasses to Mr. and Mrs. Tom Cowley who were celebrating their Golden Wedding this month.'

Recreation Ground: 'It was not a surprise to read in last month's magazine that the Playing Fields scored ten out of ten for Sonning in the Best Kept Village competition. For this we can thank Mr. Arthur Notcutt, the groundsman and Mr. Harry Prismall, a member of the Parish Council who has particularly concerned himself with the Rec.'

December 1983

Street Lighting: 'Sonning Parish Council is facing a large bill for new street lighting amounting to some £10,000. The existing oak columns are reaching the end of their service life. The lighting units themselves are of obsolete design and consume nearly ten times more electricity than ones of modern design. The Council wants to adopt a standard design wherever possible, the first example being the replacement at the junction of Pearson Road and Thames Street. Comments from residents will be welcome, including references to location, colour of paint used etc.'

Choir News: David Duvall noted that several new "recruits" had joined the Sonning choir: 'We have seven new boys and girls – Lucy and Joe Mitchell, Julian and Suzanne Phillips, Philip Brooker, Emma and Alex Hayward. No less welcome is Val (soprano) the mother of Emma and Alex, also Mark Treherne and Mark Hayter (tenors). We are now in the happy position of being "full up".'

January 1984

Vicar's Notes: 'it is often that one hears the words "Christmas is for the children". This is a completely mistaken idea as even the very scantiest acquaintance with the Gospels demonstrate. Christmas is for the whole of human kind. Christians rejoice in the "sure and certain hope of the Resurrection to Eternal Life", won for mankind by Jesus, born in a stable, crucified on a gallows, and "raised up" by God.

Warm enough in Church? Our heating system is about at the end of its life. It is wasteful and costs about £60 to heat the Church at weekends for Sunday Services. A new boiler is essential and will cost about £2,000. Any offers from kindly disposed parishioners? Please!'

Forthcoming Events: 'With this issue we are experimenting with a list of the forthcoming events in village life which are outside the regular meeting held by village organisations for their members. The entries will be kept brief and fuller information will usually be found in the main body of the Magazine.'

February 1984

Vicar's Notes: 'Our Christmas was fabulous so far as the Church was concerned. Large congregations all paying their reverence to God-made-Man in the Bethlehem stable.

Thanks be to God that our damaged stained glass window on the south wall, has been beautifully restored by G. Maile and Sons of Canterbury. Have a good look at it. The cost is about £750.

The P.C.C. has decided to accept the tender for almost £2,000 to renew the boiler in St Andrew's. Further work on the pipes and chimney may well cost another £800. But it must be done.'

Sonning C. of E. School: 'At the end of the Autumn Term we said farewell to Mr. Stubbs, who has emigrated to Australia. This term we welcomed Miss Susan Joyner to the School to teach the third and fourth year Juniors.'

Sonning Sunday School: 'Our annual party was held in the Pearson Hall on January 14. This year's theme was "Tramps" and naturally we had to feed our young hobos with hot soup, hot-dogs and other goodies.'

March 1984

Vicar's Notes: 'It is proposed that from May 1984 to May 1985 there will be a year of celebration of our Christian Heritage. On May 9, there will be a National Inaugural Service in Westminster Abbey at which the Archbishop of Canterbury will preach. On Sunday, May 13, we are invited to remember the Christian witness of our local and national forebears and to pray for the nation and its future.'

The Parish Magazine: 'The Magazine continues to run at a loss (£527 in 1982), which is borne by the Church, but the deficit may be somewhat less for 1983. Therefore, it should be possible to hold the price at 15p for the time being. We are grateful to many subscribers who pay £2 a year for twelve issues instead of the exact £1. 80.

It is regretted that some long-standing advertisers have withdrawn their custom but we have gained some new advertisers, whom readers are asked to support.

The Charvil representative considers there is scope for increased sales among the expanding population of Charvil. The Editors would welcome more reporting contributions from Charvil in order to make the Magazine more relevant to Charvil readers.'

April 1984

Sonning Parochial Church Council: The Treasurer's report together with the accounts for the year 1983 appeared in this issue: 'Whilst the accounts show a healthy surplus for the year 1983, this has been derived mainly from gifts, donations and interest on our investments. However, the level of gifts and donations cannot be assured every year. It would be pleasing to see an upsurge in income both from collections and from covenants, especially covenants as the Church recovers from the Inland Revenue 43p for every £1 covenanted.' There followed estimated costs of various necessary work which would be required in the foreseeable future, including urgent restoration of the large stained glass window in the east wall of St Andrew's. It was emphasised that little financial provision had been made for much of this likely expenditure.

Murder at the Vicarage: 'From the moment that the Vicar sat down to luncheon with his household, we knew "Murder at the Vicarage" would be another Sonning Village Players' success. Barbara Carr and Betty Stokes rightly produced the play at a good pace, sparking-off characters one against another, making the performance thoroughly enjoyable.'

May 1984

Sonning Sunday School: 'We at present number about thirty-five youngsters, some of the older ones having left Sunday School since their Confirmation, but we are extremely pleased to see the five to seven year old class expanding. We recently took part in the Scripture Union Bible Contest and of the nine children who gained certificates six obtained Distinction and, of those, three had ninety-five per cent. This made the six-week extra effort and the conscientious preparation and attendance of the teachers well worthwhile.'

The Church Flagpole: 'Observant parishioners will have noticed that the flagpole is now back in place, after major repairs and painting. Thanks are particularly due to Cyril Harris for his skilled work and to a few members of the congregation for their sterling efforts in providing the required muscle power.'

June 1984

Sonning Parish Council: 'The Annual Parish Meeting was held in the Pearson Hall on May 11. The Chairman, Mark Bodley Scott, described the Council's main activities during the past year, of which the following is a summary:

The ever increasing flow of traffic through the village has been forcefully represented to our local M.P. and many other authorities. We continue to advocate provision of a third Reading bridge, probably as an extension of the A329(M), to relieve traffic pressure over Sonning Bridge.

Renewal and improvement of street lighting has been started.

Planning applications have continued to cause problems especially the new sports complex for Reading Cricket and Hockey Club.

The Best Kept Village competition will be judged during the coming weeks. In 1983 Sonning came a close second in its class. With a little more effort from everyone we ought to be winners.

Mr. Bodley Scott said that after nine years as Chairman, he was not standing for re-election. Mr. John Edmonds was elected the new Chairman. Mr. Nigel Rose was elected as Vice-Chairman.'

Fire Damage: 'The early evening peace of the Vicarage was shattered on May 11, when a walker, passing through the churchyard saw some smoke coming from the outbuildings used to store tools and garden equipment. Fortunately, the Vicar was on hand to dial 999; he then hurried to the scene and most bravely rescued two of the mowers. Sadly, several other items and also the roof of the building were badly damaged. Fire Officers suspect vandalism as the lock had been smashed and the fire started in two separate areas.'

July 1984

First Communions: 'On June 15, our Bishop of Reading confirmed thirty-two members of the parish, young and older. Their first communions will be on Sunday July 1. This is an important day in their lives as full members of the Church. It is part of the initiation ceremonies and they are entitled to the support of all Christians in the parish.'

St Patrick's Sunday School: 'On Saturday, May 19, there was a "Sing-in" evening at the church. About thirty-five people came to sing their favourite hymns and listen to Charvil guides and Sunday School children singing some of their favourite choruses. We had an enjoyable evening and raised £16 for Christian Aid Week.'

Make-up Workshop: 'Catherine Penny will organise a Make-up Workshop in the Pearson Hall on July 10, at 8pm. Those interested in learning the technique of stage make-up please contact her.'

August 1984

Sonning Working Men's Club: 'On June 23, the Club held a Barbecue Dance to celebrate the 80th anniversary of its move into its present premises. Previously the Club was located in the High Street, in the house now called Cleaver Cottage, which it took over when founded in 1876 after the Butcher's Arms was closed down.'

Sonning Fire Brigade Trust: An article which provided a brief history of the trust appeared in this issue: 'Until the 1938 Fire Brigade Act, the Sonning Brigade was financed by local public subscription and by contributions from insurance companies. The 1938 Act placed the onus of fire protection on the shoulders of Rural District Councils. Later, in 1943 all Fire Brigades were taken over by the Government and Sonning was known as Station 15 A.I.S. Following the 1943 reorganisation the Sonning Fire Brigade continued to own the Fire Station premises in Pound Lane, but the equipment was sold to the Government and the proceeds were invested. In 1948/49 an agreement was reached with the Charity Commissioners whereby a small proportion of the fund then held should be distributed to the fire men who had earned the money, while the remainder was place under Trustees – For any public purpose for the benefit of the inhabitants of the Parish of Sonning, and not provided out of rates or other public funds.'

September 1984

Vicar's Notes: 'I announced my retirement to the P.C.C. at its meeting on August 21. It is never easy for a priest to retire when there is no dead-line, but there comes a time in life when the decision has to be made for the good both of ourselves at the Vicarage and also the parish. The date of our leaving is not fixed yet but will be some time in January, giving us one more Christmas in this beautiful church, house and village. We are to retire to a modern house in Steeple Aston in Oxfordshire and quite close to my wife's brother.'

Best Kept Village Competition: 'Sonning again came second (88.75%) to Bray (93%) in this year's competition. Full marks were given to the churchyard and playing fields. Unfortunately, untidy bus shelters and advertisements let us down.'

October 1984

Sonning Parish Council: 'The iron bridges on the Oxfordshire side of the river (known as the Sonning Backwater Bridges) are to be completely replaced. Work is expected to start in February 1985 and will probably last about eighteen months. The five tonne weight limit at present imposed will no longer apply when the bridges are replaced. However, the two Parish Councils will be pressing the two County Councils to ensure that a similar limit remains in force to discourage heavy traffic.'

Sonning C. of E. School: 'Following the end of the Summer term, we said farewell to Miss Joyner, who has taken up a teaching post in Worcester. This term we welcomed Mr. David Smith to the School to teach the third and fourth year Juniors. We hope his time spent at Sonning School will be a long and happy one.

The new School year has started with a busy term ahead for both children and parents. On October 5, the children will be bringing flowers and produce to the School for their own Harvest Festival.'

Mobile Library: 'The Berkshire County Library is now sending out a new and larger library van on the Sonning and Charvil route, which has more room for the staff and customers as well as more shelf space for books. The service is free but a charge is made for reserving books or obtaining them from another branch.'

November 1984
Sonning Glebe Women's Institute: 'We celebrated our twentieth birthday on October 15. Our President, Mrs. Joanna Allaway, was very pleased to announce that Val Walker and Janet Bailey had joined our ranks and welcomed them to membership of the Institution. Congratulations were given to our General Knowledge Quiz team who had fought so well to reach the semi-finals of the Berkshire competition.'

Sonning Stores: 'We are sure that we speak for the whole village when we say "Thank you" to Della and Glen for their years of service to the community while running Sonning Stores. We extend a warm welcome to Malcolm and Christine Dorward, hoping that they find fulfilment running the Stores and being amongst us.'

December 1984
From the Churchwardens: 'The Bishop of Reading met the Parochial Church Council at the end of October to discuss the appointment of an incumbent of St Andrew's in succession to Rev. George Stokes. We are to have another Vicar of Sonning, but the appointment will be combined with that of Principal of the Berkshire Christian Training Scheme. This vacancy has already been advertised and it is unlikely that the new Vicar will be in residence before April.'

Royal British Legion: 'At the Armistice Day Parade it was noticeable that the ranks of the veterans were sparse this year. There were many who conceded with regret that the years now prevent them from marching to St Andrew's, among them Bill Shepherd who, after innumerable years as our President, has decided to make way for Hugh Stewart. Our Treasurer, Bernard Langley, has also stepped down and we now have Adrian Atkinson to look after our finances.'

January 1985
Vicar's Notes: 'The time has come when I have to write my last letter to you in the Parish Magazine. We are leaving Sonning during the week following January 20, having spent eleven years here, the longest period I have ever served in one place during my forty-seven years of active ministry. We have been very happy here and it has been very hard to decide to leave you all. I am sure that you know how much I owe to the support of my wife Betty, she has involved herself in so many parish activities.

You have no doubt heard that the Rev. Christopher Morgan is to be your new Vicar. He brings to the parish his wife and their two young children. I warmly commend him to you and ask you to remember him in your prayers, and to make him and his family as welcome as you made us.

So with much love and affection, we wish you good-bye – Betty, Libby, and all the other members of the family.'

Sonning Guides: 'I would like to take this opportunity to thank everyone who helped our company during 1984. Without all our supporters and badge testers our guides would not be so successful. 1984 saw three girls gain their Queen's Guide Badges and the patrols have all gained interest pennants. In all over seventy different badges have been awarded.'

Scout and Guide Building: 'The "Hut" has caused much concern over recent years and the management committee are now ready to instigate the first phase of our new building programme – and we need your support. Everyone interested in seeing our plans and helping with this project are invited to an opening evening on Tuesday, January 29.'

February 1985

Churchwardens' Notes: 'We understand that all Church services can continue as normal with the help of our two Readers (Mr. Hudson and Mr. Sanders), the Rev. John Crawford and visiting clergy.

We would like to thank all of those who so generously contributed towards the Vicar's retirement gift. As a result we are able to make a suitable presentation to him.

During this interregnum period, should you wish to make arrangements for Baptisms, Weddings or Funerals please get to touch with one of the Churchwardens.'

The Vicar's Retirement Party: 'A lovely crowd of friends and parishioners gathered in Way Hall on Saturday, January 19, to say goodbye to George and Betty Stokes. Nobody was actually counting but the general consensus seems to have been that some two hundred and fifty people attended. Tom Feak made a short and very apposite speech which was responded to by George Stokes. Nicola Sanders presented a handsome bouquet to Betty Stokes, and this was followed by the presentation to George Stokes of a cheque for £1,000 and a book of photographs recalling memorable happenings in the village during the period of his incumbency.'

March 1985

The Pearson Hall: 'The hall was kept busy in 1984 with the usual parties, discos, jumble sales, receptions, entertainments and celebrations – but there are still plenty of free evenings and afternoons; if anyone has a new venture in mind, please talk to the caretaker, Jenny Adams. If the hall is not in constant use there will not be enough income to maintain it, so, as with the Post Office, use it or lose it.'

Sonning Flower Club: 'What a feast of good things we had for St Valentine's Day! The Pearson Hall was packed with members and visitors to witness the ordeal of three aspiring demonstrators being examined by Area Judges. Mrs. Jane Rowton-Lee, conducting the proceedings, thanked the Club for hosting the afternoon's event and Mrs. Ann Turner, our Chairman, said in her reply that we were very pleased and privileged to be chosen for the purpose.'

April 1985

Churchwardens' Notes: This is probably our last note before the new Vicar arrives, we should like to thank the many parishioners who have made the interregnum period run smoothly – those who have polished and kept the church clean, looked after the linen, arranged the flowers etc., and those who have quietly continued to do the many other jobs about the church.

Some parishioners have said they would like to know more about the Rev. Christopher Morgan, so here are a few notes: He was born in 1947 at South Shields, Co. Durham, and lived subsequently in Norway, Sussex and Somerset. He was educated at the City of Bath Boys School and began his training for the Ministry at Kelham, and completed it at the University of Lancaster where he gained a first class Honours degree in Religious Studies and Politics. Ordained in 1973 he has been Curate at Birstall, Leics; Assistant Chaplain in Brussels; Priest in Charge and a Team Vicar both at Redditch. He is married to Anne, who is a speech therapist, and they have two children, Claire and James.'

The Third Thames Bridge: The Sonning Parish Council reported that the Berkshire County Council is conducting a Public Consultation upon the "Third Bridge". 'There appears to be four possible crossings, two are west of Reading, which would have no benefit to Sonning, and two to the east – the Sonning preferred route would be from the A329(M) at the A4 junction at Suttons Corner to the junction of the Henley Road with Caversham Park Road.'

Sonning Parochial Church Council: The Treasurer in his report for the year ended December 31, 1984 mentioned that the surplus for the year of £1,549 compared with the previous year's surplus of £4,133. It was pointed out that the reduction was due substantially to a drop in donations and a plea was made that more deeds of covenants were required in order to consolidate the P.C.C's income.

'The loss on the Parish Magazine is £533 and consideration will be given to reducing this deficit, if necessary by increasing the cover price in 1986. The price has been held at 15p for several years and effectively the Magazine provides a service and a news outlet not only for the Church but for the village as a whole.'

May 1985

The Vicar Writes: 'We have been living in Sonning for just one week; However, I am very glad of this early opportunity to write to you all and express my gratitude and warm good wishes.' Christopher Morgan continued by acknowledging the assistance he and his wife had received since their arrival, and emphasised his eagerness to begin his work and to meet as many parishioners as soon as possible.

Sonning Glebe Women's Institute: 'Despite the fact that our first meeting of the new W. I. year coincided with the induction of the new Vicar, those members who attended were treated to an excellent talk by Mrs. Mates on "A Victorian Lady Doctor".'

June 1985

Sonning Parish Council: 'The Annual Parish Meeting was held in the Pearson Hall on May 10. The following is a summary of the report by the Chairman, John Edmonds, of the past year's main activities:
'The Council's total income is still only just over £14,000. Current expenditure on the Recreation Ground accounts for about £6,000 and village street lighting about £2,000.
Perhaps the most important issue is to press for the proposed Third Thames Bridge to be positioned as an extension of the A329(M) road. It was seen as important that as many people as possible should support this option and make their view known to the County Council.
The Chairman asked everyone to make the village as tidy as possible in advance of the judging for the forthcoming Best Kept Village competition.'

July 1985

Sonning C. of E. School: 'This year, London has been the destination for the School's annual outings. On June 13, the Lower Juniors spent an enjoyable day visiting the Natural History Museum, befriending the dinosaurs and following the ecology trail among other things. The Upper Infants visited the London Museum and St Paul's Cathedral.'

Darby and Joan Club: 'We were pleased to welcome Mr. Harold Sharp from Calcot on June 10, who played the piano and encouraged us to sing. His cheerful manner did us all good and Mrs. Leyton thanked him for coming. Tea was provided with homemade scones and cakes.'

August 1985

Wanted – More Sunday School Teachers: 'Starting in September a new arrangement will be adopted for the teaching of children on Sunday mornings. There will be two teams of teachers who will each be responsible for no more than two Sundays in a month of four or five Sundays. We are looking for four adults, so if you think you can help please contact the Vicar or Dawne Vincent.'

Sonning Lawn Tennis Club: 'After a successful day's tennis at the annual American Tournament, we all sat round the pavilion on June 8, in blankets and anoraks trying to warm ourselves. Twelve couples signed on and, surprisingly, the day stayed, if not warm, at least dry. We were happy to see a few new faces and the standard of play was very good. The finalists played nervously but the worthy winners were Julie Richardson and Tony Murdock.'

September 1985

The Vicar Writes: An extensive letter from the vicar, Christopher Morgan, announced that Allan Sanders, who had joined the Reading Blue Coat School some ten years earlier, was to be ordained deacon. Allan Sanders was well connected with St Andrew's as he had performed the roll of a lay reader at the church during many past years. The ceremony was to be conducted by the Bishop of Reading in Sunningdale parish church and would be followed by an evening service in Sonning church and a reception afterwards at the vicarage.

New Bus Service: 'A new service to Woodley and Lower Earley will be introduced from September 10, on a trial basis. The route in Sonning will be via Sonning Lane, Pearson Road and Pound Lane. The adult single fare will be 30p to Woodley (Chequers) and 50p to Lower Earley (ASDA). This service has been arranged by Berkshire County Council and Reading Transport as a direct result of the Parish Council's transport survey in March. As with other services in villages nowadays, the watchword is "Use it or lose it".'

[*Incidents of mob rioting had been occurring in many British cities for some time. On September 29 rioting by mainly youths in Brixton, London resulted in 209 arrests.*]

October 1985

The Vicar Writes: 'This is the season of prize onions and marrows, of bright displays of dahlias, of berry picking and jam making – it is the season of Harvest Festival. Many people who cannot put an exact name to their feelings are aware of "the hand of providence" and think that we cannot be quite alone in this productive and yet mysterious world. For reasons like these, Harvest Festival services maintain a popular appeal, and I for one am glad that our parish church will welcome a real cross-section of parishioners at a time like this.'

Sunday School Teachers: 'In response to the Vicar's request for more teachers, we are pleased to welcome – Betty Sweet, Margaret Booen and Kay Dawes with whom we commence a new rota in October. Pam Glasspool, Brian Brooker and Peter Goodacre have agreed to help us on an occasional basis.'

November 1985

Sonning Parish Magazine: 'The charge for each issue of the Magazine has remained at 15p for several years despite continually increasing costs. The Magazine provides information relating to many village activities as well as the church itself. It has always run at a loss and the P.C.C. accepts the principle that the Church should try as far as possible to absorb this loss, within reasonable limits. Regrettably, the losses have now become so large that a review of the cost has needed to be made and with effect from January 1986 the cost for each issue will be 20p. A realistic charge would have been 25p per copy and this is the charge made in many other Parishes (unless they have their own printing facilities).'

Sonning Produce Show 1985: 'The decision to hold this year's show a week later than usual paid off. With villagers back from holidays and children back at school, attendances were up, and there were more entrants in the competitions. Even the rain almost held off! The barbecue was a sell-out with some 250 people enjoying an evening with music. Another change this year was that the afternoon fete was run independently by the committee raising funds for the new Scouts and Guides Hut, with novelties such as a pet show and horses to ride.'

December 1985

The Vicar Writes: 'I invite you all warmly to join in the Christmas celebrations in church at this time. It seems to me that this festival without Christian worship is indeed Xmas – where "X" equals an unknown quantity, a space, a shapeless gap. A way in which we can save our Christmas celebration from being haphazard or thoughtless is to freshly recognise the tremendous love of God in Christ. A carol verse which expresses this very attractively is:'

"What can I give Him, poor as I am?
If I were a shepherd I would bring a lamb;
If I were a wise man I would do my part;
Yet what I can give Him – give my heart"

The Parish Magazine: The small letterpress printing business based in Woodley, and operated by John Heppell and his wife, had been producing this parish magazine for many years. John Heppell had died recently and now his wife had decided to close down the business:
'For many years the Heppell business has given fine service as printers of Sonning's Parish Magazine. Now that Mrs. Heppell is taking her well-earned retirement, discussions are under way to join forces with a new printer, news of which will be in the January 1986 issue . . .'

The Parish Magazine . . . and into the future!

The size, design and general appearance of this magazine had hardly changed since the end of World War II, during the incumbency of four Sonning vicars. Had William Caxton (c.1422-1492), considered by many to be the father of English printing, been alive during those years he would have surely "felt at home" in most small printing works. However, with the ending of the Heppell business those responsible for the publishing of this magazine would clearly be encouraged to take advantage of new composing and printing techniques which were now available.

During the next thirty years further vast technological advancement for the printed word would see this magazine undergo a transformation, that Hugh Pearson could never have dreamed of, but would surely have approved of, when he conceived the idea to launch the magazine in 1869.

Vicars of St. Andrew's Church, Sonning 1946–1985

Sidney John Selby Groves
1942-1965

Robert (Robin) Springett Brutton
1965-1974

George Smithson Garbutt Stokes
1974-1985

Christopher Heudebourck Morgan
1985-1997

Vicars of St. John the Evangelist Church, Woodley 1946 –1985

K. F. WAY 1945 – 1948
H. W. H. WILKINSON 1948 – 1974
J. EASTGATE 1974 – 1983
J. CONGDON 1984 – 1991

Vicars of All Saints' Church, Dunsden 1946 –1985

H WIGAN 1904 – 1947
J F AMIES 1948 – 1963
H CUTLER 1964 – 1970
J BIDDLESTONE 1971 – 1977
N PRINT 1978 - 1990

Vicars of Earley St. Peter's Church 1946 –1985

S C ROBINSON 1943 – 1970
J C HUTTON 1970 – 1975
W D S LARK 1975 – 1985
P L BATSON 1985 - 1993

British Sovereigns 1946-1985

KING GEORGE VI 1936 – 1952
QUEEN ELIZABETH II 1952 –

British Prime Ministers 1946-1985

CLEMENT ATTLEE (Lab) 1945 – 1951
WINSTON CHURCHILL (Con) 1951 – 1955
ANTHONY EDEN (Con) 1955 – 1957
HAROLD MACMILLAN (Con) 1957 – 1963
ALEC DOUGLAS HOME (Con) 1963 – 1964
HAROLD WILSON (Lab) 1964 – 1970
EDWARD HEATH (Con) 1970 – 1974
HAROLD WILSON (Lab) 1974 – 1976
JAMES CALLAGHAN (Lab) 1976 – 1979
MARGARET THATCHER (Con) 1979 – 1990

INDEX

1946 – 1985